Measuring and Assessing Well-being in Israel

BETTER POLICIES FOR BETTER LIVES

Please cite this publication as:
OECD (2015), *Measuring and Assessing Well-being in Israel*, OECD Publishing, Paris.
http://dx.doi.org/10.1787/9789264246034-en

ISBN 978-92-64-24602-7 (print)
ISBN 978-92-64-24603-4 (PDF)

Photo credits: ©

Corrigenda to OECD publications may be found on line at: *www.oecd.org/publishing/corrigenda*.

Foreword

Since 2011 the OECD has played a major role in carrying forward work on the measurement of well-being and on how well-being measures can be used to inform better policy-making. Under the aegis of the Better Life Initiative, reports such as How's Life? *have pioneered the analysis of how outcomes on the different elements of well-being vary across countries, while other reports such as the* OECD Guidelines on Measuring Subjective Well-being *have proved instrumental in extending the range of well-being indicators available from official sources. The Better Life Index illustrates how good data visualisation can be effective in engaging the wider public in thinking about what constitutes a better society, and has also generated useful information on how people in different countries value the different dimensions of well-being.*

In all of the OECD's efforts to advance the measurement of well-being, the active engagement of OECD member countries has been crucial. In refining the choice of measures for How's Life? *or in testing different approaches to collect data, member countries have been at the core of the OECD work on well-being. This report on* Measuring and Assessing Well-being in Israel *represents another step in working with member countries to incorporate the analysis of well-being into the OECD's analysis, and in supporting member countries to develop policies that will improve the well-being of their citizens.*

Although short sections on well-being are now regularly included in the OECD's economic surveys, and a well-being perspective has been fully integrated into the Multi-Dimensional Country Reviews led by the OECD Development Centre, Measuring and Assessing Well-being in Israel *is the first OECD country monograph specifically focused on well-being. The OECD hopes that this monograph will support, and contribute to, Israel's national programme to develop indicators of well-being, resilience, and sustainability, launched in 2012, by providing an international comparative picture, and by sharing its experience in the policy applications of well-being data.*

Beyond complementing Israel's own national efforts to measure well-being , Measuring and Assessing Well-being in Israel *is also intended to be of interest to a broader international audience. As a small, rapidly changing country, the picture of well-being that emerges in Israel is of potential interest well beyond Israel itself. In particular, the greater depth of analysis possible in a country monograph means that* Measuring and Assessing Well-being in Israel *is able to go further than many other OECD reports in looking at key specific issues such as the sustainability of well-being.*

Israel has taken a bold step forward in engaging with the OECD to produce Measuring and Assessing Well-being in Israel *to support and complement its national project to measure well-being, resilience, and sustainability. Achieving better policies for better lives requires that well-being be mainstreamed within the broader policy process, therefore it is hoped that Israel's initiative will set a best practice that will be followed by many other OECD countries.*

Acknowledgements

The OECD is very grateful to colleagues in Israel who contributed to this report and particularly to the team drawn from the National Economic Council, Ministry for Environmental Protection, and Central Bureau of Statistics who provided detailed comments and feedback on many aspects of the report, and who were a primary source of information on Israel's project to develop indicators of well-being, resilience, and sustainability. Staff at the Central Bureau of Statistics and National Insurance Institute and Central Bank of Israel also provided data for the report and responded to numerous enquiries about the data. Finally, we would also like to thank the many people in different parts of Israel who, during our visit and meetings, gave their time to welcome us and answered our questions. This report was prepared by Fabrice Murtin, Kate Scrivens and Conal Smith, with assistance from Romina Boarini for Annex A, of the Well-being and Progress Unit of the OECD Statistics Directorate.

Table of contents

Tables

Figures

Executive summary

In December 2012 Israel embarked on one of the most ambitious initiatives in the world to publish information on well-being in order to better inform citizens and policy makers. In itself, the Israeli government's decision to produce indicators of "well-being, resilience, and sustainability" (the heading chosen by the Israeli authorities for their initiative) places it in the company of several other OECD countries and follows growingly accepted international best practice. Australia, Austria, Italy, and the United Kingdom, for example, have all undertaken high-profile national initiatives to improve the measurement of "what matters to people". This, in turn, reflects a growing global awareness of the importance of measuring well-being and integrating these indicators into the policy process.

Measuring and Assessing Well-being in Israel is a well-being focused country monograph intended to complement the Israeli process. The goal is to be useful to Israeli policy makers and citizens by providing a view of the methodological issues at stake in measuring well-being, to assist the Israeli government in the process of establishing its own set of well-being indicators relevant for Israel, and to provide the international comparison on a set of outcomes across all OECD member countries.

By applying the OECD well-being framework to Israel, *Measuring and Assessing Well-being in Israel* aims to bring OECD expertise in the measurement of well-being to bear on the situation of a single country and to both describe the level and distribution of well-being in Israel as well as to go beyond this to look at the sustainability of well-being over time, how well-being measures can be used to inform policy, and to identify the key data gaps associated with measuring well-being in Israel.

Key findings

In some dimensions of well-being Israel is among the top performers in the OECD, but in other dimensions Israel performs relatively poorly.

While on some aggregate measures, the country performs well – and is among the best in the OECD, particularly in terms of life satisfaction, health status and educational attainment – Israel also presents some of the poorest outcomes in the OECD in areas such as income poverty, housing and air quality. Some paradoxes are also present within individual well-being domains, such as in education, where high upper secondary and tertiary educational attainment rates contrast with comparatively low learning outcomes of students, as measured by PISA scores.

Average measures alone do not give a complete picture of well-being conditions.

Assessing well-being outcomes at the level of a national community requires taking into account differences between people and population groups. Israel is a highly diverse society with large differences in well-being outcomes between the Jewish and the Arab population, and also between different sub-groups within each population. Arabs are unambiguously disadvantaged across all dimensions for which measures are available, experiencing higher rates of poverty, and lower levels of labour force participation, educational attainment and health status. These multiple disadvantages are likely to be mutually reinforcing, with low educational attainment leading to unfavourable labour market outcomes. In contrast, while Haredi Jews also experience higher levels of income poverty and lower levels of labour force participation and educational attainment, they tend to report much higher levels of satisfaction with their life, economic situation, housing, and health.

The drivers of well-being are largely the same for Arab Israelis and secular Jews, but differ for Haredi Jews.

An analysis based on the Israeli Social Survey suggests that Haredi outcomes reflect differences in preferences, and thus suggests that bringing outcomes for this population group in terms of income, education and jobs, up to the level of Israeli society as a whole will be challenging. In contrast, Arab Israeli preferences mirror those of mainstream Jews relatively closely, suggesting that if the social and economic causes of poor Arab outcomes are addressed, there is scope for relatively rapid convergence.

The levels of the capital stocks underpinning the sustainability of well-being in Israel show a mixed picture.

Although Israel has relatively low per capita levels of produced capital compared to other OECD countries, this stock has been steadily increasing over time. Unlike many OECD countries, the 2008 financial crisis had relatively little impact on either the stock of produced capital or its rate of growth. Israel needs to boost its human capital, which is significantly below OECD average, mostly due to low labour market participation among Arab-Israelis and Haredi Jews. It is difficult to draw a clear overall picture of the state of natural capital in Israel and how this compares with other countries given the limited set of internationally comparable information available. Within the limited range of information available, however, Israel fares relatively well. The picture with regards to social capital in Israel is mixed. Levels of generalised trust are relatively high. However, perceived corruption in Israel is high, which is a cause for concern and is in contrast to confidence in the national government.

Israel has a sound base of statistical information for measuring well-being.

This information is grounded in a strong official statistical system collecting information on a broad array of relevant dimensions. The Central Bureau of Statistics (CBS) collects a wide range of data relevant to measuring well-being, and much of this is published in a format very close to that required for effectively monitoring well-being. However, there are a number of areas where the Israeli statistical system could be improved from the perspective of measuring well-being and sustainability. In particular there are significant measurement gaps in the area of natural capital, and it is difficult to make international comparisons or look at change over time for many of the indicators relating to the other capital stocks. This is an area where Israel is well positioned to make significant progress if relevant measures are identified among the indicators of well-being, resilience and sustainability and the Israeli statistical office is resourced to collect them.

Chapter 1

Measuring well-being in Israel: An introduction

The question of how to measure people's well-being and societal progress has always been at the heart of what the OECD does. As an international organisation focused on providing evidence-based advice on the full range of country's policies, the OECD has an intrinsic interest in measuring the high-level outcomes that policies are intended to achieve. This chapter outlines the OECD framework for measuring well-being and sets out the goals of this country monograph on well-being in Israel. The relationship of Measuring and Assessing Well-being in Israel *to the Israeli indicators of well-being, resilience, and sustainability is discussed. In particular, the chapter articulates how* Measuring and Assessing Well-being in Israel *can complement existing Israeli initiatives to measure well-being by providing an international and comparative perspective.*

The statistical data for Israel are supplied by and under the responsibility of the relevant Israeli authorities. The use of such data by the OECD is without prejudice to the status of the Golan heights, East Jerusalem and Israeli settlements in the West Bank under the terms of international law.

Introduction

In December 2012 Israel embarked on one of the most ambitious initiatives in the world to measure and publish information on well-being in order to better inform citizens and policy makers. In itself, the Israeli government's decision to produce indicators of "well-being, resilience, and sustainability" (the heading chosen by the Israeli authorities for their initiative) places it in the company of several other OECD countries and follows growingly accepted international best practice. Australia, Austria, Italy, and the United Kingdom, for example, have all undertaken high-profile national initiatives to improve the measurement of "what matters to people". This, in turn, reflects a growing global awareness of the importance of measuring well-being and integrating these indicators into the policy process.

Global efforts to measure well-being and to integrate well-being indicators into the policy process were given addition weight by the global financial crisis, but have their roots in several long-standing criticisms with the way economic performance, social progress and their sustainability are measured. These concerns were strengthened with the publication in 2009 of the *Report of the Commission on the Measurement of Economic Performance and Social Progress* led by Amartya Sen, Joseph Stiglitz, and Jean-Paul Fitoussi, who argued in favour of reorienting statistical efforts from economic production to people's well-being and articulated a concrete agenda for better measurement in this field. This agenda formed the basis of the pioneering OECD work pursued in the context of its *Better Life Initiative*.

The Israeli indicators of well-being, resilience, and sustainability

The Israeli project to develop indicators of "well-being, resilience, and sustainability" builds on these global trends, taking international best practice and extending it within a uniquely Israeli context. Following a government resolution to develop measures of "well-being, resilience and sustainability" in December 2012, work has been undertaken to develop a suite of indicators in order to:

> "provide decision makers and the public the data required to create a comprehensible, updated and sound picture of the well-being of Israeli citizens, in terms of economic, social and environmental factors"

The aim of the Israeli indicators is to allow decision makers to design and evaluate policy with a clear view of the desirable outcomes that policies are intended to achieve, and a clear framework for evaluating whether conditions in Israel are improving over time. A second, equally important objective is to provide the public with the information necessary to assess the state of Israel and progress over time across all of the relevant dimensions of well-being. Although much of the information used to measure people's well-being is already available – such as information on incomes from the system of national accounts – the well-being indicator system complements this by bringing commonly used economic indicators together with information from other sources on non-market outcomes to provide a broad view of well-being in Israel.

Another key feature of the Israeli project is that it goes beyond looking at current well-being outcomes to measure the sustainability of these outcomes over time and the resilience of Israeli society in the face of potential shocks. Building on the capital stocks framework, which is now widely accepted as best practice for monitoring sustainability (OECD, 2013b, 2015; UNECE, 2009), the Israeli initiative is developing a set of indicators to monitor sustainability that complement the measures of current well-being.

Although there is now a wide literature discussing the outcomes that matter to people's well-being, for a set of well-being measures to have real legitimacy it is essential that they are grounded in the values and outcomes that matter the most for the people whose well-being is being measured. Following the experience of other countries that have launched processes to measure well-being, the Israeli indicators were developed after consultation with a wide variety of stakeholders, from across the government, the private sector, non-governmental organisations (NGOs) and representative organizations, as well as academia. These stakeholders provided expert input into the identification of the well-being outcomes that matter to Israeli citizens. Beyond this expert consultation, the development of the Israeli well-being measures was grounded in a consultation with the Israeli public. This took place through a variety of different channels, and was undertaken to ensure that the process of selecting the indicators reflected the views of Israeli people.

A particular strength of the Israeli project has been the close involvement of the main policy agencies in defining the outcome domains to be measured and in selecting the indicators to measure them. The Israeli project is led by the Prime Minister's office, the Ministry of Environmental Protection, the Bank of Israel, and the Central Bureau of Statistics. Under this leadership group, the development of indicators for each of the eleven domains of well-being identified by the Israeli authorities has been done by senior officials from all of the relevant policy agencies for each domain. This has ensured that the outcomes measured can be related directly to policy, and has proved an effective way of getting government agencies to consider the impacts of their policy beyond their immediate remit on a broader range of well-being outcomes.

The final result of the Israeli project is an agreed set of outcome areas and statistical indicators that will be published annually by the Central Bureau of Statistics. These indicators will also be a major input to the strategic outlook presented to the government each year by the National Economic Council.

The OECD Better Life Initiative

The question of how to measure people's well-being and societal progress has always been at the heart of what the OECD does. As an international organization focused on providing evidence-based advice on the full range of country's policies, the OECD has an intrinsic interest in measuring the high-level outcomes that policies are intended to achieve. Since 2011, this has been reflected in the OECD's mission statement – "better policies for better lives" – and pursued through the OECD *Better Life Initiative*. The OECD focus on "better lives" emphasizes that, while the health of the economy is of fundamental importance, a strong economy is ultimately only a means to another end: it is important to the extent that delivers better lives to the country's citizens. It is people's well-being that is the ultimate goal for all types of policies.

The *Better Life Initiative* focuses on measuring well-being outcomes: the aspects of life that matter to people and that, together, shape their lives. It comprises a bi-annual publication benchmarking and monitoring well-being across the OECD area as a whole (*How's Life? Measuring Well-being*), as well as analysing the drivers of these well-being outcomes and their links to other dimensions; and an interactive web-application allowing people to examine how countries' average achievements compare based on the weights that users attach to the different dimensions of well-being (*Your Better Life Index*).[1] These two components are complemented by an ongoing series of methodological and research projects aimed at improving the measurement of different aspects of well-being and the understanding of their trends and drivers.[2]

The *OECD Better Life Initiative* had a meaningful impact on the Israeli government's decision to undertake the task of creating a framework for measuring well-being in Israel. In light of this, the Israeli government invited the OECD to prepare a report on well-being in Israel. This country monograph on well-being in Israel is the first of its type, and is intended to complement the Israeli domestic process.

Country monographs

Although well-being has been a theme in a number of the OECD's country reviews (e.g. the OECD *Economic Survey* of Austria in 2013, the 2014 *Economic Survey* of the United States in 2014, and the series of Multi-Dimensional Country Reviews coordinated by the OECD Development Centre), *Measuring and assessing well-being in Israel* is the first country monograph entirely focused on well-being produced by the OECD. It is particularly important, therefore, to be clear about the objectives of this report, and how it contributes both to the OECD's wider agenda, and to the initiatives undertaken by various stakeholders in Israel.

At the core of the OECD mission is the idea that it is possible to learn from comparing the experiences of different countries. When it is not possible to experiment with policy changes in experimental settings, analysis of how outcomes vary across countries provides one way to learn about what works in national policy. Much of the OECD's work reflects this perspective. Thematic reports draw together what is known about a specific topic looking across OECD countries, while country surveys apply knowledge gained from comparative studies to make country-specific recommendations, allowing for a more in-depth analysis of the lessons to be learned from a particular country's experiences.

How's Life? Measuring Well-being, first published in 2011, looks at well-being across OECD countries. It aims to respond to the needs of citizens for better information on well-being, and to provide a more accurate picture of societal progress across the OECD area. *Measuring and assessing well-being in Israel* focuses specifically on one country. The intent is to be useful to Israeli policy makers and citizens by providing a view of the methodological issues at stake, to assist the Israeli government in the process of establishing its own set of well-being indicators relevant for Israel, and to provide the international comparison on a set of parameters across all OECD member countries. Clearly such a report cannot and should not be considered a substitute for performance measures developed in Israel and validated through the democratic process but rather as a useful complement.

Beyond any value to stakeholders, *Measuring and assessing well-being in Israel* is also intended to be useful to the OECD itself and to other member states. Although much about Israel is unique, there is also wide scope for other OECD nations to learn from Israel's experience. As a small, export-oriented, multi-ethnic democracy, Israel shares much with a range of other OECD countries.[3] Finally, the production of well-being country monographs supports the broader strategic goal of the organisation to encourage OECD members to evaluate policy in an explicitly multi-dimensional framework. By demonstrating that the well-being of Israeli citizens can be meaningfully measured, and that doing so highlights issues that might be missed if the focus remained silo-based, the report helps demonstrate the value added of applying a well-being approach to policy-making.

A framework for measuring well-being

To go beyond a list of disparate indicators, there needs to be a clear conceptual framework identifying what is meant by well-being and illustrating how well-being relates to other concepts. This is not straightforward. Providing a simple definition of well-being is challenging because the concept is inherently multi-dimensional and requires looking at many different aspects of people's lives.

Despite these difficulties, the core concept of well-being is relatively intuitive: well-being involves those aspects that most people around the world would agree are crucial to meeting human needs, as well as the ability to pursue one's goals, to thrive, and to feel satisfied with their life. While different people will place differing weights on the various elements of well-being, there is a remarkable level of agreement among experts and ordinary people across countries on the basic elements of a "good life" (Alkire, 2002).

Figure 1.1 below presents the OECD well-being framework. In this framework, current well-being is described in terms of eleven dimensions covering the aspects of both material living conditions (i.e. people's command over commodities) and quality of life that people value (i.e. peoples' "doings and beings" in Sen's terminology). These dimensions are intended to be conceptually distinct (i.e. they capture fundamentally different aspects of well-being), intrinsically valuable to people and, taken together, comprehensive (i.e. they capture all the important aspects of well-being). Conceptually, these dimensions of well-being can be seen as grounded in the capabilities that individuals have to transform resources into given ends (Sen, 1998).

In addition to the current well-being of individuals, the OECD well-being framework separately considers future well-being: this implies valuing the well-being of future generations as well as that of the current population, and is thus concerned with the sustainability of well-being through time. While future well-being outcomes are obviously not observable today, they are shaped by many of todays' actions, which impact today on those resources that will be required to ensure well-being tomorrow. These resources can be described in terms of the four capital stocks that underlie how different well-being outcomes are produced: economic, natural, human and social capital.

Beyond the detailed dimensions that define well-being today and in the future, the well-being framework outlined above shares a number of other characteristics. First, it is concerned with the well-being of *individuals and households* rather than on aggregate economic conditions; second, it focuses on well-being *outcomes* rather than programme outputs or inputs; third, it considers the *distribution of well-being* as well as its aggregate level; and fourth, it considers both *objective aspects of well-being* (i.e. those that can be observed by a third party) and those *subjective aspects* that can only be reported by the person concerned. Together, these four characteristic recognises the fact that aggregate economic conditions do not necessarily capture the experience of households, and that their outcomes may be imperfectly correlated with the resources devoted to achieving them. It also acknowledges that inequalities in outcomes matter, particularly when these

Figure 1.1. **The OECD Well-being Framework**

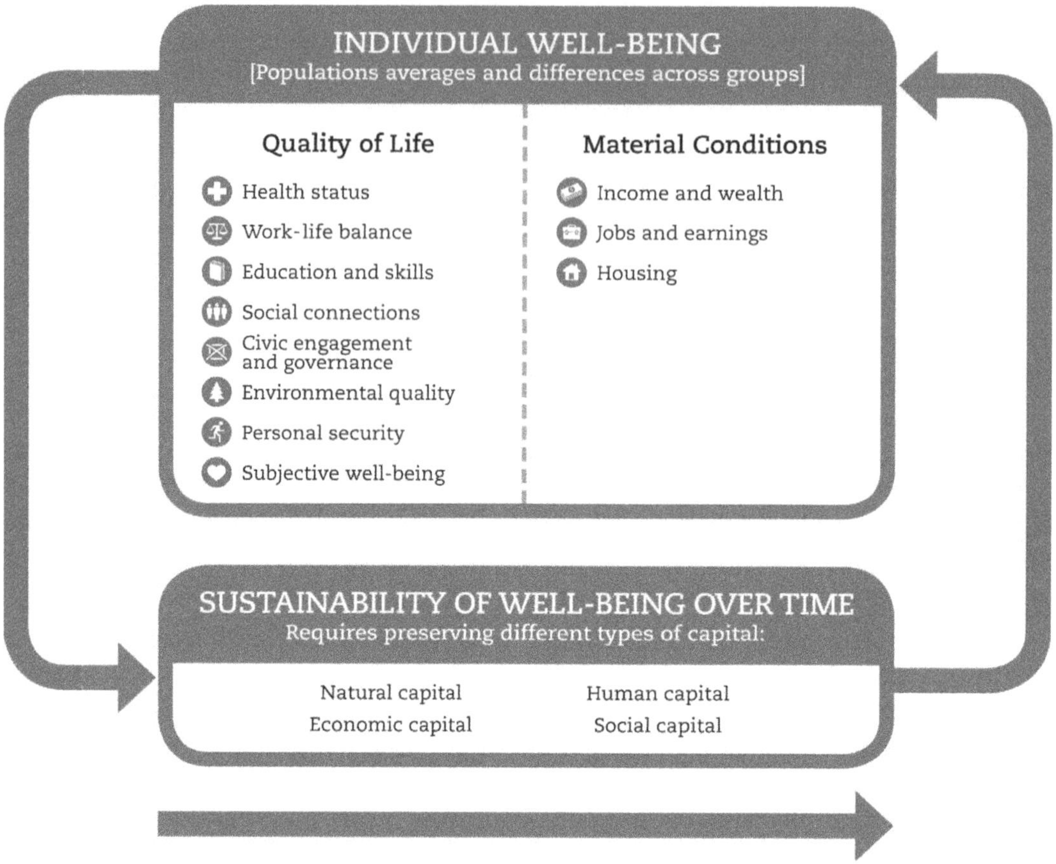

Source: OECD (2011), *How's Life?*, OECD Publishing, Paris.

inequalities are concentrated in specific population groups or span multiple outcome areas. Finally, both objective and subjective aspects of well-being are included in the framework because they both matter: while the objective conditions in which people live are essential to assess well-being, it is also important to assess people's own evaluations and feelings about their lives: through this aspect, people's voices became integral to any assessment of well-being.

A comparison of the Israeli and OECD approaches to measuring well-being

The *How's Life?* well-being framework applies to all OECD countries. There is now an extensive body of evidence based on cross-country surveys of measurement initiatives, analysis of the determinants of subjective well-being (Alkire, 2002, Boarini et al., 2012; Dolan, Peasgood, and White, 2008; Helliwell, 2013) and theoretical accounts of well-being (Nussbaum, 2013) to support the view that well-being is inherently multi-dimensional. However, while there is good evidence to support the relevance of the eleven well-being dimensions included in the *How's Life?* framework, it is important to test its validity and applicability to Israel.

Three recent efforts have investigated what well-being means to Israeli citizens. The Erech project (Erech is the Hebrew word for "value") was an NGO project to measure progress in Israel developed in the wake of the second OECD World Forum on Statistics, Knowledge, and Policy, held in Istanbul in 2009. To establish what was important to the quality of life of Israeli citizens, the Erech project held workshops involving over 400 people with a range of different backgrounds, occupations, and interests from across Israel (Daniel, 2012). Domains discussed during the workshops covered education, health, security, employment, the economy, family and community, the environment, policy, and consumption. Seven of the nine domains endorsed by the Erech project map directly onto the *How's Life?* framework.

A second major effort was the report of the Trajtenberg *Committee for Socio-Economic Change*, that was convened by the government after the street protests of 2011. Although the Committee's report made no effort to set out a comprehensive framework for evaluating well-being, it did identify the main broad goals of socio-economic policy. These included economic growth, quality of life (health, environmental quality), housing, employment, and inequality as issues of particular importance. Amongst other things, the Trajetenberg report recommended that the government should "define and periodically update social objectives together with traditional macroeconomic objectives, including quantitative targets". In particular, the report noted that:

> *"Important aspects of* ***quality of life*** *are not factored into it (GDP), including the extent of inequality, health conditions, environmental quality, and so on. Thus the canvas must be stretched when defining the parameters for measuring the economy's performance and the policy should be steered accordingly".*

The most important evidence for what constitutes well-being in Israel, however, is to be found in the process undertaken to develop the Israeli indicators of "well-being, resilience, and sustainability".

As noted earlier, the Israeli process started in December 2012 when the government passed a resolution to develop indicators of "well-being, resilience, and sustainability". A steering committee jointly chaired by the Director Generals of the Prime Minister's Office, the Ministry of Finance, the Ministry of Environmental Protection the Head of the National Economic Council, and the Chief Statistician of the Central Bureau of Statistics was established to direct the project.

In June 2013 the steering committee approved the recommendations to develop indicators for 9 domains: health, personal security, quality of employment, housing and infrastructure, education and skills, civic engagement and governance, personal and social welfare, environment, and material standard of living. In the government resolution approving the indicators in April 2015, two more domains were added: leisure, culture and community and information technology, bringing the total number of domains to 11. The steering committee also determined the methodological guidelines and principles for the process. A key element of this was an extensive programme of public consultation on the proposed indicators (see Box 1.1).

Box 1.1. **Consultation on indicators of well-being, resilience, and sustainability**

In December 2012, the Israeli government adopted a resolution to develop indicators on well-being, sustainability and resilience To that end, the government instructed the Director General of the Ministry of Environmental Protection, in consultation with the Director General of the Prime Minister's Office, the Director General of the Ministry of Finance, the Head of the National Economic Council and the Chief Statistician of the Central Bureau of Statistics, to prepare a proposal for developing such indicators. Within the framework of the decision, a three-part process was initiated in 2013:

Box 1.1. **Consultation on indicators of well-being, resilience, and sustainability** *(cont.)*

- A consultation forum was set up to formulate, among others, recommendations on domains, indicators, methodologies, and public participation.
- Inter-sectoral teams were appointed to identify sub-domains and indicators for each of the nine domains identified by the consultation forum.
- A public participation process was initiated to present the recommended domains, sub-domains and indicators to the public for review and feedback.

The first part of the indicator development process is described in the report "Well-being, Sustainability and Resilience Indicators for Israel", published by the Ministry of Environmental Protection in October 2013. The report describes the guiding principles for selecting complementary indicators for Israel; recommends nine well-being domains for measurement; discusses methodological issues; recommends a method for using the indicators within the framework of national strategic planning; discusses public participation processes; and outlines a road map for deciding on the indicators and collaborating with the OECD on the subject.

In the second part of the process, teams of experts from relevant government departments, NGOs, academia and private sector met to review the contribution of each domain to well-being and to identify the gaps that would need to be filled. These inter-sectoral teams made recommendations about the choice of indicators for each domain.

The inclusion of the public in the process of deciding on well-being indicators aimed to ensure that the system being developed would truly reflect the diversity of voices in Israel's society. This third stage of the process therefore involved online questionnaires to help finalize the indicators recommended by the inter-sectoral teams. These questionnaires invited the public to rank the recommended sub-domains by their importance to quality of life, both of the individual and of society as a whole. Furthermore, they invited the public to propose additional domains that may impact on quality of life and to indicate how the indicators should be used by government, business and society. Over 2000 participants filled these questionnaires. One of the major influence on the process was adding a tenth domain: "leisure, culture and community".

In addition to the online questionnaires, workshops that were designed to examine the suggested sub-domains and other aspects of well-being were held with audiences that have less accessibility to internet resources. In total, approximately 400 participants took part in workshops organised throughout Israel, and which were especially targeted at different groups within the Israeli population.

To choose indicators for each of the domain, the steering committee assembled 9 professional teams – one team for each domain. Each team was led by a senior government representative from the relevant ministry and composed of representatives from government, academia, NGOs, representative organizations, local municipalities and the Central Bureau of Statistics. The role of these teams was to flesh out the definition and scope of the relevant outcome domain, and to identify an ordered list of 12 indicators to measure the relevant aspects of the outcome domain. This list of indicators was submitted to the steering group, and 8 indicators from each domain were then selected for inclusion in the final indicator set. The final indicator set was reviewed and approved by the government in April 2015, and the government also set out a new task for the steering committee: to recommend indicators for two new domains of "leisure, culture and community" and "information technology". The steering committee has established teams of experts, in the same form as the previous domain teams, to examine and recommend indicators in each new domain.

In the process of choosing the indicators the teams consulted with the Statistics Directorate of the OECD, to learn from international experience and their methodological expertise. The OECD team reviewed and commented on the indicators suggested by the domain teams, and their input was part of the consideration of the steering committee's final selection of indicators.

The OECD and Israeli frameworks are quite similar. Both distinguish between current well-being and the sustainability of well-being over time. Well-being itself is conceived in very similar terms. Both the OECD and the Israeli indicators of well-being, resilience, and sustainability analyse well-being in terms of eleven distinct dimensions. With a small number of relatively minor differences the two sets of dimensions map onto each other very closely (Box 1.2). The main conceptual difference between the two frameworks lies in the focus on resilience in the Israeli government indicators, and the inclusion of a dimension related to "information technology" in the Israeli framework.

Box 1.2. **The OECD Well-being Framework and Israel's indicators of well-being, resilience, and sustainability**

The OECD *How's Life?* framework and the one underpinning Israel's indicators of well-being, resilience and sustainability are similar in scope. Both frameworks are outcome focused and recognize well-being as a multi-dimensional concept capturing those aspects of life that people value. Both the OECD and Israeli frameworks have 11 dimensions and these generally map onto each other very closely as is shown in Figure 1.2 below. Compared to the OECD framework, the Israeli framework combines the content of the OECD's "jobs and earnings" and "work and life balance" dimensions into a single dimension labelled "employment and work-leisure balance". Similarly, the Israeli "personal and social well-being" dimension covers roughly the same area as the OECD "social connections" and "subjective well-being" dimensions. The Israeli domain on "leisure, community, and culture" captures some of the elements of the OECD domains relating to "work and life balance" and "social connections". The only really significant difference in the dimensions of well-being measured is the Israeli domain relating to "information technology", which has no parallel in the OECD framework and would be considered a potential driver of well-being rather than a constituent element of it. Beyond this, the dimensions are essentially the same.

While the two frameworks are very similar at the level of outcome domains, there are some more significant differences in terms of the indicators used. Where *How's Life?* usually has 2 headline indicators for each domain, supplemented by a small group of secondary indicators to flesh out elements of that domain not captured well by the headline measures. The Israeli framework, however, uses 8 indicators for each domain in order to capture the multi-dimensional nature of each outcome area in greater detail. The process for selecting indicators was also different for the two well-being frameworks. While both frameworks use a set of criteria for indicator selection based on international good practice, the Israeli initiative had more freedom to focus on the optimal indicators. Further, the Israeli indicators were selected with a view to new data being collected by the CBS to fill key data gaps, while the OECD was constrained by a desire to use indicators for which international comparisons are possible and the need to use existing data sources. As a result, about half of the indicators approved by the government for the Israeli framework represent new measures, and a five year plan has been developed by the CBS to collect the relevant data. It is also worth noting that the Israeli indicators are grounded in extensive public consultation to supplement the technical judgment of experts, while the OECD indicators were chosen through a more narrowly technical process.

Box 1.2. **The OECD Well-being Framework and Israel's indicators of well-being, resilience, and sustainability** *(cont.)*

Figure 1.2. **A comparison of the OECD and Israeli Framework**

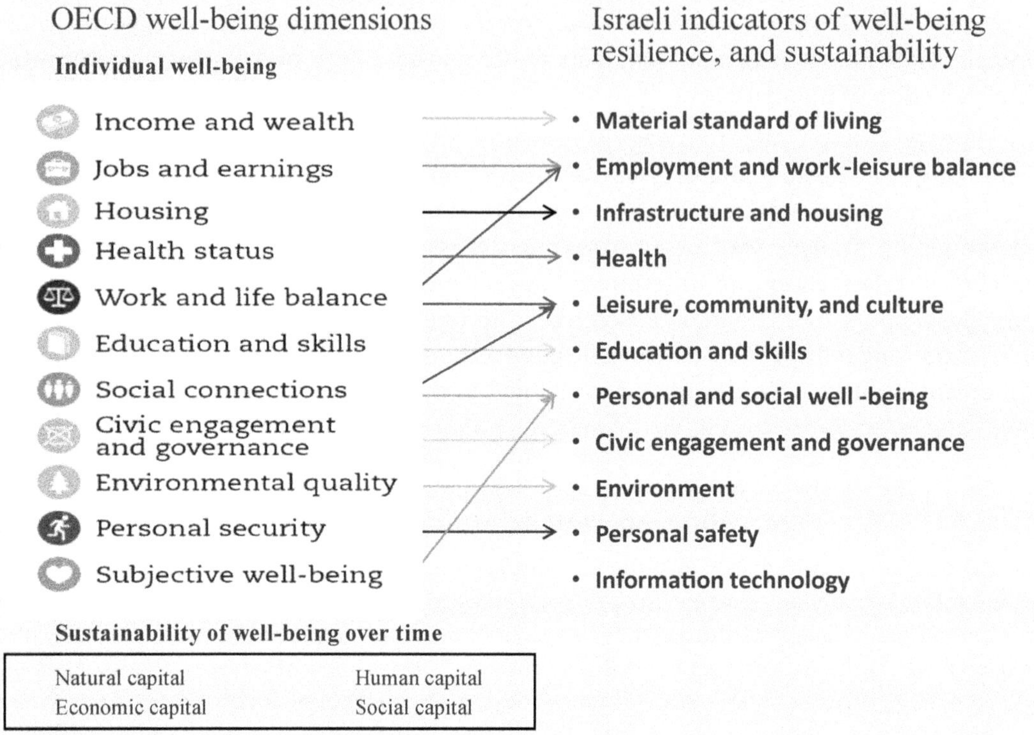

Selecting indicators

Identifying the broad dimensions of well-being is a necessary starting point for any measurement initiative, but is clearly not sufficient. In order to compare outcomes across countries and to track well-being over time it is necessary to identify specific measures for each of the relevant dimensions, and to assess their statistical qualities. A robust picture of well-being in Israel requires valid and reliable indicators. As part of the *Better Life Initiative*, the OECD developed a set of criteria for selecting indicators of well-being (Box 1.3). These criteria were developed originally for the *How's Life?* report in 2011, and are used in *Measuring and assessing well-being in Israel*. The main change in applying them to a country-specific context has been to drop the criterion about "ensuring maximum country coverage" as this is less important for a report focused primarily on one country. In addition, the weight put on some criteria in the case of *Measuring and assessing well-being in Israel* may differ from the one used in the comparative report *How's Life?* in placing more emphasis on the quality of data for Israel specifically. In particular, *Measuring and assessing well-being in Israel* endeavours to make the maximum use of Israeli data where possible, to look at the distribution of outcomes within Israeli society and over time. In addition, the criterion that data "are collected through a recurrent instrument" becomes much more important for a report focused on one specific country.

Box 1.3. The choice of indicators for *Measuring and assessing well-being in Israel*

Critical criteria for the selection of well-being indicators used in this report have been that indicators: i) capture well-being achievements at the individual or household level; ii) measure well-being outcomes; iii) allow disaggregation, so as to assess the well-being of different population groups; and iv) are drawn from a dataset containing other outcome measures as well, so that it is possible to gauge the joint distributions of achievements (e.g. whether a person with a disadvantage in one dimension also experiences poor outcomes in another). The indicators have also been chosen so as to fulfil standard statistical requirements, such as:

- ***Having face validity,*** i.e. the capacity to capture what is intended to be measured. Face validity is defined with respect to the target concept that one seeks to measure, i.e. substantive interpretations of the dimensions of well-being that matter to people's lives, according to a large body of evidence and practices.
- ***Focusing on summary outcomes,*** i.e. on *relatively* broad achievements (such as "good health status") that can be easily understood (e.g. displaying no ambiguity in interpretation, showing either good/bad performance when compared across countries or population groups, or progress/regress when looking at changes over time).
- ***Being amenable to change and sensitive to policy interventions,*** which is important from the perspective of improving the design of policies that bear on well-being and, ultimately, on people's lives.
- ***Being commonly used and accepted*** as well-being good indicators within the statistical and academic communities. This is more often the case for indicators relying on statistical instruments developed within the official statistical system but it can also be the case for indicators based on surveys conducted by other institutions.
- ***Ensuring comparability across countries.*** Comparability is ensured when concepts and definitions follow internationally agreed standards, and when the surveys/instruments from which data are collected are based on a harmonised questionnaire and similar implementation design. However, comparability can also be achieved by putting together broadly comparable instruments *ex post*; this latter approach is used by the OECD in a number of fields (e.g. *Health at a Glance*).
- ***Being collected through a recurrent instrument,*** which is important for monitoring changes in well-being over time.

Together, these criteria define the characteristics of an "ideal" set of indicators for monitoring well-being across countries and over time. In practice, finding indicators that meet all these criteria equally well is challenging. For this report, the criteria above have been mapped against the available information for Israel. This has led to the identification of the indicators shown in this report, most of which meet most of the criteria listed above. For instance, all indicators focus on summary outcomes that can be easily understood and interpreted. A majority of indicators have full face-validity, while a few others meet this criterion only partially. Most indicators can be influenced by policies and all of them change over time, although to different degrees. Finally, almost all the indicators rely on definitions that are comparable across countries.

While the current choice of indicators represents a good balance between the available information on Israel and international comparability, there is considerable scope for improvement. Both of the substantive chapters of this report (on current well-being and its sustainability respectively) identify gaps in the existing suite of well-being indicators available for Israel and make some suggestions as to priorities for improving the Israel's system of well-being statistics. A stocktaking of these gaps and of the steps that could be envisaged to address them is provided in the concluding chapter of this review.

Conclusion

This report is a response to the demand for better measures of well-being and sustainability in Israel, and is intended to complement Israel's national project to measure well-being, resilience, and sustainability. It is essentially an experimental methodology by the OECD, an additional step in the efforts to streamline well-being indicators into policy and public discussions. In particular, the main goals of the report are to:

- Draw on OECD expertise to place information on the level, distribution, and sustainability of well-being in Israel in an international context
- Highlight the dimensions of well-being where the country does well and those where it performs more poorly compared to other OECD countries.
- Bring OECD expertise to bear on the measurement of aspects of well-being and sustainability that have traditionally been hard to measure, such as subjective well-being, human and social capital, and multi-dimensional inequality.
- Illustrate ways in which evidence on well-being could be used to inform policy-making

Measuring and assessing well-being in Israel is organised in 5 chapters. The first chapter – this introduction – discusses the OECD well-being framework and compares it to that developed for Israel's national project to measure well-being, resilience, and sustainability. Chapter 2 focuses on the level and distribution of individual well-being outcomes: the first part of the chapter looks at how average outcomes in Israel compare to those in other countries, while the second part focuses on differences in outcomes among the main population groups in Israel. Chapter 3 looks at future well-being and its sustainability, providing a brief descriptive picture of what is known about the stocks of natural, human, economic, and social capital in Israel.

Both Chapters 2 and 3 of this report rely on a dashboard of indicators to describe current and future well-being in Israel. This captures the multi-dimensional nature of well-being, but it does not presume to present a single picture of whether Israel is doing "well" overall or not. The focus of Chapter 4 is to draw together information from the range of different measures used in the two previous chapters into a summary overview that is readily intelligible and that could inform policy makers in terms of identifying priorities for action and dealing with the inevitable trade-offs that will arise when using a multi-dimensional framework in policy-making. Finally, Chapter 5 discusses the statistical agenda ahead for Israel, identifying gaps in Israel's statistical system that will need to be filled to better measure well-being and sustainability. Because information only matters if it can be used, an appendix reviews the experience of other OECD countries in applying well-being indicators to their policy process.

Notes

1. *www.oecdbetterlifeindex.org.*
2. More information on these projects can be found at *www.oecd.org/progress.*
3. For example, Israel is a member of the Small Advanced Nations Initiative, an independent grouping comprising Denmark, Finland, Ireland, New Zealand and Singapore, established in 2012 in order to understand what insights small advanced countries could gain from looking at each other's experience.

References

Alkire, S. (2002), "Dimensions of Human Development", *World Development* 30 (2), pp 181-205.

Boarini, R. et al. (2012), "What Makes for a Better Life?: The Determinants of Subjective Well-Being in OECD Countries – Evidence from the Gallup World Poll", *OECD Statistics Working Papers*, No. 2012/03, OECD Publishing, Paris, *http://dx.doi.org/10.1787/5k9b9ltjm937-en.*

Daniel, R. (2012), *Project Erech*, *www.ecoeco.org.il/node/131*.

Dolan, P., T. Peasgood and White (2008), "Do we really know what makes us happy? A review of the economic literature on the factors associated with subjective well-being", *Journal of Economic Psychology*, Vol. 29(1), pp 94-122.

Helliwell, J. (2013), "World Happiness: Trends, Explanations and Distribution", *World Happiness Report 2013*, Sustainable Development Solutions Network, New York.

Ministry of Environmental Protection (2014), *Well-being Indicators for Israel*, Jerusalem, *www.sviva.gov.il/English/Indicators/Documents/Well-Being-Indicators-for-Israel-April2014.pdf*.

Nussbaum M. (2013), *Creating capabilities: the human development approach*, Cambridge, Massachusetts: The Belknap Press of Harvard University Press.

OECD (2013a), *Health at a Glance 2013: OECD Indicators*, OECD Publishing, Paris, *http://dx.doi.org/10.1787/health_glance-2013-en*.

OECD (2013b), *How's Life? 2013: Measuring Well-Being*, OECD Publishing, Paris, *http://dx.doi.org/10.1787/9789264201392-en*.

OECD (2013c), *OECD Economic Surveys: Austria 2013*, OECD Publishing, Paris, *http://dx.doi.org/10.1787/eco_surveys-aut-2013-en*.

OECD (2011), *How's Life?*, OECD Publishing, Paris, *http://dx.doi.org/10.1787/9789264121164-en*.

Sen, A. (1998), *Development as Freedom*, Oxford University Press 1999.

Trajtenburg, M. (2012), Trajtenburg Report: *Creating a More Just Israeli Society*, Israeli Prime Minister's Office, *www.bjpa.org/Publications/details.cfm?PublicationID=13862*.

UNECE (2014), *Conference of European Statisticians Recommendations on Measuring Sustainable Development*, United Nations, New York and Geneva, *www.unece.org/fileadmin/DAM/stats/publications/2013/CES_SD_web.pdf*.

UNECE, OECD, and Eurostat (2009), *Measuring Sustainable Development*, United Nations, Geneva, *www.unece.org/fileadmin/DAM/stats/publications/Measuring_sustainable_development.pdf*.

Chapter 2

Well-being in Israel today

This chapter describes well-being in Israel measured across the 11 dimensions of the OECD Well-being Framework. The first part of the chapter gives an overview of well-being in Israel, describing the general demographic and socio-economic situation of the country, and then presents key indicators to explore how Israel's performance compares with that of other OECD countries. The second part of the chapter then looks at the distribution of well-being within Israel, with a particular focus on differences between the three most significant population groups in the country: Jews (excluding Haredi Jews), Haredi (or Ultra-Orthodox) Jews, and Arabs.

Israel is a complex, and in many ways, unique country, given its history, geo-political situation and demographic make-up. Reflecting this complexity, aggregate well-being outcomes vary significantly depending on the measure selected, and the sub-group considered. The distribution of well-being outcomes within the country also varies significantly for the three population groups covered here, with Israeli Arabs and Haredi Jews tending to experience lower well-being than the majority non-Haredi Jewish population.

The statistical data for Israel are supplied by and under the responsibility of the relevant Israeli authorities. The use of such data by the OECD is without prejudice to the status of the Golan heights, East Jerusalem and Israeli settlements in the West Bank under the terms of international law.

Introduction

This chapter describes well-being in Israel measured across the 11 dimensions of the OECD Well-being Framework (see Chapter 1, Box 1.2). The headline indicators selected for *How's Life?* (OECD 2011a, 2013a, 2015a) provide the starting point for analysis in each dimension. As described in Chapter 1, these indicators were selected according to a number of criteria, with an emphasis on international comparability. As the aim of this report is to provide an in-depth picture of life for Israeli citizens, where relevant, the headline indicators are supplemented by additional indicators that shed more light on aspects of well-being in Israel. Thus, the indicators in this chapter have been selected not only for their international comparability but also for the quality of data and their applicability to Israeli life. Box 2.1 provides for a short explanation of the data sources used in this chapter and the reasoning behind their selection.

Box 2.1. **Data sources used in this chapter**

Comparing well-being across countries is challenging. Official data are not yet available for all indicators included in this chapter, but efforts have been made to use the most appropriate data source for each measure.

International comparisons

For the first part of the chapter, focusing on the performance of Israel in comparison with other OECD countries, the international comparability of the data is an important concern, and similar data sources have been used to those used in *How's Life?* (OECD 2011a, 2013a, 2015a). In most cases, these data come from national statistical offices and other official sources in OECD countries, and are collected together in a harmonised way in various OECD databases, which are available at OECD Statistical Portal at *http://stats.oecd.org/*.

However, as the *How's Life?* framework covers many areas of well-being that are not yet measured in a comprehensive or comparable manner by official statistics, several indicators are presented using Gallup World Poll data, particularly those referring to subjective, or self-reported, assessments of dimensions of well-being. While subjective measurement has been widely recognised in recent years as a necessary complement to the use of more established, objective measures, the availability of good data from official sources is uneven. The Gallup World Poll has been selected as the best-available source of internationally comparable data in the absence of official statistics for several indicators. Gallup data tends to have a smaller sample size than most official surveys (with a sample of around 1 000 people per country and per year) but the quality of the data is deemed to be of a sufficient standard to reliably indicate real differences in well-being outcomes between countries. Wherever possible, data were chosen to cover all 34 OECD countries. However, for two measures of social connections, data from the European Social Survey have been used (which only covers 22 OECD countries), as this source provides interesting measures that are not available in the Gallup World Poll. For a small selection of indicators, specialist data from external sources that have been judged to be of sufficient quality, have

Box 2.1. **Data sources used in this chapter** *(cont.)*

also been used, such as data from the International Institute for Democracy and Electoral Assistance (IDEA) on voting participation rates.

Israeli national statistical sources

Israel has a well-developed official statistical system. This includes an annual General Social Survey (GSS) which covers many of the *How's Life?* Indicators. GSS data are not used for international comparisons due to differences in methodology between the GSS and other sources (e.g. Gallup). However, for the second part of the chapter that focuses on distribution of well-being outcomes between different population groups, a preference is given to data from the Central Bureau of Statistics (CBS) and other Israeli institutions. In most cases, data were provided to the OECD by the Israeli CBS and the National Insurance Institute (for data on poverty rates in Israel).

The indicators are intended to be relevant to policies while not directly measuring them; so, they describe a desirable outcome rather than the inputs and outputs of government policy. It is also important to emphasise that the indicators used in the report (and in this chapter in particular) present a complementary picture to that provided by Israel's own indicators of well-being, resilience and sustainability.

The first part of the chapter gives an overview of well-being in Israel, describing the general demographic and socio-economic situation of the country, and then presenting key indicators to explore how Israel's performance compares with that of other OECD countries in the 11 dimensions of current well-being from the *How's Life?* framework: income and wealth, jobs and earnings, housing, education, health, work and life balance, social connections, civic engagement and governance, environmental quality, personal security, and subjective well-being.

The second part of the chapter then looks at the distribution of well-being within Israel, with a particular focus on differences between the three most significant population groups in the country: Jews (excluding Ultra-Orthodox Jews), Ultra-Orthodox Jews, and Arabs.

Overview

Setting the scene: Israel today

Israel is a complex country, with a history, geo-political situation and demographic make-up which are in many ways very different from other OECD countries. Historically, immigration has played an important role in Israeli society, accounting for a large share of population growth in the country since its establishment in 1948. While Israel remains a relatively small nation – with a population of 8.1 million in 2014 (CBS, 2014) – it is also very diverse. In 2014, 75% of Israelis were Jews and 20.7% were Arabs, with the remaining 4.3% coming from other population groups (CBS, 2014). Within the Jewish and Arab populations, there is also significant cultural and religious diversity. According to the 2013 Israeli General Social Survey, 43.4% of Israeli Jews identify themselves as non-religious or secular, while a substantial minority (8.9%) identify as "Haredim" or Ultra-Orthodox. While the majority of Israeli Arabs are Muslim, the Arab population also includes Christian and Druze sub-groups. A significant minority of Muslim Arabs in Israel are Bedouin, mostly living in the region of the Negev in the South of Israel.[1]

Israel has by far the highest fertility rate in the OECD, with an average of 3 children per woman: this is almost double the OECD average of 1.7 children per woman (OECD, 2014b), giving Israel a much younger population than is typically the case for other OECD countries. In 2014, over one-third of the population (36%) was under 20 years of age in Israel, compared to an OECD average of 24%, according to the OECD Demography and Population Statistics database. Fertility rates amongst Arabs and the Haredim are particularly high, and it is large family sizes in these sub-groups that are likely to shape the composition of Israel's population in the future. Based on the Central Bureau of Statistics' projections, the Arab population will increase slightly from 20% to 23% of the population over the next 25 years before stabilising. The Haredi population is projected to increase from roughly 9% of the population now, to 17% in 2034 and 27% of the population by 2059 (Figure 2.1).

Figure 2.1. **Projections of population distribution for Israel, 2009-59**

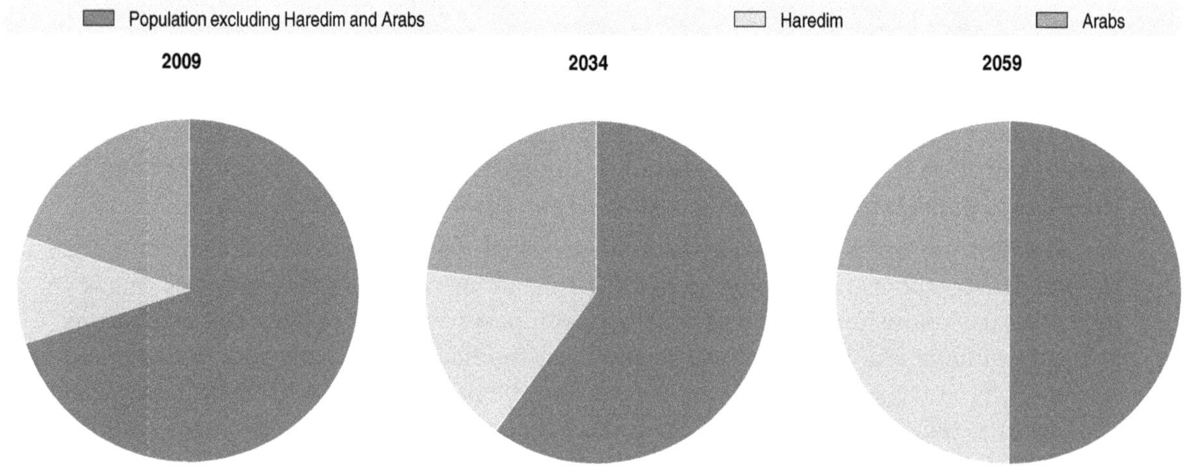

Source: Central Bureau of Statistics (CBS) (2012).

StatLink http://dx.doi.org/10.1787/888933293218

Israel is a middle-income country, with a GDP per capita of 33 462 USD in 2014 (at current purchasing power parity prices), compared to an OECD average of 38 937 USD. Like a number of other OECD countries, Israel undertook substantial economic reforms from the late 1980s onwards and emerged as an open, trade-oriented economy. Often characterised as the "start-up nation", Israel has a vibrant high-tech sector. Geo-political and strategic concerns have a significant impact on Israeli society, and are responsible for a number of ways in which it differs from other OECD countries. Most notably, Israel has a large defence force that absorbs a large share of GDP (almost 6% in 2013, compared to around 1.5% across OECD countries as a whole, OECD 2016). Most of the Jewish population, and some of the male Druze and Bedouin population, spends 2 or 3 years (women and men respectively) in compulsory military service after completing school. Civilian public welfare expenditure is low by international comparison, in part due to high levels of military defence expenditure.

Well-being at a glance

The OECD framework has been developed to emphasise the multidimensionality of well-being, and as such avoids providing a single summary measure. However, when looking across headline indicators for all the 11 dimensions of current well-being, Israel provides an interesting picture. Whereas some countries such as Australia, Denmark, and Canada perform fairly consistently above the OECD average across dimensions, and other countries such as Mexico and Turkey tend to fall below the average, the picture in Israel is more complex.

Figure 2.2 gives an overview of Israel's performance on selected well-being measures in comparison to the OECD average. The indicators chosen are similar to the headline indicators in the *How's Life?* framework (OECD 2011a, 2013a, 2015a). To measure Israel's situation relative to the OECD average, the difference between Israel's outcomes and the OECD average is reported in terms of standard deviations of the outcome measure in question and normalised so that an improvement in the score always indicates a better outcome (e.g. an improvement in the score show a decrease in deaths by assault but an increase in life expectancy).

Figure 2.2. **Selected well-being outcomes in Israel compared to the OECD average**

Performance in selected indicators, 2014 or latest year available.

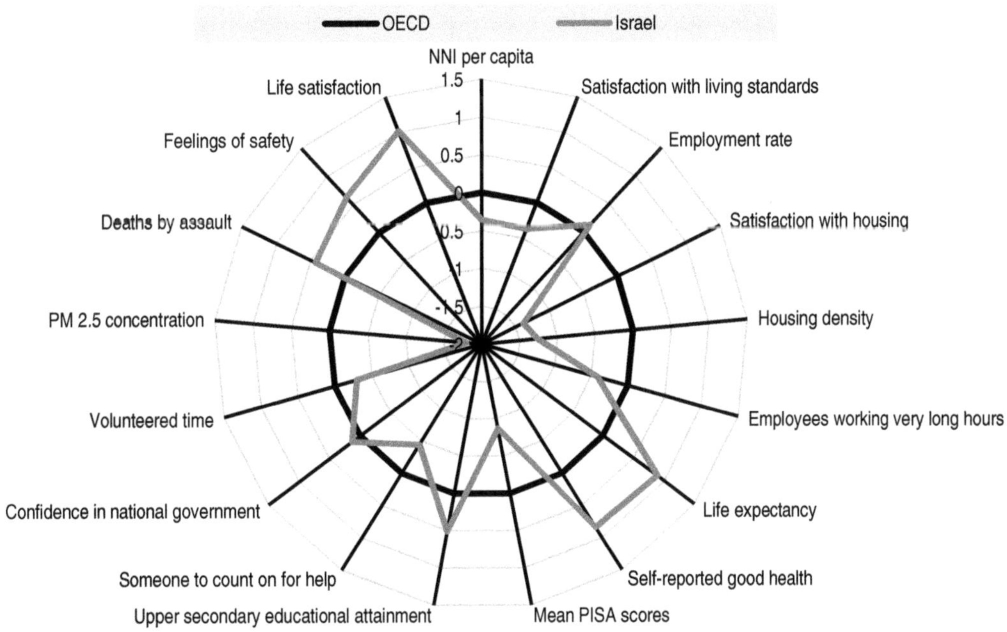

Note: Well-being outcomes for Israel are expressed as a ratio of OECD average outcomes, measured in standard deviations. All indicators have been normalised so that a higher score implies a better outcome. The circular black line indicates the OECD average, while the blue line indicates Israel's performance. Movement away from the centre of the circle indicates an improvement in outcomes. Outcomes in Israel are above the OECD average when the blue line lies outside the black circle.

Source: Gallup World Poll; "Labour Force Statistics", *OECD Employment and Labour Market Statistics Database, http://dx.doi.org/10.1787/lfs-lfs-data-en; OECD Health Database, http://dx.doi.org/10.1787/health-data-en; OECD PISA Database, http://dx.doi.org/10.1787/19963777;* "Regional Well-being statistics", *OECD Regional Statistics Database, http://dx.doi.org/10.1787/region-data-en.*

StatLink http://dx.doi.org/10.1787/888933293226

Israel's performance is well above the OECD average in the areas of health status (measured by life expectancy at birth and by the share of people saying they are in good health), personal safety (measured by the rate of deaths by assault as well as the share of people saying they feel safe walking alone in their area at night) and life satisfaction. In other dimensions, the performance is mixed or below-average. For example, in the area of education, Israel performs well above the OECD average in terms of upper secondary educational attainment, but performs almost an entire standard deviation unit below the OECD average in terms of learning outcomes for 15-years old students (as measured by the OECD Programme for International Student Assessment, PISA).

While the employment rate in Israel is slightly above the OECD average, both net national income per capita and satisfaction with living standards are slightly below average, and an above-average share of the population work very long hours (over 50 hours per week), leaving comparatively less time for leisure and family. The share of the Israeli population who spend time volunteering, or who say they have someone to count on for help – measures of social connectedness – are slightly lower than OECD average, but confidence in the national government is slightly above average. Finally, Israel performs significantly below the OECD average in two areas: housing (measured by the share of people saying they are satisfied with the availability of good, affordable housing, and by housing density, i.e. the number of people per room) and the environment (measured by $PM_{2.5}$ concentration in the air).

Headline indicators can only provide a snapshot of the situation within the country, and performance in different dimensions can often vary depending on the indicators selected. While the *How's Life?* indicators have been selected as the best-available internationally-comparable measures of key aspects of well-being, it is necessary to look at each dimension in more detail in order to better understand the situation in a country. The remainder of this section looks at each dimension of the OECD *How's Life?* framework in turn, comparing performance in Israel with other OECD countries.

Income and wealth

Household income and wealth are essential components of individual well-being. The ability to command economic resources allows people to satisfy basic needs and to pursue many other goals that they deem important to their lives. Economic resources enhance people's freedom to choose the lives that they want to live, and protect them against economic and personal risks.

Household living standards within a country are to a great extent dependent on the state of the economy. Israel weathered the economic crisis much better than other OECD countries and the country's performance on macro-economic indicators has been relatively strong in recent years (OECD, 2013b). In particular, Israel has developed exceptionally high levels of entrepreneurship and innovation. It has the second-highest level of business expenditure on research and development in the OECD (OECD 2014a), and a 2012 report on start-up ecosystems ranked Tel Aviv as the second-largest source of innovation after Silicon Valley in terms of the value of its start-ups (Startup Genome, 2012). These are impressive achievements in the face of the challenges Israel faces as a small, relatively young country, with few natural resources and an ongoing geopolitical conflict. In fact, Israel's high levels of immigration and compulsory military service for much of the population may help to explain the rise of the so-called "start-up nation" by contributing to a supply of skills and knowledge that transfer readily to the business sector (Senor and Singer, 2011).

Despite strong economic growth in recent years, net national income per capita remains below OECD average and places Israel in the bottom third of countries (Figure 2.3.a). In the decade 2004-14, net national income per capita grew from 20 327 USD to 27 577 USD in Israel, a rate of increase which is exactly in line with the OECD average of 36% during this period. The picture for household net financial wealth per capita in Israel

Figure 2.3. **Levels of income and wealth**

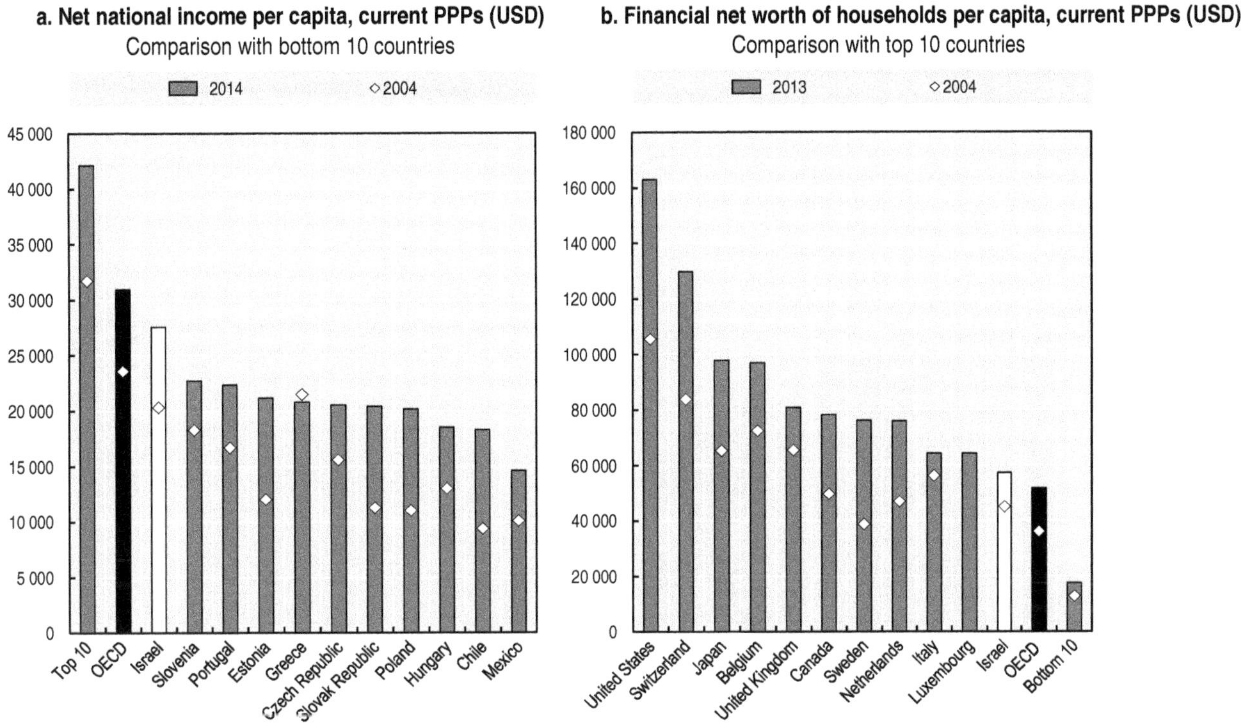

Note: Net national income is defined as gross domestic product (GDP) plus net receipt of wages, salaries and property income from abroad, minus the depreciation of fixed capital assets. Household net financial wealth is defined as the financial net worth of households and non-profit institutions serving households per capita. Both measures are expressed in US dollars at current purchasing power parities (PPPs).
Source: OECD National Accounts Database, http://dx.doi.org/10.1787/na-data-en.

StatLink http://dx.doi.org/10.1787/888933293238

is quite different, however, with Israel ranking in the top third of OECD countries and above the OECD average, with an average value of household financial net worth per capita of 57 330 USD (in current purchasing power parities, PPPs) in 2013. Indeed, Israel is the OECD country that has experienced the largest increase in this measure since 1995 (OECD, 2013a), with the bulk of household wealth being held in pension funds.

Poverty rates and income inequality in Israel are amongst the highest in the OECD (see later in this chapter) and in recent years there has been an increasing perception amongst many Israelis, particularly amongst the young middle class, that living standards are stagnating or even falling (Rosenhek and Shalev, 2013). In 2011, widespread social protests brought hundreds of thousands of Israelis to the streets, in part as a result of perceived rising costs of living.

In 2014, 67% of Israelis reported that they were satisfied with their living standards, a share which is 5 percentage-points below the OECD average of 72% and that puts Israel in the bottom third of OECD countries on this measure (Figure 2.4a). The level of satisfaction with living standards in Israel has remained fairly stable in the period 2006-14, dropping by 3 percentage points overall from 70% in 2006 (Figure 2.4b). The OECD average rate has also remained fairly stable in this period, although the situation in individual countries looks very different depending on economic circumstances, with satisfaction dropping by 31 percentage points in Greece, 19 percentage points in Spain, and increasing by 8 percentage points in Germany. While Israel has not experienced the clear decline in satisfaction with

Figure 2.4. **Satisfaction with living standards**

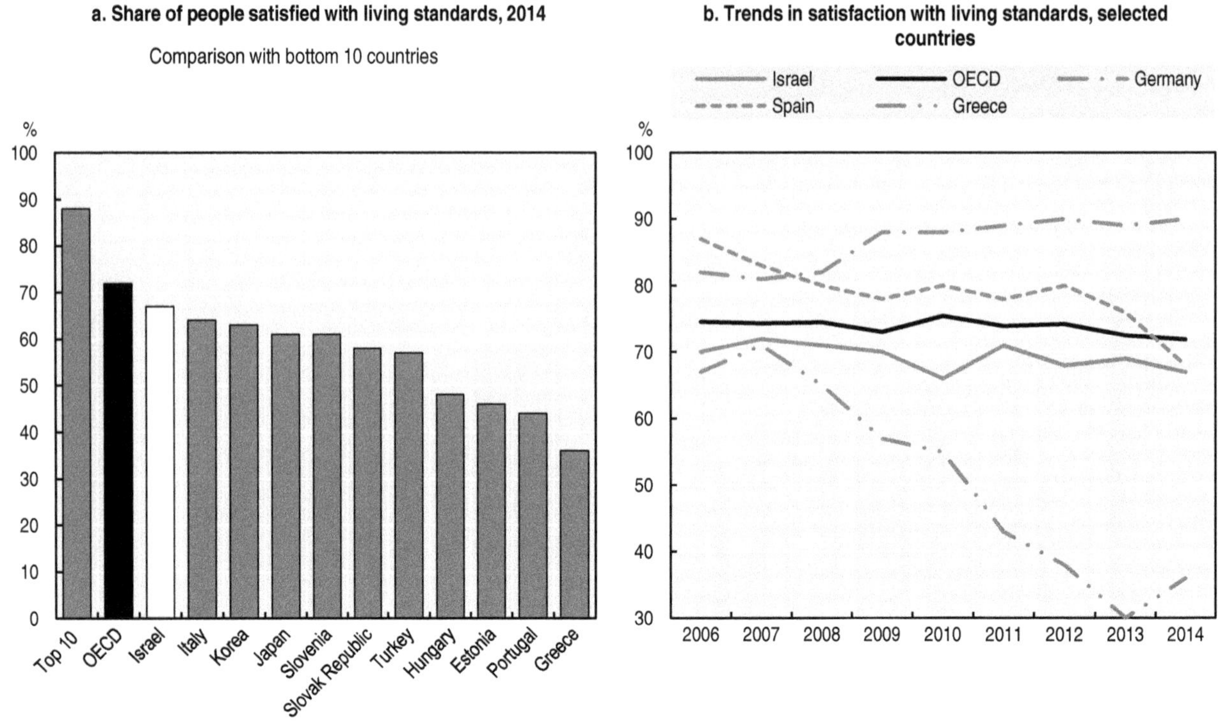

Note: Share of people responding "yes" to the question: "Are you satisfied or dissatisfied with your standard of living, all the things you can buy and do?".

Source: Gallup World Poll.

StatLink http://dx.doi.org/10.1787/888933293247

living standards observed in some countries most affected by the crisis, neither has it seen a significant increase or convergence with the OECD average.

Overall, the economic situation of Israelis looks mixed, with incomes just below the OECD average, high levels of wealth (as measured by household financial net worth), and constant levels of satisfaction with living standards compared to the OECD average. Furthermore, while the economy performs well on key macro-economic indicators such as GDP growth, the affluence generated by certain sectors of the economy has not benefitted all, and poverty and inequality levels are high, as will be discussed in the second part of this chapter.

Jobs and Earnings

Having a job that matches one's own aspirations and skills and that provides adequate earnings is a fundamental component of workers' well-being. Generally, being unemployed has a large negative effect on both physical and mental health as well as on people's subjective well-being, with very little adaptation as the length of the unemployment spell increases. Unemployment also has a negative impact on other members of a household, not just the unemployed person.

Labour force participation has been rising steadily in Israel and the employment rate of 68% is today 2 percentage-points above the OECD average (Figure 2.5a). Indeed, Israel has seen one of the largest increases in employment in the period 2009-14, with the employment rate raising by 3.5 percentage-points, compared to 0.6 percentage-points on

Figure 2.5. **Selected measures of jobs and earnings**

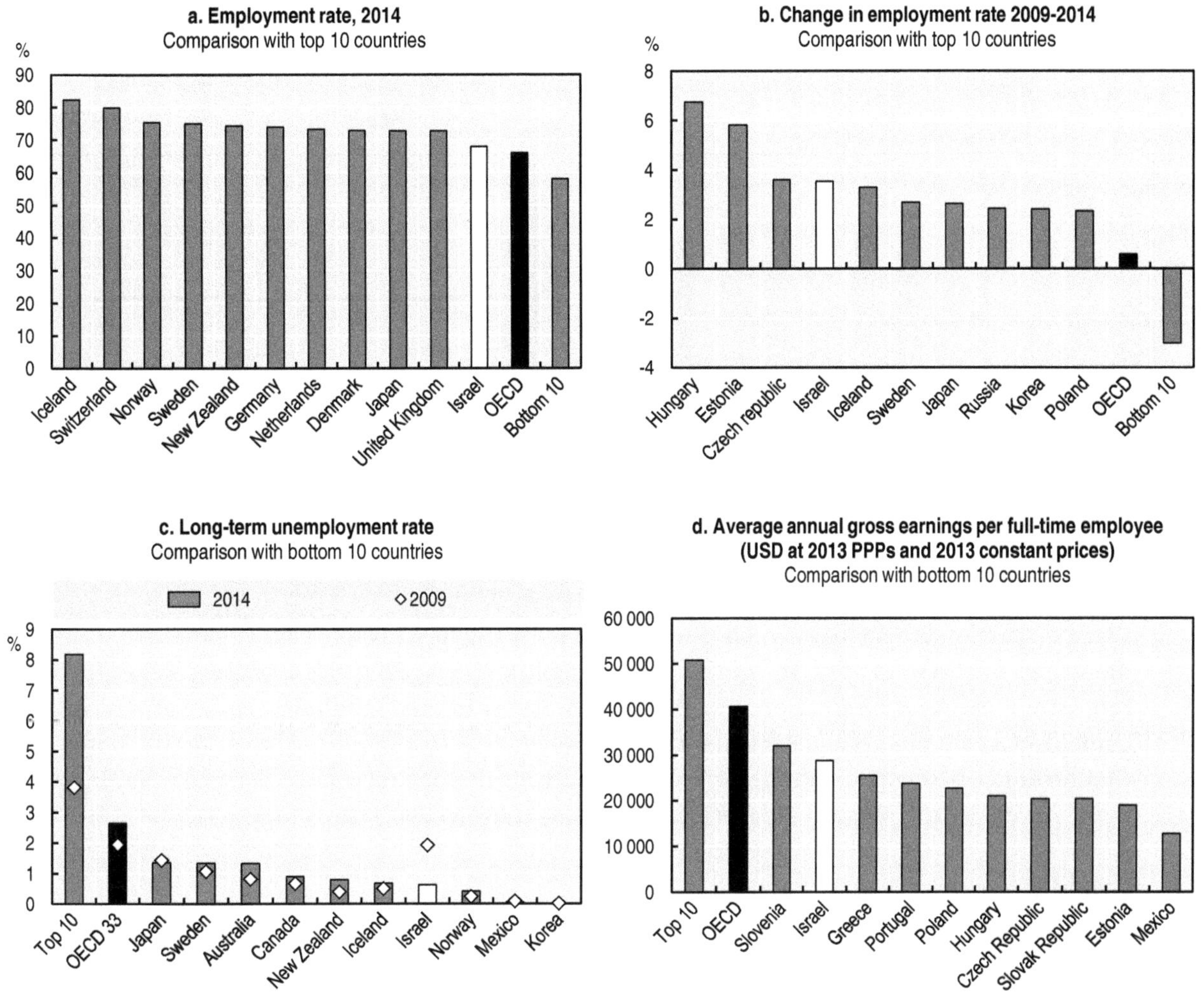

Note: OECD averages are population-weighted.

Source: "Labour Force Statistics", *OECD Employment and Labour Market Statistics Database*, *http://dx.doi.org/10.1787/lfs-lfs-data-en*; for earnings, OECD calculations combining data from the *OECD Earnings Distribution Database* and *OECD Average Annual Earnings per Full-time and Full-year Equivalent Dependent Employee Database*.

StatLink http://dx.doi.org/10.1787/888933293252

average in the OECD (Figure 2.5b). Unemployment, at around 6.2% of the labour force in 2014, was lower than the OECD average of 7.3%, and the long-term unemployment rate (the share of the labour force who have been unemployed for at least one year) is the 4th-lowest in the OECD, at only 0.6% compared to an OECD average of 2.6% (Figure 2.5c). However, gross annual earnings of full-time employees are well below the OECD average, at 28 817 USD in 2013 (as measured in 2013 PPPs at constant prices) compared to 40 640 USD on average in the OECD (Figure 2.5d).

While unemployment is relatively low, the Israeli labour force is characterised by a high share of non-standard work (i.e. temporary, part-time and self-employed work taken together), which tends to be associated with low-paying jobs and low levels of job security (OECD 2013c). Israel has one of the highest minimum wages in the OECD but there are some issues with enforcement (OECD, 2013c). Indeed, in 2012, Israel had the fourth-highest share of low-wage workers in the OECD, after the United States, Korea and Estonia (Figure 2.6.a).

Figure 2.6. **Israel has many low-income workers and a high level of wage inequality**

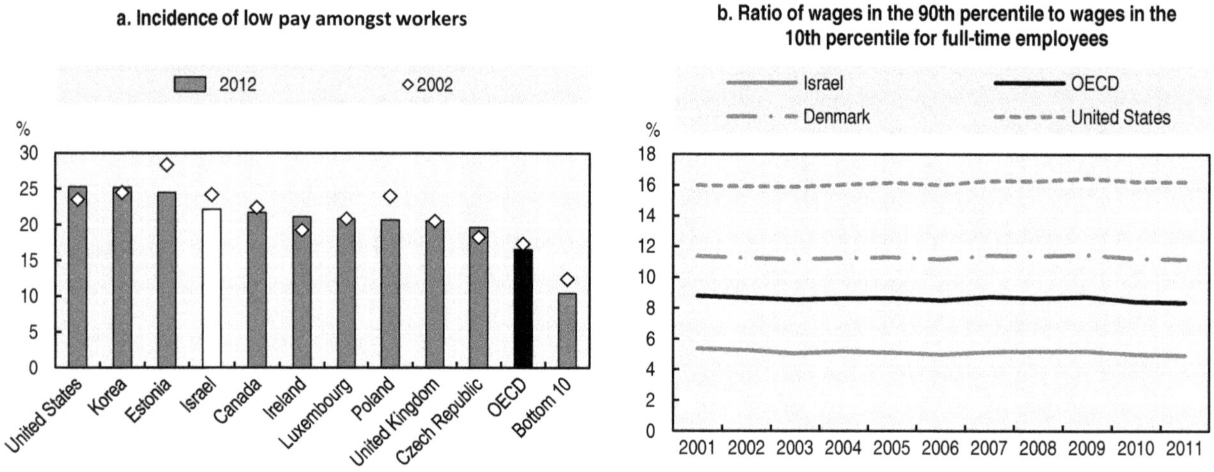

Note: Incidence of low pay is defined as the share of full-time workers with earnings less than two-thirds of gross median earnings of all full-time workers.
Source: *OECD Database on Earnings Distribution.*

StatLink http://dx.doi.org/10.1787/888933293262

Wage dispersion is also high, and Israel had one of the highest levels of wage inequality (as measured by the ratio of wages in the 90th percentile to wages in the 10th percentile) for full-time employees, second only to the United States in 2011, the latest year for which comparable data are available (Figure 2.6.b). However, it is also important to note that both the incidence of low pay and the 90th to 10th percentile wage ratio have both been falling in recent years, and showed an overall downwards trend in 2002-12.

Housing

Access to decent housing is a fundamental component of the material conditions that make up well-being. Beyond providing shelter and safety, home ownership is also the primary means of accumulating wealth for most families, thereby contributing to long-term economic security. For households who cannot afford or choose not to buy their residence, access to affordable rental property or public housing is a pre-condition for achieving an adequate standard of living.

Housing has become an issue of particular significance within Israel in recent years, and the lack of affordable housing is often cited as a trigger for the 2011 social protests (Bank of Israel, 2012; Shalev, 2012). Israel has one of the lowest shares of people saying that they are satisfied with the availability of good, affordable housing in the city or area where they live, according to Gallup World Poll data. In 2014, only 36% of people reported being satisfied with the availability of housing, the third-lowest share after Slovenia and Poland in the OECD, and below the OECD average of 52% (Figure 2.7.a). While levels of satisfaction with the availability of good, affordable housing have remained fairly stable across the OECD area, on average, Israel experienced a downwards trend since 2009, with a particularly large drop to only 28% in 2011, the year of the social protests (Figure 2.7.b).

Housing prices have risen sharply in Israel in recent years in comparison with the OECD average, which is likely to be a major driver of these low levels in satisfaction. For many years in the early 2000s, Israeli house prices remained fairly stable, but beginning in 2008 there was a rapid rise, with the Israeli consumer price index for housing increasing at

Figure 2.7. **Satisfaction with housing**

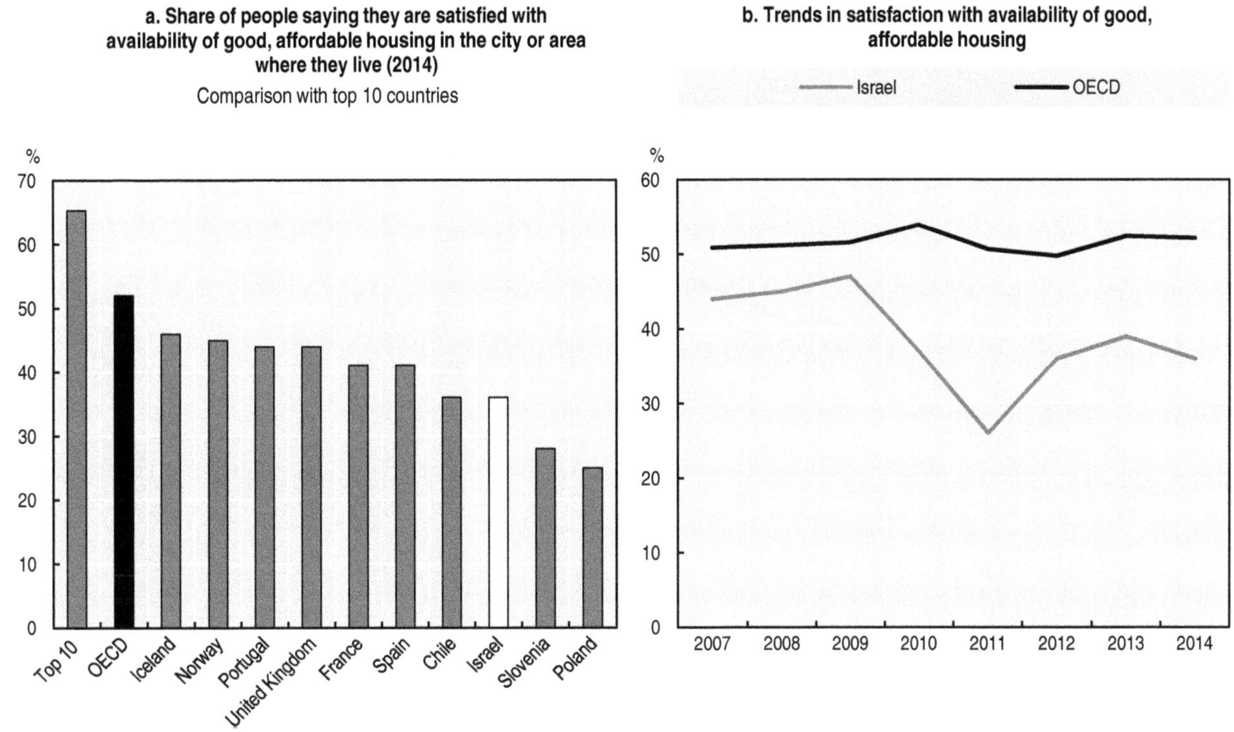

Note: Share of people responding "yes" to the question: "In the city or area where you live, are you satisfied or dissatisfied with the availability of good, affordable housing?". Data for Iceland are from 2013.
Source: Gallup World Poll.

StatLink http://dx.doi.org/10.1787/888933293272

a much more rapid rate than the OECD average (Figure 2.8.a). According to the Demographia Housing Affordability Survey, which estimates the number of years of work needed to buy a house in different countries, Israel is one of the most expensive countries in the world where to purchase a home (Figure 2.8.b), requiring 7.7 years of median annual income to buy a median-priced apartment in 2009. The survey classifies levels above 5.1 years of work as "severely unaffordable", and Israel is placed well above other OECD countries known for high house prices such as Australia, New Zealand and the United Kingdom. In fact, according to data from the same survey (Ben-David, 2012), the cost of housing relative to income in Israel is higher than in England's 33 metropolitan areas (including London) and more expensive than in 174 of America's 175 metropolitan areas (including New York City).

Rental prices have also increased in Israel in recent years, although at a slower rate than house prices (Gruber, 2014). Between 2008 and 2012, the share of rental expenditure out of household income rose from 20% to 23% in Israel (Figure 2.11.a). The share of rental expenditure is much higher for people in the lower income quintiles, increasing from 25% to 31% in the 4 years to 2012 for the bottom quintile (Figure 2.9.a). In the European Union, households that spend more than 40% of their disposable income on housing costs are considered to suffer from housing cost overburden. According to this definition, the rates of housing cost overburden for households renting their home is higher in Israel that in most EU countries (Figure 2.9.b). In 2012, 37.5% of households renting their home on the open market suffered from housing cost overburden, compared with only 26.5% in the Eurozone.

Figure 2.8. **Housing costs**

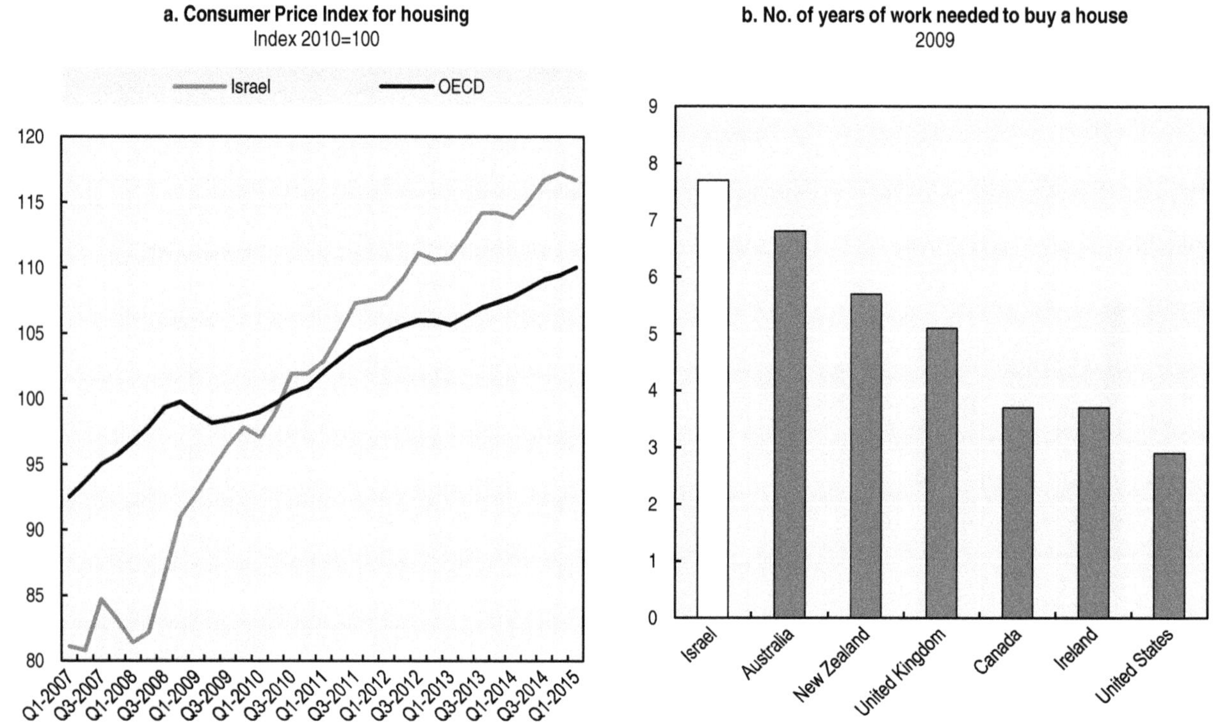

Note: The number of years of work needed to buy a house is calculated on the basis of the years of median annual income to buy a median-priced apartment.

Source: OECD Consumer Price Database, http://dx.doi.org/10.1787/data-00047-en; Ben-David (2012), based on data from the Demographia International Housing Affordability Survey.

StatLink http://dx.doi.org/10.1787/888933293288

Government assistance, through the provision of public housing or rental subsidies, is a means to increase housing affordability amongst those without the means to purchase a home or who spend a large share of their income on rents. While Israel is in the middle of OECD rankings in terms of the share of people receiving rental assistance (Andrews et al., 2011), it only spent 0.16% of GDP on such assistance, compared to an average of 0.28% of GDP in EU countries (Bank of Israel, 2014). Furthermore, the stock of public housing available in Israel has been reduced in recent decades; in 2009, dwellings in public housing made up only 4% of total dwellings, compared to 8% on average in the European Union (Bank of Israel, 2014).

One of the most important aspects of adequate housing is that the dwelling provides sufficient space for all household members. Housing density is high in Israel, with an average of only 1.16 rooms per person in Israel, compared to an OECD average of 1.7 rooms (Figure 2.10). The large family size in Israel, especially amongst Arab and Haredi households, is likely to be the main driver of the high housing density seen in the country. Housing density rates differ significantly between these population groups and non-Haredi Jews, as described later in this chapter (Figure 2.36).

Aside from issues of housing affordability, the quality of housing matters for people's well-being. Internationally comparable data on housing quality, covering issues such as adequacy of construction materials or amenities (e.g. water and room heating, the presence/absence of separate spaces for food preparation and personal hygiene) are not readily available. The Israeli General Social Survey does include some questions on

Figure 2.9. **Rental costs**

a. Share of rental expenditure out of household income in Israel, by income quintile

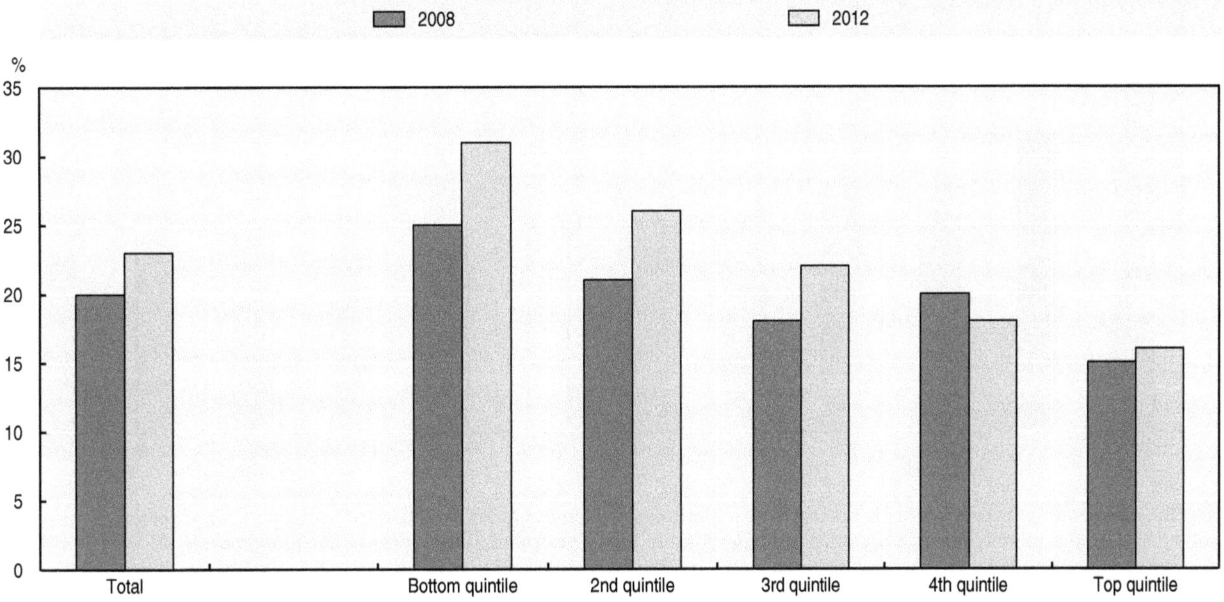

b. Share of households renting a home in the open market whose housing expenditures exceed 40% of their disposable income

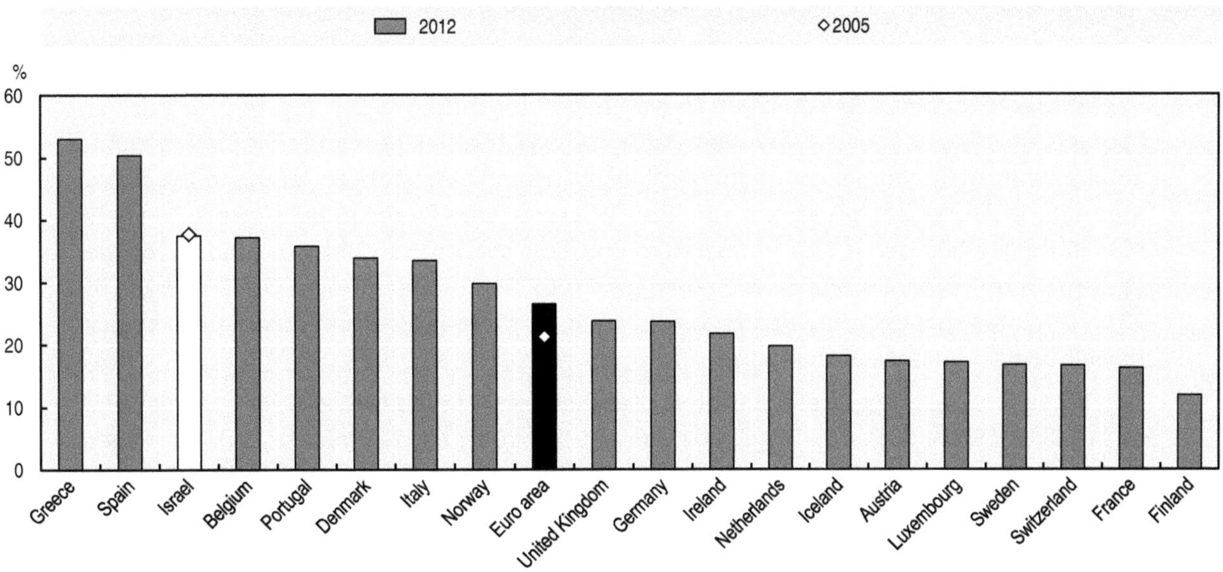

Notes: a) Rental expenditure is calculated as median rent expenditure out of net cash income among renting households, for households where head of household is aged over 25; b) Housing expenditures include utilities (electricity, water, gas and heating), current maintenance expenses, home insurance, municipal tax and building committee payments. Household disposable income (adjusted to the Eurostat definition) is defined as net household monetary income plus imputed income from employer's vehicle minus current transfers to other households (in Israel and abroad).

Source: Gruber (2014) based on CBS Household Expenditure Survey data and Eurostat data.

StatLink http://dx.doi.org/10.1787/888933293298

satisfaction with different aspects of housing, but these are unfortunately not comparable with measures existing elsewhere. A discussion of housing quality in Israel using measures from the Israeli General Social Survey is presented in the second part of this chapter on inequalities and distribution of well-being outcomes.

Figure 2.10. **Average number of rooms per person, 2013 or latest available year**
Comparison with bottom 10 countries

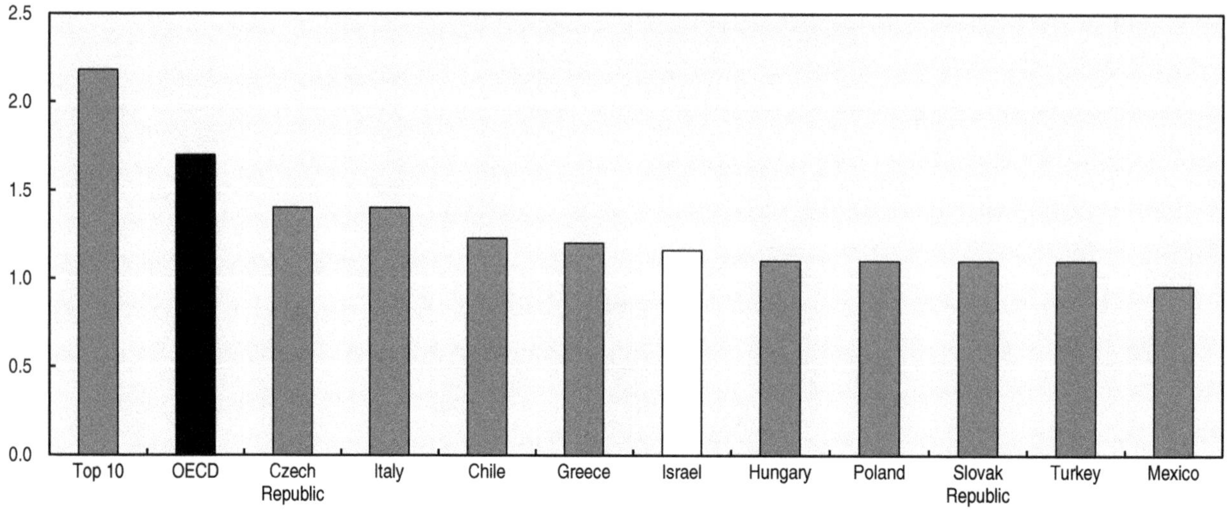

Note: The number of rooms per person is measured as the number of rooms in a dwelling, divided by the number of persons living in the dwelling. It excludes rooms such as a kitchenette, scullery/utility room, bathroom, toilet, garage, consulting rooms, office or shop. OECD estimates for Israel and Chile are based on national data. The latest available year is 2012 for Israel; 2011 for Turkey; 2010 for Mexico; and 2002 for Chile. The OECD average is population-weighted.
Source: European Union Statistics on Income and Living Conditions (EU-SILC) for EU countries; INE Censo 2002 for Chile; Israeli Household Expenditure Survey for Israel; INEGI Censo de Población y Vivienda 2010 for Mexico; Population and Housing Census for Turkey.

StatLink http://dx.doi.org/10.1787/888933293307

Education

Access to high-quality education is essential for individual well-being, both as a driver of other outcomes such as employment status, income, health status and civic participation, and as an intrinsic component of human flourishing and personal development. Israel has a young population: it ranks second amongst OECD countries for the proportion of 5-14 years olds in the population (at 18% compared to an OECD average of 12.5%) and fourth for the proportion of 15-29 year-olds in the population (at 23%, compared to an OECD average of 20%). It follows that ensuring access to education for these large youth cohorts will be key to well-being outcomes in the future.

When looking at aggregate indicators, Israel has one of the most educated populations in the OECD. Since 2011, the Israeli government has subsidised public education for ages 3 to 5, and education is compulsory from age 5 to 18, making Israel's period of compulsory education one of the longest in the world. Israel ranks second among OECD countries (tied with Japan and after Canada) for the percentage of 25-64 year olds who have completed tertiary education (at 46% compared with an OECD average of 32%). Also, 83% of 25-64 year olds have achieved at least upper secondary education, which is much higher than the OECD average of 75%. Finally, the proportion of those with only an elementary education (at 17%) is well below the OECD average (of 25%; OECD, 2013d).

Educational performance is less positive as measured by the Programme for International Student Assessment (PISA), which assesses the cognitive skills of 15-year olds students in mathematics, reading and science. Israel's performance is below the OECD average, with a combined score across the three subjects of 474, compared to the OECD average of 497 (Figure 2.11). However, Israel's performance has greatly improved in recent years, at a much faster rate than the OECD average. PISA scores also show that there is a

Figure 2.11. **Average performance in PISA testing**

Combined scores of mathematics, reading and science assessments

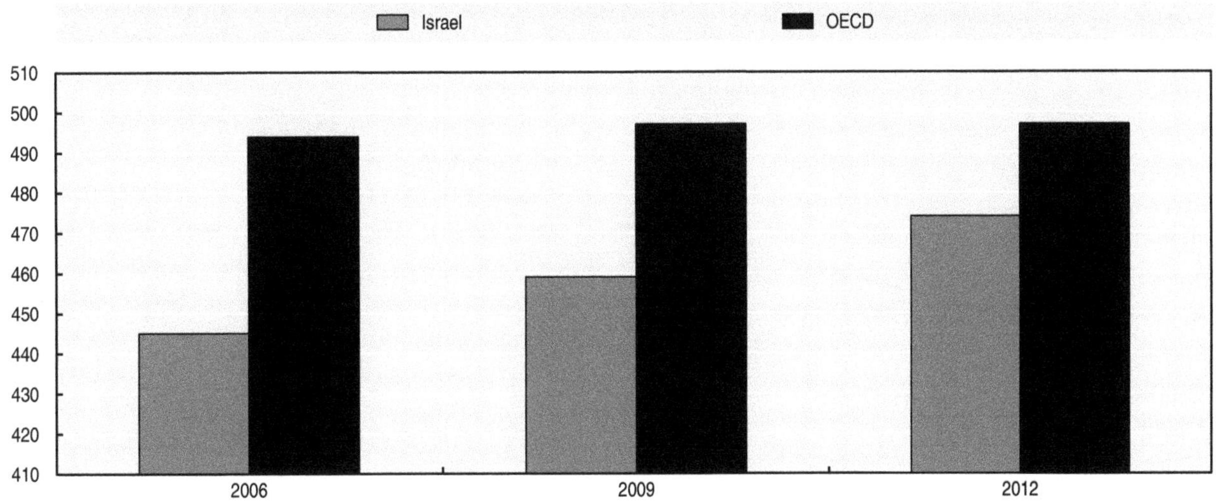

Source: OECD PISA 2012 Database.

StatLink http://dx.doi.org/10.1787/888933293319

wide spread of abilities in the Israeli education system, with one of the highest rates of score dispersion amongst the 64 participating countries. In terms of the size of the difference in scores between the top 10% of students and the bottom 10% of students, Israel ranked third in the dispersion of mathematics scores, second for that in reading scores, and first for that in science scores in the 2012 PISA round, according to the OECD Education GPS Database.

Health

Good health – living a long life free of illness and disability – is essential to well-being, not only because of its intrinsic value, but also because being healthy affects a person's chances of being employed, earning an adequate income, and actively participating in a wide range of valued social activities. In Israel, self-reported health outcomes are well above the OECD average, with 80% of Israelis saying they were satisfied with their health in 2013, compared to 69% on average in the OECD, according to the OECD Health Database.

Life expectancy is also higher than the OECD average, and has been so since the early 1990s, with the gap further increasing over time (Figure 2.12).

This strong performance of Israel in health outcomes is particularly impressive as Israeli healthcare expenditure, both per capita and as a share of GDP, is lower than the OECD average (OECD, 2013). Israel has a particularly effective primary care system, based on an affordable, accessible and well-managed network of community clinics, which is an important driver of positive health outcomes in the country (OECD, 2012).

Lifestyle factors also play a role, as Israelis have generally healthy lifestyle behaviours compared with the OECD average. They consume less sugar and alcohol, more fruit and vegetables, and are less likely to be smokers or obese than the OECD average (Figure 2.13). However, according to European Social Survey data, 38% of Israelis report that they did no exercise in the previous week in 2012, by far the least active country among the 22 countries surveyed, against an average of 10% (ESS, 2012).

Figure 2.12. **Life expectancy at birth**

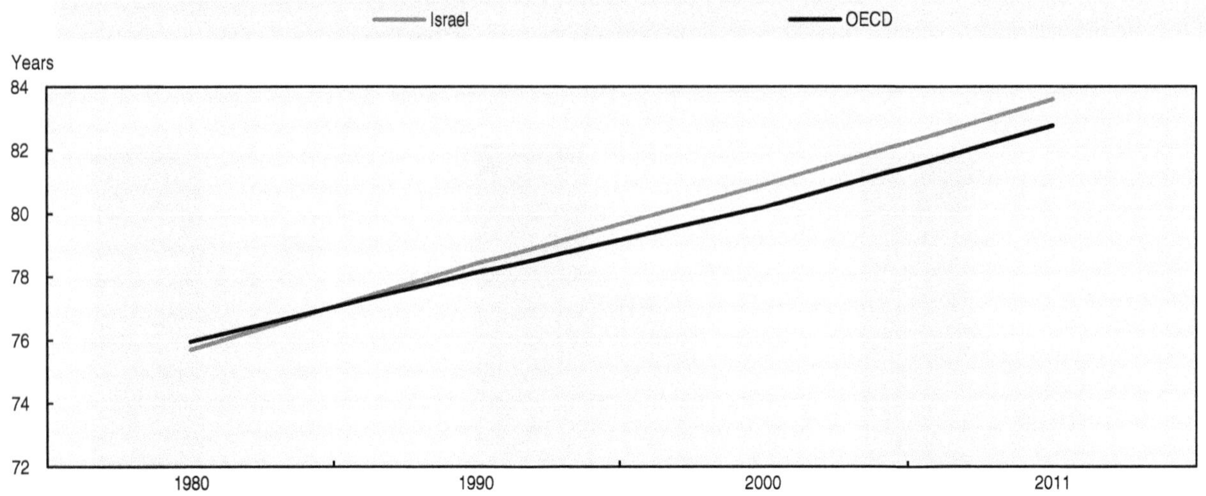

Source: "OECD Health Statistics", *OECD Health Database, http://dx.doi.org/10.1787/health-data-en.*

StatLink http://dx.doi.org/10.1787/888933293324

Figure 2.13. **Selected non-medical health determinants**

Ratio of Israeli to OECD levels on selected indicators

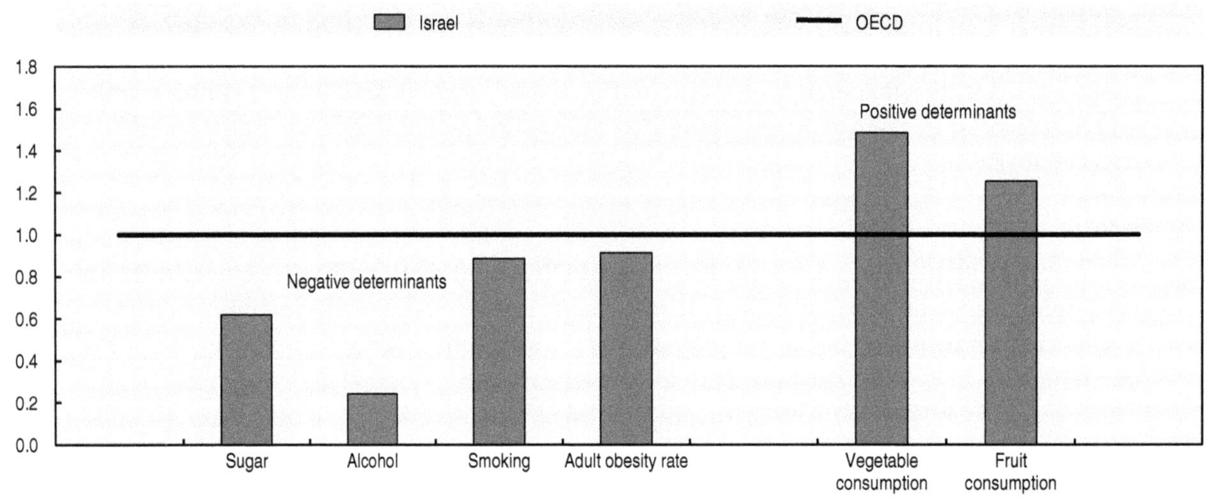

Source: OECD calculations based on FAOSTAT (database); *OECD Health Database, http://dx.doi.org/10.1787/health-data-en.*

StatLink http://dx.doi.org/10.1787/888933293338

Work and Life Balance

Achieving the right balance between work and life is a key component of people's well-being: if too little work may prevent people from earning enough to attain the desired standard of living, too much work may also impact negatively on their well-being (and that of their families) if their health or relationships suffer as a consequence.

Israelis tend to work longer hours than in other OECD countries, with an average of 40.9 hours per week compared with 38.4 in the OECD average in 2014, according to the OECD Labour Force database. 16% of employees in Israel regularly worked over 50 hours per week in 2013 (compared to an OECD average of 12.5%), which is the third-highest share of workers working over 50 hours per week amongst OECD countries for which data are available, after Turkey and Mexico (Figure 2.14).

Figure 2.14. **Share of people working very long hours**

Employees regularly working over 50 hours per week

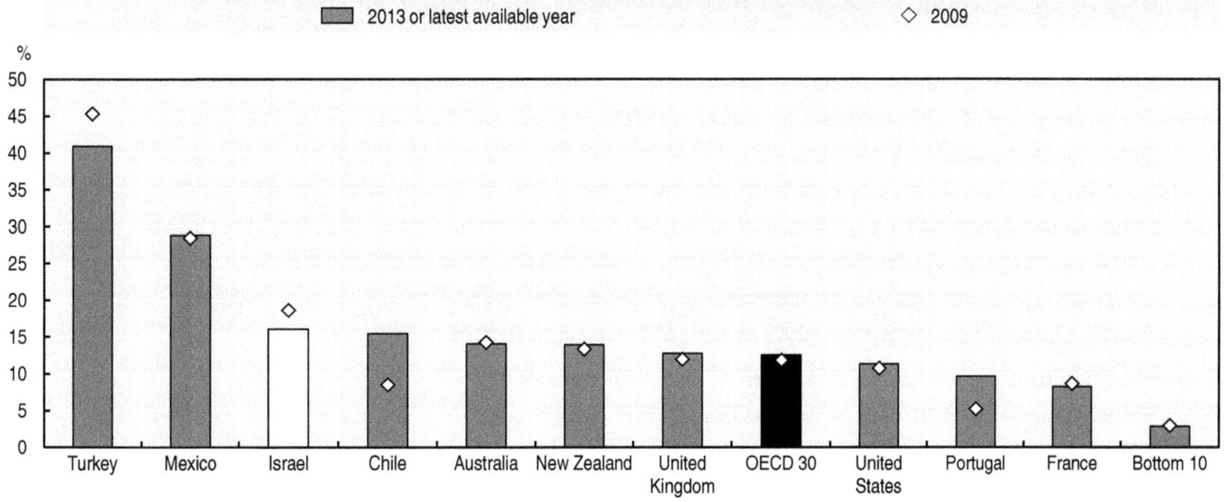

Note: Data refer to the percentage of all employees usually working 50 hours or more per week. Data refer to 2012 for Chile. The OECD average is population-weighted.

Source: "Labour Force Statistics", *OECD Employment and Labour Market Statistics Database, http://dx.doi.org/10.1787/lfs-lfs-data-en.*

StatLink http://dx.doi.org/10.1787/888933293345

Travel to and from work is amongst the least enjoyable activities in a worker's day (Kahneman and Krueger, 2006). While fully comparable data on commuting time are lacking, there is some indication that commuting times are high in Israel compared to other countries. According to the Israeli General Social Survey, 32% of workers took at least 30 minutes to get to work. This compares with a European average of 13% of workers saying it took them at least 60 minutes to get to work and back (which is roughly equivalent to 30 minutes for a one-way journey; European Survey on Working Conditions, 2010). While these data should be treated with caution, as they are not directly comparable across countries, they give some indication that Israeli commuting times are longer than in most European countries.

Length of paid work and commuting time is not the only aspect of work-life balance. Unpaid work (such as child care, meal preparation and housework) also has an important impact on people's work/life balance. However, an accurate assessment of time devoted to these activities requires time use data, and no time use survey has been conducted in Israel since 1991. Time use data are particularly needed to assess gender inequalities in work-life balance, as women are much more likely to spend longer hours in unpaid rather than paid work compared to men. This is particularly the case amongst the Arab and Haredi population, where female labour force participation rates are low and fertility rates are high.

In order to get a better picture of work-life balance, it is necessary to look at the quality of leisure time as well as its duration. Israel's indicators of well-being, resilience and sustainability include a separate domain on leisure, which will help to develop better measurement and understanding of this key aspect of well-being.

Social connections

Social connections have positive spill-over effects for individual and societal well-being, beyond the intrinsic pleasure that people derive from spending time with others. People with extensive and supportive networks have better health, tend to live longer, and are more likely to be employed. At a society-wide level, social connections can generate shared values – such as trust in others and norms of reciprocity – which influence a range of outcomes, including economic growth, democratic participation, and crime levels.

Social connections are one of the areas where the evidence base for measuring well-being is weakest, both internationally and in Israel. In Israel, the General Social Survey provides a useful set of measures relating to social contact, which are, unfortunately, not directly comparable with those collected elsewhere. Although there is no international standard for measuring social contact, changes to the question wording and scale could improve comparability, and the Israeli well-being, resilience and sustainability initiative is working to improve measurement in this area. Finally, a time use survey would provide detailed, and internationally comparable, information on the quantity and nature of social contact that would significantly improve information in this area.

In order to obtain a picture of how social connections in Israel compare to those in other countries, there are nonetheless, a number of measures available from non-official sources such as the Gallup World Poll and the European Social Survey.

In the *How's Life?* framework, the headline indicator for social connections is the share of people saying that they have someone to count on for help when needed, as the support provided by people's networks is an important measure of the strength of social connections. In Israel, according to Gallup World Poll data, 87% of people report having someone to count on for help, which is just below the OECD average of 89%, and close to the rates shown by European countries such as France and Portugal (Figure 2.15).

Figure 2.15. **People saying they have someone to count on for help when needed, 2014**

Comparison with bottom 10 OECD countries

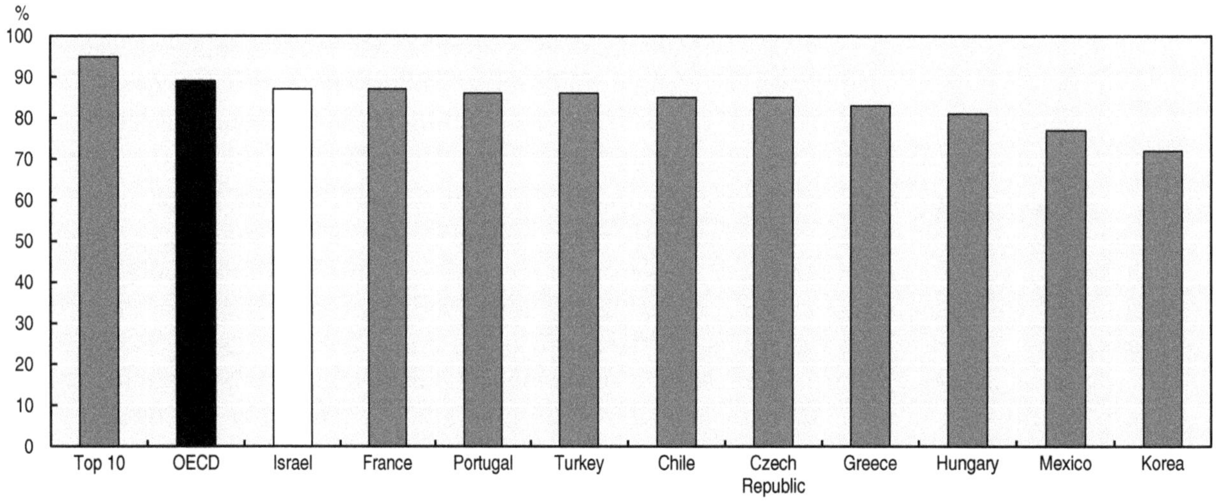

Note: The share of people responding "yes" to the question "If you were in trouble, do you have relatives or friends you can count on to help you whenever you need them, or not?".

Source: Gallup World Poll.

StatLink http://dx.doi.org/10.1787/888933293353

Further information is needed to understand social connections within a country, and comparable data on key indicators such as frequency of socialising are not available for all OECD countries. However, the European Social Survey does collect comparable data for 22 OECD countries, including Israel, which can help to provide more detail on this dimension of well-being. Regular contact with friends and loved ones is an essential aspect of social connections. According to this measure, Israelis tend to be very sociable, with around 74% of people in Israel saying that they socialise with friends, relatives or colleagues at least once a week (Figure 2.16, Panel a). This is one of the highest rates among the countries covered by the European Social Survey, similar to that seen in Sweden, Norway and the Netherlands, and 12 percentage-points higher than the average of the 22 OECD countries included in the survey (62%). However, an alternative measure of the quality of people's relationships – the number of close friends or loved ones with whom people can discuss intimate or personal matters – shows a slightly different picture (Figure 2.16, Panel b). According to this measure, 8.5% of Israelis say they have no-one to talk to about private issues, one of the highest shares among the countries sampled and almost double the average share in the 22 OECD countries surveyed (4.6%).

Figure 2.16. **Socialising and discussing personal matters, 2012**

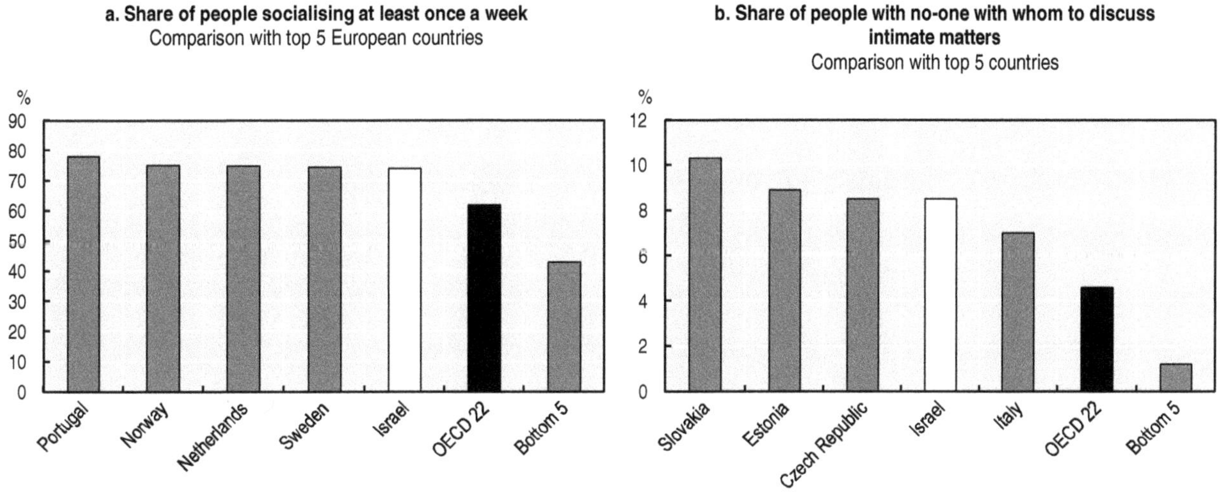

Notes: a) The share of people responding "every day", "several times a week" or "once a week" to the question: "How often do you meet socially with friends, relatives or work colleagues?" b) The share of people responding "none" to the question: "How many people, if any, are there with whom you can discuss intimate and personal matters?". OECD 22 refers to the 22 OECD countries included in the European Social Survey.

Source: European Social Survey, 2012: *http://nesstar.ess.nsd.uib.no/webview/.*

StatLink http://dx.doi.org/10.1787/888933293362

The measures presented here suggest that while Israelis tend to be very sociable, a comparatively large share of Israelis have no-one to count on for help or talk to about personal matters. Social relationships are very complex, however, and improvements in the measurement of social connections are needed to better understand the situation. It is also worth mentioning that social connections between people who know each other well are not the same thing as social capital, which instead refers to trust and cooperation *across* social groups (i.e. between people who do not know each other well; Scrivens and Smith, 2013). Social capital is an important driver of long-term well-being within a country and, while also very challenging to measure, will be discussed in Chapter 3 in the context of the sustainability of well-being in Israel.

Civic engagement and governance

Civic engagement allows people to express their political voice and contribute actively to the functioning of society. In turn, open and transparent governance contributes to the functioning of institutions and to the provision of public services that support material well-being and quality of life.

There are many forms of civic engagement and little standardisation of measurement across countries. The most fundamental form democratic engagement is participation in national elections. Voter turnout differs widely across countries, partially reflecting differences in electoral systems, including the existence of compulsory voting in some OECD countries such as Australia, Belgium, Luxembourg and Turkey. Figure 2.17 shows rates of voter turnout, expressed as a share of both the voting-age population and the population registers to vote. The differences in the two measures reflect country differences in voter registration, how electoral registers are maintained, non-resident voting and the numbers of residents who are not eligible to vote in national elections. Israel is one of a small number of countries, along with Greece, Chile and Korea, where the number of voters registered exceeds the voting-age population (VAP) within the country, likely reflecting the large proportion of Israelis living overseas who are registered to vote. As Israeli voting policy does not permit voting outside the country, the VAP-based measure is probably a better reflection of democratic participation in the country. On this measure, Israel ranks amongst the top ten countries with 73% of voters participating in national elections, compared to an OECD average of 63%.

Figure 2.17. **Voter turnout at national elections**

2014 or latest available year

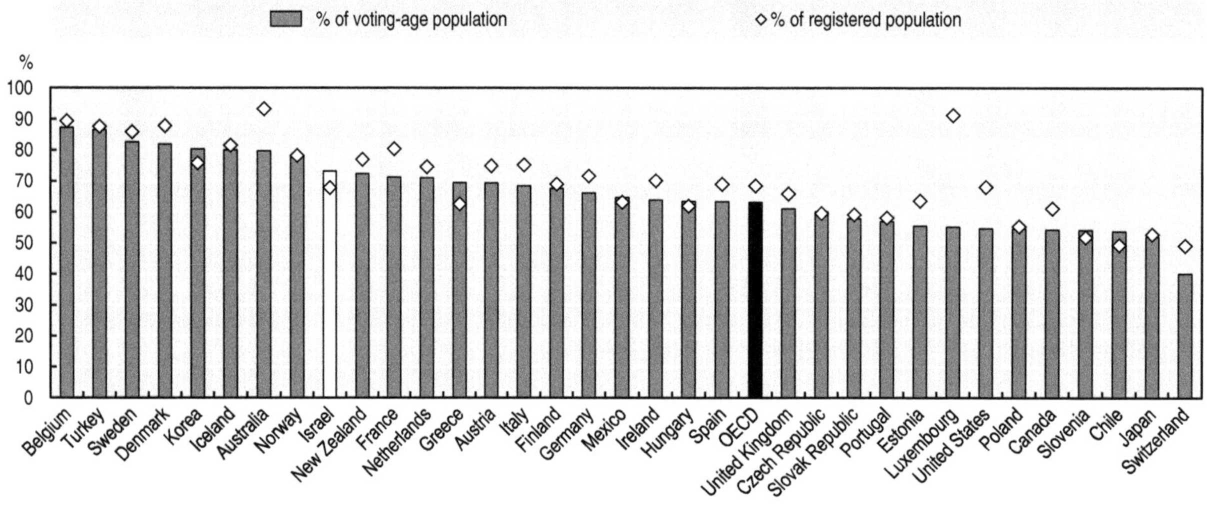

Note: National elections refer to parliamentary elections, with the exceptions of Finland, France, Korea, Mexico, Poland, the United States, Brazil and the Russian Federation, where Presidential elections are considered. The latest available year is 2014 for Slovenia, Japan, New Zealand, Hungary, Sweden, Brazil and Belgium; 2013 for Luxembourg, Chile, Germany, Norway, Austria, the Czech Republic, Italy, Australia and Iceland; 2012 for the United States, the Russian Federation, Israel, the Netherlands, the Slovak Republic, Finland, Mexico, Greece, France and Korea; 2011 for Spain, Portugal, Canada, Switzerland, Denmark, Estonia, Ireland and Turkey; and 2010 for the United Kingdom and Poland. The OECD average is population-weighted.

Source: International Institute for Democracy and Electoral Assistance (IDEA) (2015), *www.idea.int*.

StatLink http://dx.doi.org/10.1787/888933293371

The level of confidence that citizens have in their government can provide an indication of the quality of governance within a country. Around 44% of Israelis say that they have confidence in the national government, just above the OECD average of 42% (Figure 2.18, Panel a), and putting Israel in the top-third of OECD countries on this measure. It is worth noting also that Israel is one of only a handful of countries where trust in

Figure 2.18. **Confidence in government**

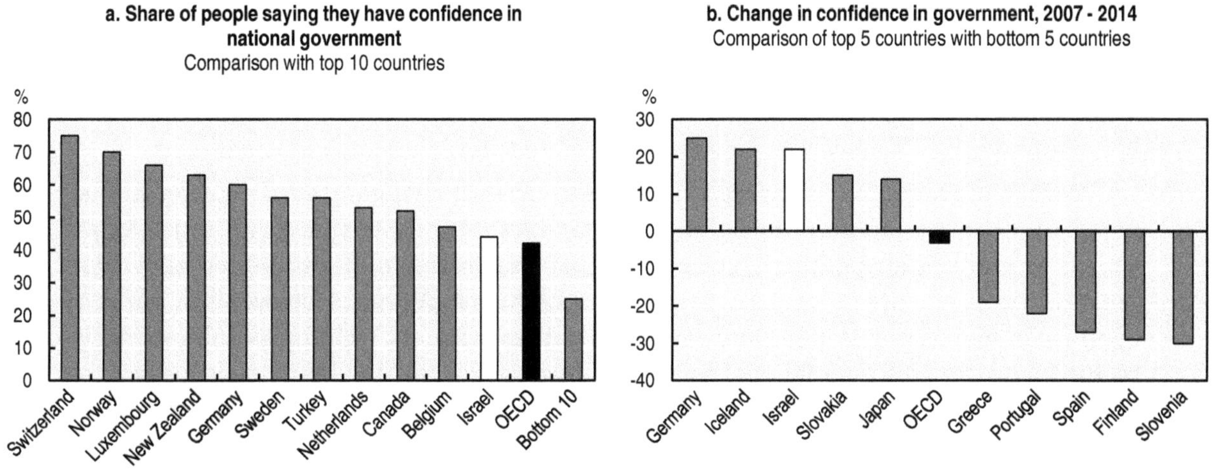

Note: Share of people responding "yes" to the question, "In this country, do you have confidence in national government?".
Source: Gallup World Poll.

StatLink http://dx.doi.org/10.1787/888933293380

government has actually increased since the crisis (Figure 2.18, Panel b), possibly reflecting Israel's relatively strong post-crisis economic performance. Across the OECD, confidence in national government fell by an average of 3 percentage points, and by as much as 30% in Slovenia, the country that saw the biggest drop in government confidence. In Israel, conversely, the share of people who have confidence in government doubled from 22% to 44% between 2007 and 2014, the third-biggest increase across OECD countries after Germany and Iceland.

Environmental quality

A clean and healthy physical environment is essential for quality of life, and the impact of environmental pollutants on people's health is sizeable. The beauty of people's natural surroundings can also bring intrinsic value to people's lives, and people tend to care about preserving natural resources to prevent the degradation of their local area, and of the planet, for future generations.

Israel is one of the most densely populated countries in the world, with a high rate of population increase due to natural growth, immigration and rising life expectancy: the population in Israel is expected to increase from around 8 million in 2014 to 11 million by 2030 (EEA, 2014). It is also a small country, with a large proportion of desert landmass and limited natural resources. Most of the population lives in urban areas, with a significant share residing along the coastal plain. The country's rapidly expanding population, accompanied by urban sprawl and high levels of industrialisation, place high environmental pressures on Israel's land, freshwater and ocean ecosystems.

Air quality is a key environmental issue with a major impact on people's health and subjective well-being. Air pollution takes a number of different forms, each having their own negative effect on human health and ecological imbalances. The greatest health risks are associated with long-term exposure to poor quality air: for example, chronic exposure to particulate matter (PM) contributes to the risk of developing cardiovascular and respiratory diseases as well as of lung cancer (OECD, 2014c). Fine particulate matter ($PM_{2.5}$) from sources such as vehicle emissions, energy production, and the burning of agricultural biomass poses a particular threat to people's health. Israel, being a desert country and surrounded by desert areas, suffers from naturally high background particulate matter from Saharan dust. However, as in many other countries, the main sources of air pollution in Israel are transport, electricity generation and industrial activities, and while air pollution has improved, hotspots remain in Haifa Bay, the Ashdod area and Ramat Hovav (OECD, 2011b). Both natural and human causes therefore contribute to low air quality in Israel.

Developing summary measures of air pollution is challenging, as air quality is the result of a complex mixture of pollutants that vary over time, space and form. Most countries monitor air pollution through ground monitoring stations, which allow for precise measurements in localised areas over short time periods. However, the uneven coverage of monitoring stations and variations in measurement techniques and reporting methods hampers the international comparability of such data. An alternative approach to measuring air pollution in an internationally-comparable manner is to rely on a new technique using satellite-based observations, which provide methodological consistency across countries and over time, globally, and including rural areas – thus enabling exposure to be estimated for a country's whole population, rather than just its urban centres (Brezzi and Sanchez-Serra, 2014). New estimates derived in this manner indicate that annual exposure to $PM_{2.5}$ in Israel is the second highest after Korea amongst OECD countries (Figure 2.19), and that air pollution levels in the country have risen in recent years. With an estimated 23 micrograms per cubic metre in the period 2010-12, annual exposure to $PM_{2.5}$ in Israel exceeds both WHO and EU air quality recommendations.[2]

Figure 2.19. **Annual exposure to $PM_{2.5}$ air pollution**

Population-weighted exposure to $PM_{2.5}$ concentrations, micrograms per cubic metre

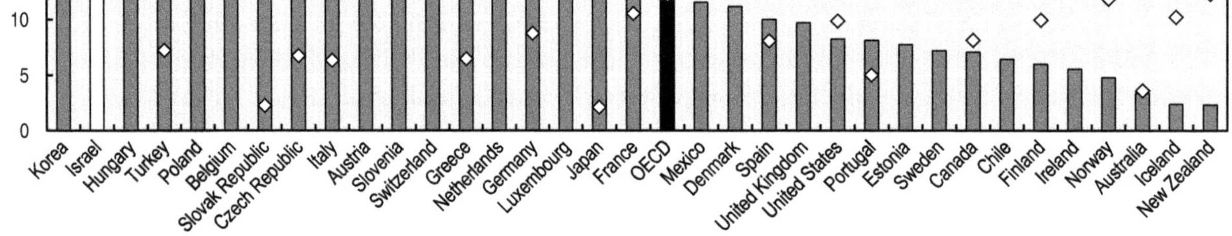

Note: The values shown are OECD estimates, averaged over three years (2010-12), based on satellite image data from van Donkelaar, A., R.V. Martin, M. Brauer and B.L. Boys (2015), "Use of Satellite Observations for Long-Term Exposure Assessment of Global Concentrations of Fine Particulate Matter", *Environmental Health Perspectives*, Vol. 123, Issue 2. A 50% relative humidity standard has been adopted for consistency with ground-level measurements. The values for each country are population-weighted averages of the annual concentration of $PM_{2.5}$. The OECD average is also population-weighted.

Source: *OECD Regional Well-being Statistics* (database), *http://dx.doi.org/10.1787/data-00707-en*.

StatLink http://dx.doi.org/10.1787/888933293391

A potential drawback of satellite-based estimates is that they can be less accurate for landmasses with bright surfaces, such as the desert which makes up much of Israeli territory. However, the results for Israel presented here from satellite observations are consistent with measures based on ground monitoring from the Israeli Ministry of Environmental Protection and made available in the WHO Ambient (outdoor) Air Pollution in Cities Database 2014 (WHO, 2014).

Sustainable water use is also a high-priority issue for Israel, given the country's arid conditions, scare natural water supplies, decreasing trends in rainfall due to climate change, and increasing demand from population increase and economic growth. In recent years, Israel has established itself as a world leader in innovative water treatment technologies for drinking water and wastewater recycling. Efficient water practices have achieved 95% water efficiency in agriculture, which is the highest ratio in the world of crop yield per water unit (EEA, 2014), while massive investments in desalination capacities mean than an estimated 80% of the country's drinking water is now provided by desalinated water, with the goal that all of Israel's water for domestic use be provided by desalination by 2013 (EEA, 2014). These are huge achievements which, when coupled with the country's successful and continuing efforts to reduce water pollution in its rivers, lakes and oceans, represent important advances for water sustainability in the country. Challenges do remain however, as desalination processes exert their own pressures on the environment, particularly on marine ecosystems, and wide use of desalination results in a much increased energy demand.

The quality of drinking water is also an issue, and while there has been a substantial improvement in the microbiological quality of drinking water in the past two decades (with the rate of non-compliance falling from 6.5% in 1991 to 0.2% in 2008), deteriorating water quality led the Ministry of Health to close 10% of the country's drinking water wells during the first decade of the 2000s (OECD, 2011b). Placing these figures in an OECD context is not straightforward as up-to-date, internationally comparable, objective information on water quality is not readily available. However, according to Gallup World Poll data, only 68% of Israelis say that they are satisfied with the quality of water in the city or area where they live, which is the fourth lowest rate in the OECD (after Turkey, Chile and Mexico) and well below the OECD average of 84%. However, the high level of public awareness of water-related issues in Israel, which is partly driven by media campaigns to encourage water conservation, may also contribute to below-average perceptions of water quality.

Personal security

Personal security is affected by a wide range of threats to people's lives, one of the most common being crime. Some forms of crime may lead to the loss of life, but even non-fatal ones can have a strong impact on the victim's mental and physical health, both in the short and long term. Crime also has large direct impacts on the well-being of non-victims, through the increase in worry and anxiety. Compared to other OECD countries, personal security in Israel is more complex than is typically the case as, in addition to the standard threats to safety from violent crime, Israel's geo-political conflicts lead to a relatively high rate of terrorist violence within the country. When measuring outcomes related to personal security, it is difficult to make a clear distinction between these different factors and their effect on the data, but the particular context of Israel needs to be borne in mind when analysing well-being in this dimension.

In 2014, the rate of deaths by assault was lower in Israel than in the OECD average, with 1.8 deaths per 100 000 people due to assault in Israel, compared to 4 per 100 000 across the OECD. However, it is worth noting that the exceptionally high levels of violence in Mexico in recent years tend to drive up the OECD average. While the rate of deaths by assault in Israel is relatively low, it is nonetheless the fifth highest rate in the OECD, and above the average rate for the 33 OECD countries other than Mexico of 1.3 per 100 000 (Figure 2.20).

Figure 2.20. **Deaths by assault per 100 000 population (standardised rates)**

Comparison with top 10 countries

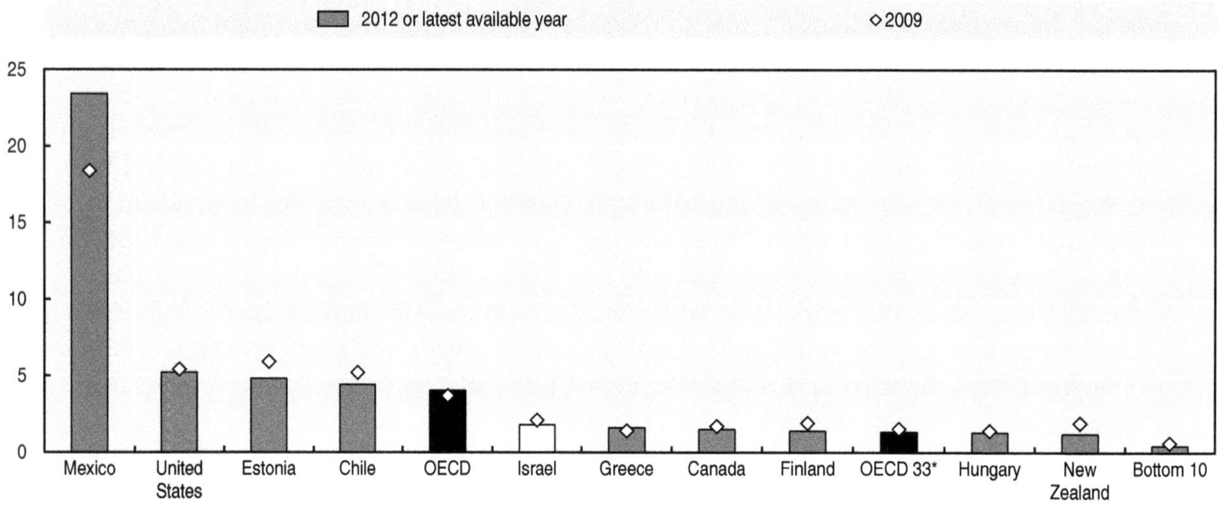

Note: The latest available year is 2011 for Chile, Greece, and Israel; 2010 for New Zealand and the United States. The OECD average is population-weighted.

Source: "OECD Health Data: Causes of Mortality", *OECD Health Statistics* (database), *http://dx.doi.org/10.1787/data-00540-en.*

StatLink http://dx.doi.org/10.1787/888933293407

Long-terms trends in violence have shown significant variation in Israel, obviously influenced by the broader geo-political context. In order to get a sense of how many deaths in Israel are caused by violent crime, as opposed to deaths related to the conflict, Figure 2.21 shows the rate of all deaths by assault compared with the homicide rate,

Figure 2.21. **Trends in total deaths by assault, and homicides excluding terror casualties in Israel**

Rate per 100 000 people

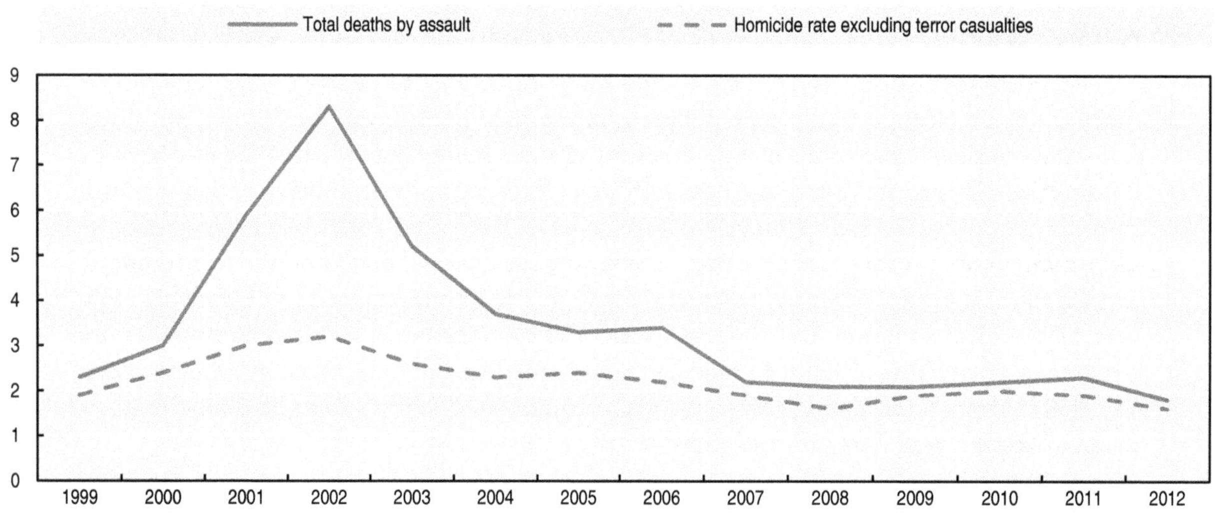

Source: "OECD Health Data: Causes of Mortality", *OECD Health Statistics (database), http://dx.doi.org/10.1787/data-00540-en*; Israeli Central Bureau of Statistics.

StatLink http://dx.doi.org/10.1787/888933293418

excluding terror casualties, in Israel from 1999 to 2012.[3] In the early 2000s, during the Second Intifada, the rate of deaths by assault skyrocketed and has fallen only in the last few years. By this measure, it is clear that without political violence, long-term trends in violent death in Israel are much lower, although in recent years the impact of terror violence has been marginal. In 2012, the latest year for which data are available, the homicide rate without terror casualties was 1.6 people per 100 000, which is still above the OECD 33 (without Mexico) population-weighted average deaths by assault rate of 1.3.

Deaths due to assault, including homicides, represent only a fraction of the total risks to personal security. Israel conducted its first victimisation survey in 2014, the results of which were not yet available at the time of publication, but which will go a long way to better understanding trends in personal security in the country. In the absence of comparable official statistics, the Gallup World Poll provides some alternative measures of personal security across the OECD, such as self-reported prevalence of assault and feelings of safety (Figure 2.22).

Based on this source, 6.5% of Israelis declared that in 2010 (the latest year available) that they had been victim of an assault in the previous 12 months, which is above the OECD average of 4% and three times the average rate reported in the 10 OECD countries with the lowest rate of assault of only 1.9% (Figure 2.22, Panel a). Israel ranks as the fourth highest in the OECD on this measure, after Mexico, Chile and Belgium. On the other hand, Israel is in the top third of OECD countries for the share of people saying they feel safe walking alone at night (Figure 2.22, Panel b), with 77% of Israelis say that they feel safe when walking alone at night compared to an OECD average of 70%.

Figure 2.22. **Self-reported measures of personal security**

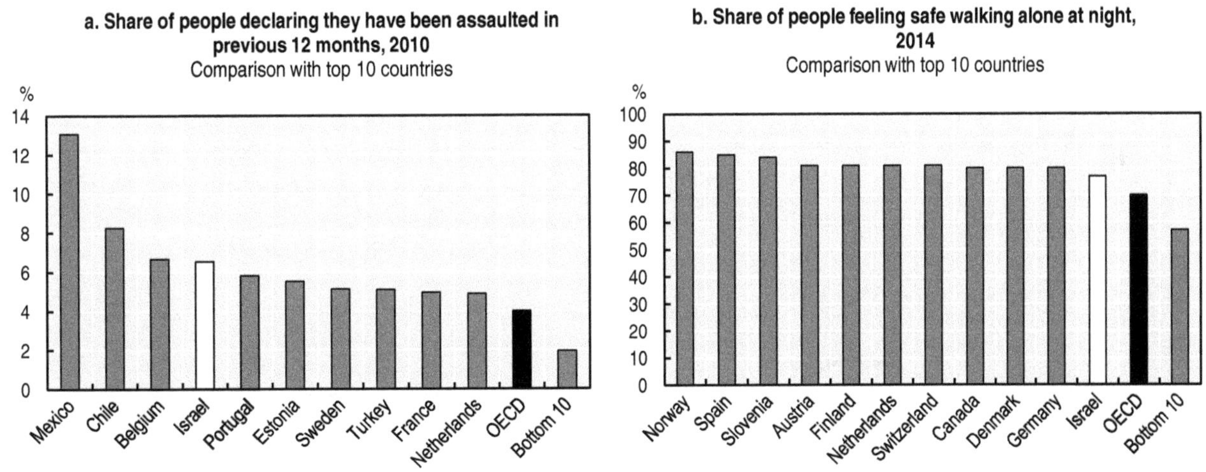

Note: b) Share of people responding "yes" to the question, "Do you feel safe walking alone at night in the city or area where you live?".
Source: Gallup World Poll.

StatLink http://dx.doi.org/10.1787/888933293423

Overall, personal security is a much more complex matter in Israel than in most other OECD countries due to the contribution of the geo-political conflict to the actual and perceived threats to people's safety. While violence is relatively high in Israel compared with the OECD average, as measured by deaths due to assault and self-reported victimisation from assault, data on homicides excluding terror casualties shows values that are much more in line with the OECD average.[4] However, perceived safety, as measured by the share of people feeling safe walking alone at night is above the OECD average.

Subjective well-being

How people evaluate and experience their lives is an important part of well-being alongside the circumstances in which people live. Measures of subjective well-being provide information on how people evaluate and experience their life, and reflect the notion that people are the best judges of how their own lives are going. Typically, a key distinction is made between different types of measure of subjective well-being. Measures of life evaluation (such as life satisfaction) capture people's cognitive reflection on how their life is going, while measures of affect (such as anger, joy, or sadness) capture moods and emotions. The two classes of measure are both of interest in their own right, as they have different drivers and provide information on different aspects of people's lives.

Self-reported life satisfaction in Israel is higher than the OECD average. The headline indicator of subjective well-being in the *How's Life?* framework is a measure of how people evaluate their lives. The Gallup World Poll collects information on the Cantril ladder, a well-established measure of life evaluation that asks respondents to rate their overall satisfaction with their lives on a scale of 0 (worst possible evaluation) to 10 (best possible evaluation). According to this measure, life satisfaction in Israel has been consistently above the OECD average in the period 2006-14, despite temporary dips in 2007 and 2012. The average score in Israel was 7.4, compared with 6.6 across the OECD area in 2014 (Figure 2.23). In 2009, the OECD average score fell, likely in response to the emergence of the crisis in the preceding year, but Israeli levels of life satisfaction remained strong during this period, a probable refection of the lessened impact of the crisis in Israel.

Figure 2.23. **Trends in life satisfaction**
Average Cantril ladder score

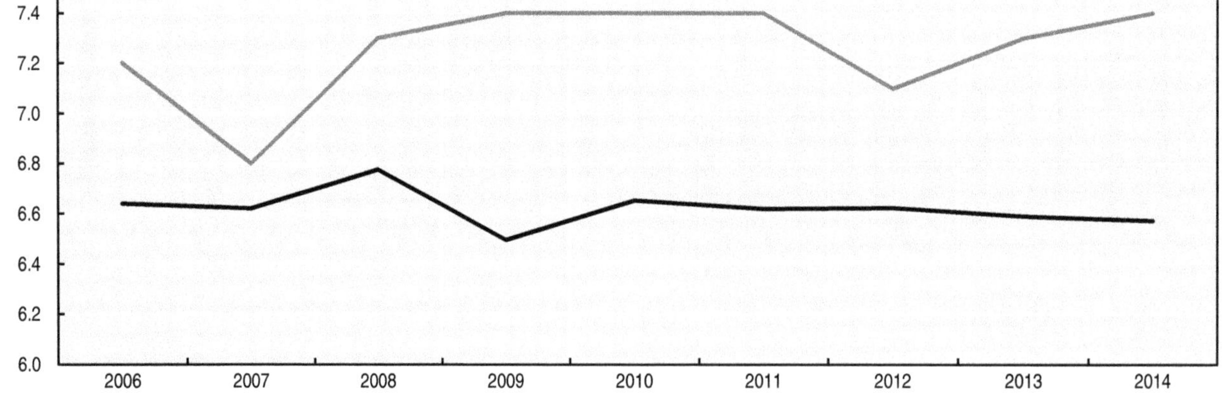

Note: The "Cantril ladder" question asks respondents to rate their overall satisfaction with their lives on a scale of 0 (worst possible evaluation) to 10 (best possible evaluation).
Source: Gallup World Poll.

StatLink http://dx.doi.org/10.1787/888933293435

Apart from people's evaluations of their lives as a whole, feelings and emotional states represent an important aspect of subjective well-being. Affect is the term psychologists use to describe a person's feelings, and measures of affect aim to capture how people experience life rather than how they remember it. Figure 2.24 shows results from the Gallup World Poll for one positive emotion (enjoyment) and a number of negative emotions (anger, stress, worry, boredom, depression), presenting the share of people saying that they experienced the emotion in question "a lot" in the previous day. According to these measures, Israelis experience the negative emotional states of anger, worry and depression with a much higher frequency than is the case in the OECD area as a whole. This is perhaps unsurprising, given the threats and realities of conflict that characterise life in Israel. High levels of negative affect are not inconsistent with high levels of overall life satisfaction in the country, as emotions are only one of the factors contributing to people's life evaluations. Other factors, such as good health, income and social contact also affect life satisfaction.

Figure 2.24. **Selected measures of the prevalence of different types of affect**

2012 or latest year available

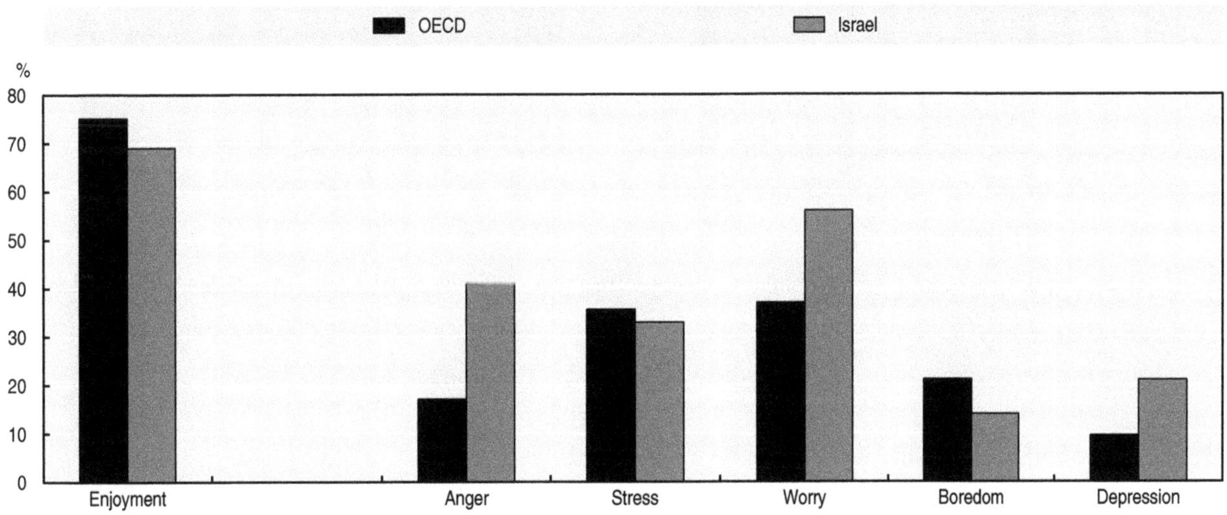

Note: Share of people saying that they experienced different feelings a lot during the previous day.
Source: Gallup World Poll.

StatLink http://dx.doi.org/10.1787/888933293440

The distribution of well-being outcomes in Israel

Assessing well-being outcomes at the level of a national community requires taking into account differences between people and population groups. Israel is a highly diverse society with large differences in well-being outcomes between the Jewish and the Arab population, and also between different sub-groups within each population.[5] Given the limited scope of this report, it focuses primarily on differences in outcomes among three groups: i) the Jewish population, excluding Haredim (or Ultra-Orthodox Jews); ii) the Haredim; and iii), the Arab population. These groups have been chosen to contrast the situation of the two most significant sub-groups in terms of size and material disadvantage (Haredim and Arabs) against that of the majority (non-Haredi Jews).

The drivers of inequalities between these three groups are complex, and often self-reinforcing, leading to a cycle of poor outcomes across multiple dimensions for the more disadvantaged. This section will first explore inequalities in material conditions and their key drivers (income and wealth, jobs and earnings, housing, and education) and then provide an overview of the distribution of outcomes across different dimensions of quality of life by population group, age and gender.

Material conditions and key drivers

In 2013, the latest year for which comparable data are available, Israel had the second highest rate of (relative) income poverty amongst OECD countries after Mexico, with 18.6% of individuals having an income of less than half of the national median (Figure 2.25, Panel a).

Figure 2.25. **Income poverty and inequality**

2013 or latest year available

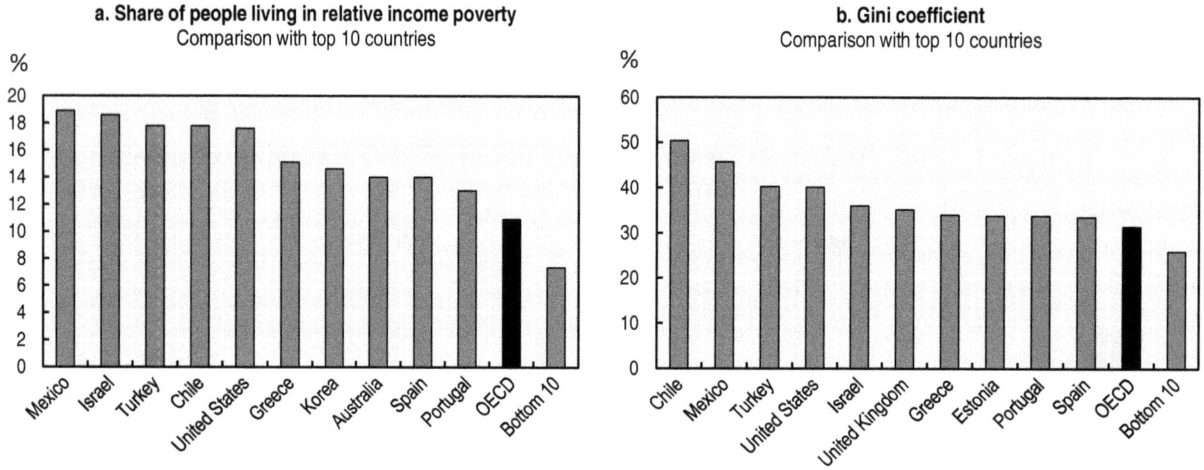

Note: The relative income poverty rate shows the share of the population with an income of less than 50% of the national median income. Income is after taxes and transfers, adjusted for difference in household size. Data in both charts are based on household disposable income after taxes and transfers. Data for Chile are from 2011, and calculated according to a slightly different income definition.

Source: OECD Income Distribution (database), http://dx.doi.org/10.1787/socwel-data-en.

StatLink http://dx.doi.org/10.1787/888933293457

Income inequality as measured by the Gini coefficient – a widely-used measure of income dispersion – is also very high in Israel (Figure 2.25, Panel b). Israel ranks as the fifth highest in the OECD after Chile, Mexico, Turkey and the United States on this measure, with a Gini coefficient of 0.36 as compared to an OECD average of 0.31 (a Gini value closer to 1 means more inequality).

Income poverty and inequality have been comparatively high in Israel for many years, although there are some indications that levels may have begun to decrease. This trend is still uncertain however, due to differences between the official Israeli method for calculating poverty rates and that used by the OECD, which result in slightly different levels and trends of the various indicators.[6]

Figure 2.26a shows long-term trends in relative poverty in Israel and in selected OECD countries. While it is difficult to calculate an overall OECD average for the period shown (1995-2011) as not all countries produce poverty data on a regular basis, the countries shown here represent examples of another high-poverty country (the United States), a low-poverty country (Norway) and a country that was around the median OECD national value in 2011 (Hungary). According to the OECD figures, the largest increase in poverty in Israel occurred in the period 2000-05; in the years 2005-11, poverty rates flattened out and even began to fall. Among the countries shown here, Israel recorded by far the largest change in poverty, with trends in the other countries being fairly stable (United States) or tending towards a slight increase (Hungary, Norway). As poverty figures are not available for all OECD countries before the mid-2000s, it is not possible to say whether Israel is unique in this regard, however.

Figure 2.26. **Trends in income poverty across countries and between Israeli population groups**

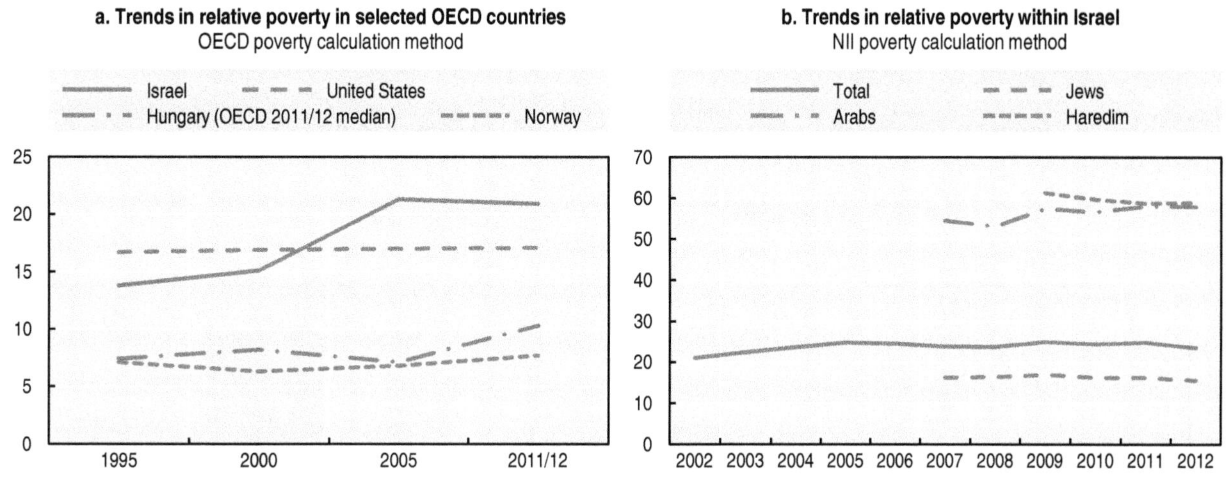

Note: NII data for Israeli Jews also include Ultra-Orthodox. The definition of Ultra-Orthodox (Haredi) Jews is according to the work of Gottlieb-Kushner (2009). OECD data are calculated using the old (pre-2012) income calculation method.

Source: OECD Income Distribution (database), http://dx.doi.org/10.1787/socwel-data-en; National Insurance Institute (NII) Annual Reports 2007-2012.

StatLink http://dx.doi.org/10.1787/888933293461

Figure 2.26b uses Israeli poverty data produced by the National Insurance Institute (NII) to look at trends by population group within the country.[7] According to these figures, which cover the period 2002-12 for the whole country, and more recent periods for the various population groups (according to data availability), the overall Israeli poverty rate has been declining since about 2009, after a number of years of rising poverty in the early to mid-2000s. What is most striking, however, are the stark differences in levels and trends of poverty among the different groups. In 2012, the latest year available, while the total poverty rate was 23.5% in Israel according to these figures (the NII figures are slightly higher than OECD figures due to the different calculation method used), only 15.5% of Jews were poor, compared with well over half of Arabs (57.9%) and a similar proportion of Haredim (58.9%). Indeed, when calculated using the OECD methodology, the poverty rate amongst Israeli Jews was only 12% in 2012 (NII 2012), which is only one percentage-point above the 2012 OECD average of 10.9%.[8] When looking at trends over time, the poverty rate for Israel as a whole and for Jews shows a slight decline in recent years. The poverty rates amongst Arabs and Haredim have converged at a similar high level, after several years of rising rates amongst Arabs and falling poverty amongst Haredim.

All the measures discussed so far are based on the concept of household disposable income, after taxes and public transfers have been taken into account. Changes in the social welfare system have played a major influence on poverty. For example, the sharp overall increase in poverty between 2000 and 2005 was due not only to an increase in market income poverty (i.e. before taxes and transfers) but also to reductions in child benefits and income support (intended to encourage increased labour force participation in the long-term), and to a weakening of the redistributive powers of the tax and benefit system during this period (OECD, 2013b). For people aged between 25-50 years, the tax and benefit system reduced income poverty by around 40% in 2000 but only by 20% in 2010 (OECD, 2013b). Social expenditure is low in Israel compared with other OECD countries, at around 15-16% of GDP since the mid-2000s, which is about 6 percentage points lower than the OECD average (OECD, 2013b).

For all groups, social transfers and taxes reduce the rate of poverty, but the effect seems to be largest for the Jewish population (Figure 2.27). In 2012, taxes and transfers resulted in a reduction in of 9 percentage points for Jews, 14.7 percentage-points for Haredi Jews and only 3.8% for Israeli Arabs.

Figure 2.27. **Poverty rate by population group in Israel, before and after taxes and transfers**

2012

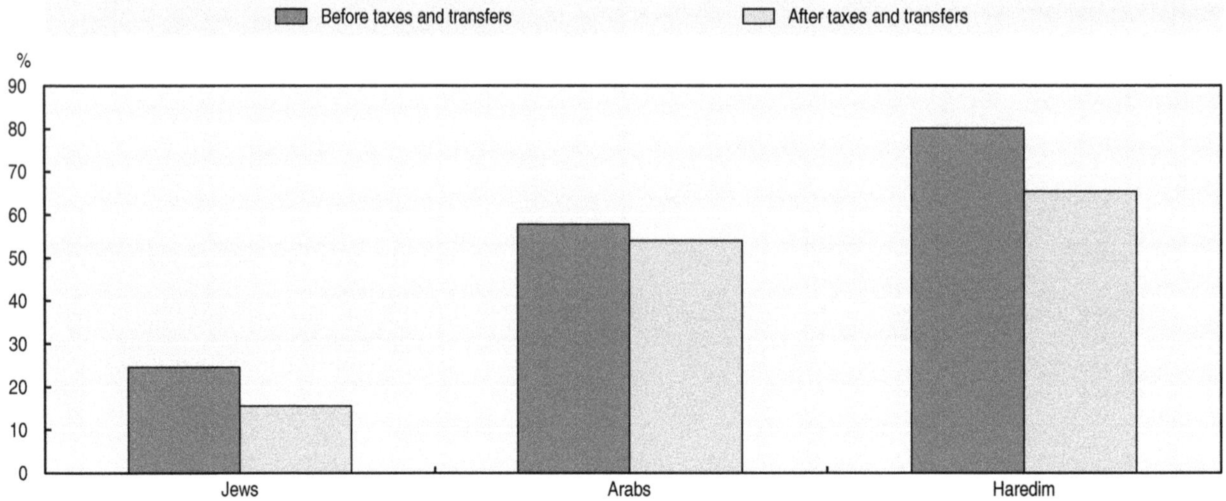

Note: Incidence of poverty refers to the share of people living below the poverty line, defined as half the median available monetary income. Public transfers are limited to those paid in cash, i.e. excluding in-kind transfers such as health and education. The Haredi population was calculated based on the Gottlieb-Kushnir method (Gottlieb and Kushnir, 2009).

Source: NII (2012).

StatLink http://dx.doi.org/10.1787/888933293477

These changing patterns of market-income and disposable-income poverty rates are likely due to recent social policy changes implemented by the Israeli government. Employment is often seen as the principal route out of poverty, and the Israeli government has put a number of measures in place to encourage entry into the labour market in recent years. In 2013, a number of measures were taken to encourage employment, including negative income tax, increases in the minimum wage and significant cuts in child welfare allowances were introduced as a means to encourage labour force participation amongst Arabs and Haredim, who tend to have larger families. The most recent poverty and employment data seem to suggest that at least amongst the Arab population, the policy may be having the desired results (NII 2013).

Employment rates amongst different population groups within Israel differ substantially, and particularly when broken down by gender (Figure 2.28). For both men and women, employment rates amongst non-Haredi Jews are very high, at around 85% of the working-age population for men and 82% for women in 2014 (compared to an OECD average of 73.6% for men and 57.9% for women). However for Arabs and Haredim, gender plays an important role in determining labour force participation, with relatively high employment rates for Arab men (75%) and Haredi women (72%), but much lower rates for Haredi men (48%) and Arab women (34%). While these patterns reflect cultural norms within the two groups, change is happening – slowly but steadily – across all groups. Increases in employment rates for all groups appear to have contributed to poverty reductions, since the early 2000s.

Figure 2.28. **Trends in employment rate by population group and gender in Israel**

Working age population

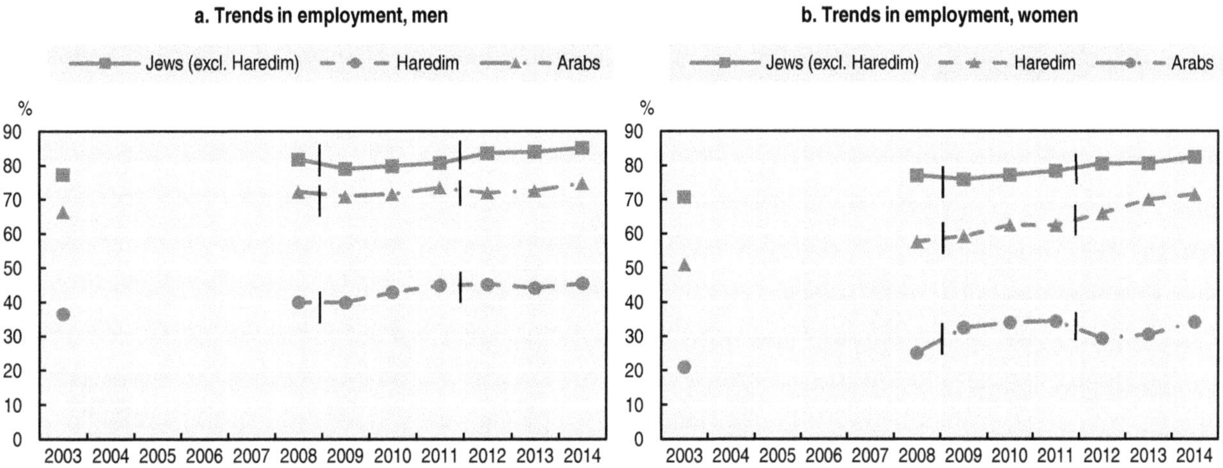

Note: There are breaks in the series between 2008-09 and between 2011-12. Before 2009, the working age population is defined according to the Israeli definition of 25-64 years for men and 25-59 years for women; after 2009 the definition of the working age population was changed to 25-66 years. As of 2012, data refer to the entire labour force (including compulsory or military service) and based on monthly labour force survey. Data not provided for 2004-07.

Source: Israeli Central Bureau of Statistics (CBS).

StatLink http://dx.doi.org/10.1787/888933293485

Education is also an important determinant of labour force participation. The employment rates amongst the least-educated part of the population remains low, with only 46% of workers aged 25-64 with less than upper secondary education being in employment in Israel, compared with an OECD average of 55% in 2011 (OECD, 2013a). For those with upper secondary education, the employment rate was 71% in 2011, 5 percentage-points lower than the OECD average, while the employment rate of those with tertiary education (at 83%) was the same as the OECD average (OECD, 2013a).

Gender and cultural background also play a role in shaping educational performance, which can then influence labour market or other well-being outcomes. Israel's school system is arranged along six different education streams, reflecting the cultural diversity of the country. Three of these streams cater to the Hebrew-speaking community (secular schools, religious schools and Haredi schools), and three cater to the Arab-speaking community (schools for the Arab, Druze and Bedouin minorities). Further, the Haredi educational curriculum is segregated by gender: while secondary education for Haredi girls broadly follows the national curriculum, the vast majority of Haredi boys attend schools that focus solely on religious studies. This means that, in general, young Haredi men do not acquire the skills in English, science or maths that they would need for successful labour market participation (OECD, 2013b). Figure 2.29 shows students' learning outcomes in 2012 for boys and girls by type of school. Data for boys studying in Haredi schools are not available, nor are breakdowns for the different streams of Arabic-speaking schools, and so only the total is presented here. For both sexes, secular Hebrew-speaking schools tend to see the best performance, followed by religious Hebrew-speaking schools and Haredi schools. Differences within the Hebrew-speaking system are much smaller than those between Hebrew and Arabic speaking schools, and the gap is more pronounced for boys than for girls. Digital reading is an area where students in the Arabic system perform particularly poorly in comparison to other streams, reflecting a digital skills gap between

Figure 2.29. **Israeli students' learning outcomes by type of school and gender**

PISA 2012 scores

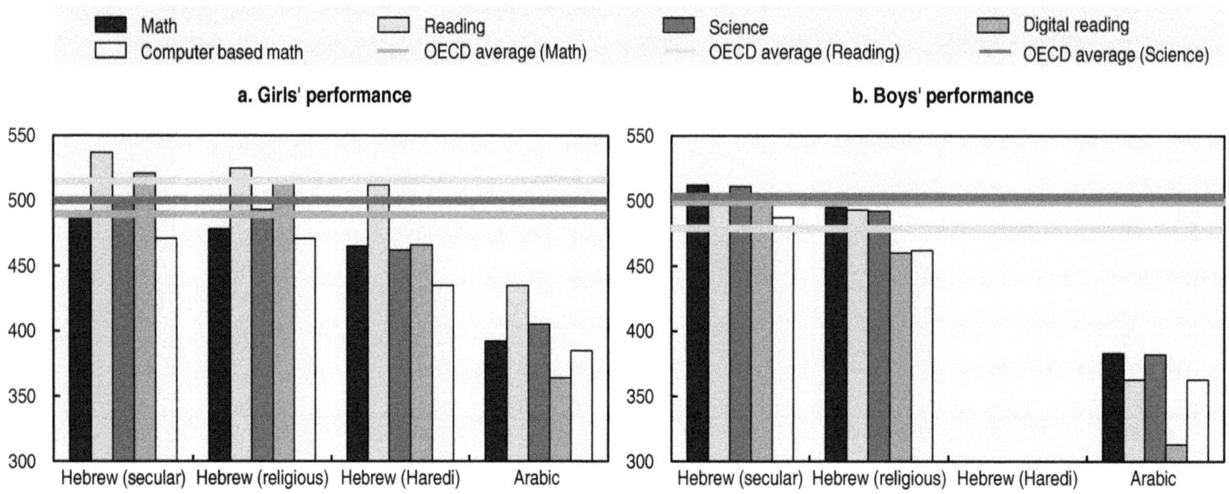

Note: No PISA data available for Haredi Boys' Schools.
Source: National Authority for Measurement and Evaluation (RAMA).

StatLink http://dx.doi.org/10.1787/888933293496

the population groups. It should also be noted that Arabic students have to effectively learn four languages: written and spoken Arabic (which are very different), Hebrew and English. This language barrier may also affect labour force participation of Arabs, as there is be a high correlation between Hebrew proficiency and employment.

While labour force participation is on the rise, the differences in human capital between the population groups are likely to influence the type of work and the level of pay received.

When looking at patterns of income distribution for the three groups, the relative disadvantage of Arabs and Haredim in relation to non-Haredi Jews is also clear (Figure 2.30). Nearly 50% of Haredim lived in households in the bottom income quintile in 2012, as did 55% of Arabs. However, a significant proportion (10%) of non-Haredi Jews are also in the lowest income quintile, accounting for more people in total than does the Haredi population (as the non-Haredi Jewish population is 70% of the total population of Israel).

Looking at the composition of the total poor population (i.e. the share of the population living on an income 50% below the median) (Figure 2.31) also shows that poverty is not a problem affecting only Arabs and Haredim. While almost half of the poor population are Arabs, and 19% are Haredi Jews, one-third of poor individuals are non-Haredi Jews.

Headcount rates do not give a picture of the severity of poverty experienced by different groups. Figure 2.32 plots the average depth of poverty (as measured by the income-gap ratio, i.e. the average "distance" from the poverty line for each group) against the share of total poverty accounted for by each group. The area of each box is directly proportional to the total cost of eliminating poverty for the population group in question (i.e. the total amount of income transfers that would be required to eliminate poverty for that population group). In contrast to Figures 2.29 and 2.30, which provide information about the probability of someone from each population group to live in poverty, Figure 2.32 provides information about the total burden of poverty. From this perspective, it can be seen that the total cost of eliminating Arab poverty is greater than that for all Jews combined: this reflects the large share of the Arab population in poverty and their greater depth of poverty.

Figure 2.30. **Income distribution by population group in Israel**

Percentages

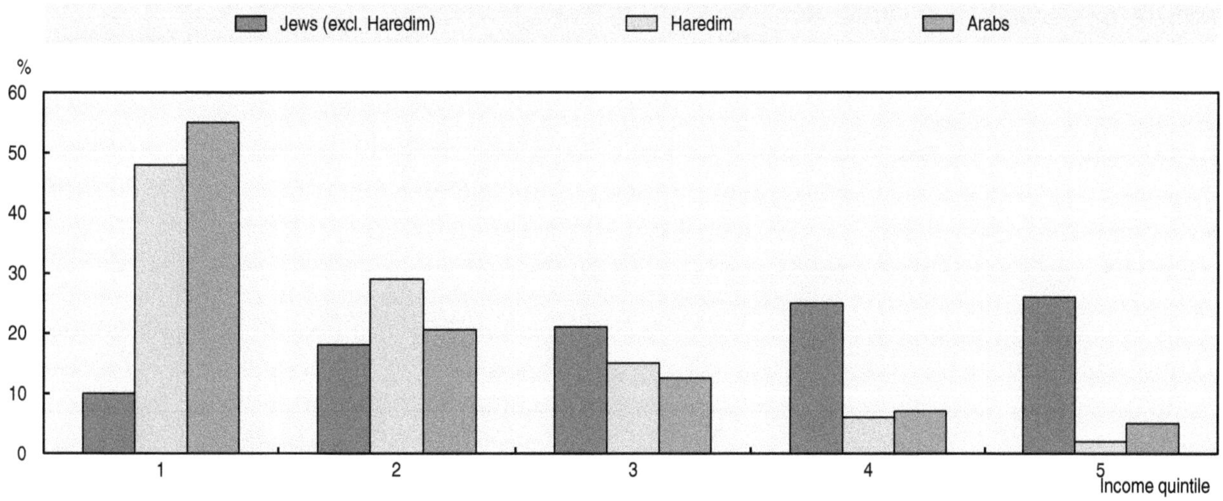

Source: Israeli General Social Survey 2012.

StatLink http://dx.doi.org/10.1787/888933293504

Figure 2.31. **Share of all poor individuals accounted for each population group in Israel, 2012**

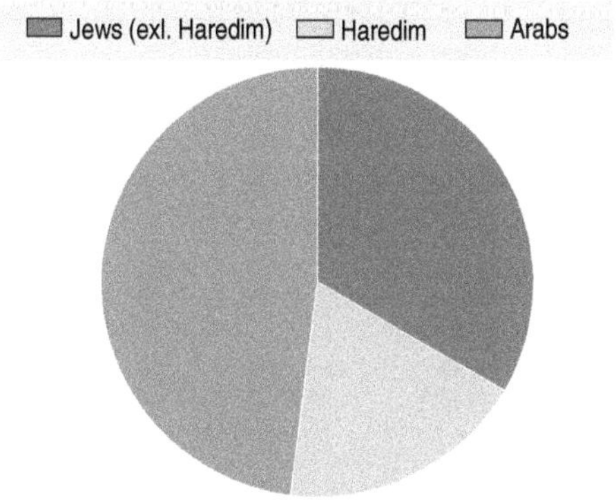

Source: OECD calculations based on National Insurance Institute (2013).

StatLink http://dx.doi.org/10.1787/888933293518

The high fertility rates among the comparatively disadvantaged Israeli Arabs and Haredim implies that child poverty is extremely high in Israel. In fact, according to Luxembourg Income Study data from the mid-2000s, Israel had the highest rates of child poverty among the 22 OECD countries for which data are available, with over a third of the country's children living below the poverty line, even after welfare assistance was taken into account. This is well above levels seen in the country with the second-highest rates of child poverty – the United States – which had a quarter of its children living under the poverty line after welfare assistance in the same period (Ben-David and Bleikh, 2013). However, high rates of child poverty cannot be solely attributed to large family sizes among the most disadvantaged population groups. Figure 2.33 shows that, even when Haredi and Arab children are excluded from the sample, over 1 in 5 Israeli children live in households that are below the poverty line in disposable income terms. This compares to an OECD average of 13% of children living in poverty in 2010, according to the OECD Family

Figure 2.32. **The total burden of poverty in Israel, by population group**

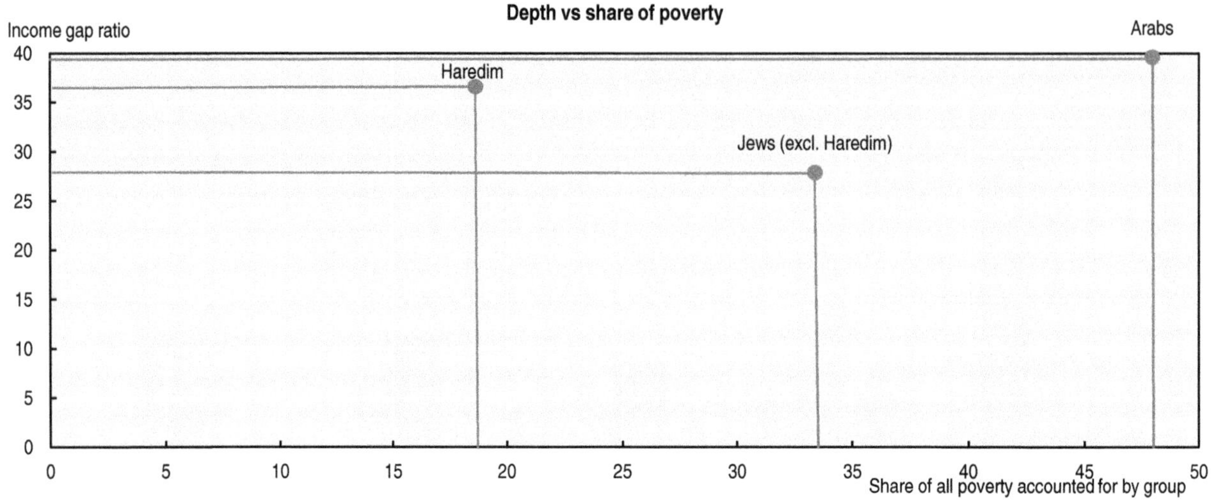

Source: OECD calculations based on National Insurance Institute (2012).

StatLink http://dx.doi.org/10.1787/888933293523

Figure 2.33. **Share of children living under the poverty line in Israel**

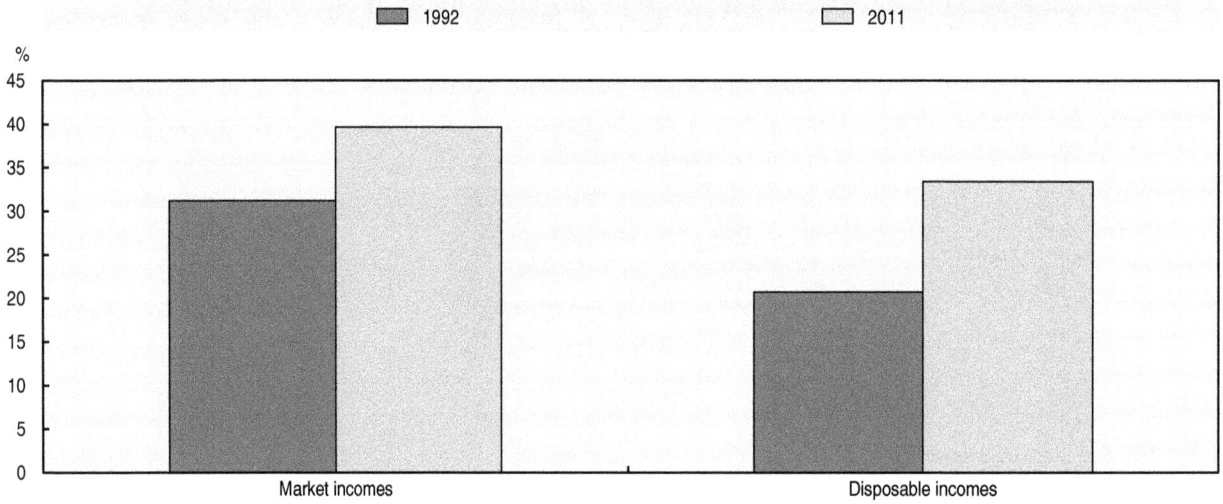

Source: Ben-David and Bleikh (2013), based on Central Bureau of Statistics data.

StatLink http://dx.doi.org/10.1787/888933293537

Database.[9] These data also show that child poverty rates have risen significantly over time, although the latest data from the National Insurance Institute suggest that this trend has started to reverse, with the share of children living in poor families falling from 33.7% in 2012 to 30.8% in 2013 (NII, 2013).

Israel's elderly population is relatively small, with only 10.6% of the population aged over 65 in 2013, especially when compared with European countries such as Sweden, Italy and Germany (with the share of the population around or exceeding 20%). The poverty rate among the elderly is high in Israel, as is common in OECD countries, and social benefits in Israel seems to have comparatively much less impact in reducing poverty in this group. The international comparison of the market income in Israel and other developed countries is somewhat problematic due to the fact Israel has a policy of encouraging private pension saving and from 2008 mandatory pension while pension in most developed countries is based mostly on government social insurance. According to the OECD Income Distribution database, in 2013, 46% of Israel's elderly population would fall under the poverty line based on market income, which exclude pension payments (Figure 2.34). While this is a large share, it is actually much smaller than the average rate of market-income elderly poverty across OECD countries (70%). However, once taxes and public transfers are taken into account, Israel had in 2013 the fourth highest rate of (disposable-income) relative poverty among the elderly in the OECD, after Korea, Australia and Mexico. High levels of immigration of retired and elderly people in Israel are a likely contributing factor to elderly poverty, especially when immigrants come from countries that do not pay pensions such as Former Soviet Union countries or Ethiopia.

Figure 2.34. **Relative income poverty amongst the elderly**

2013 or latest available year

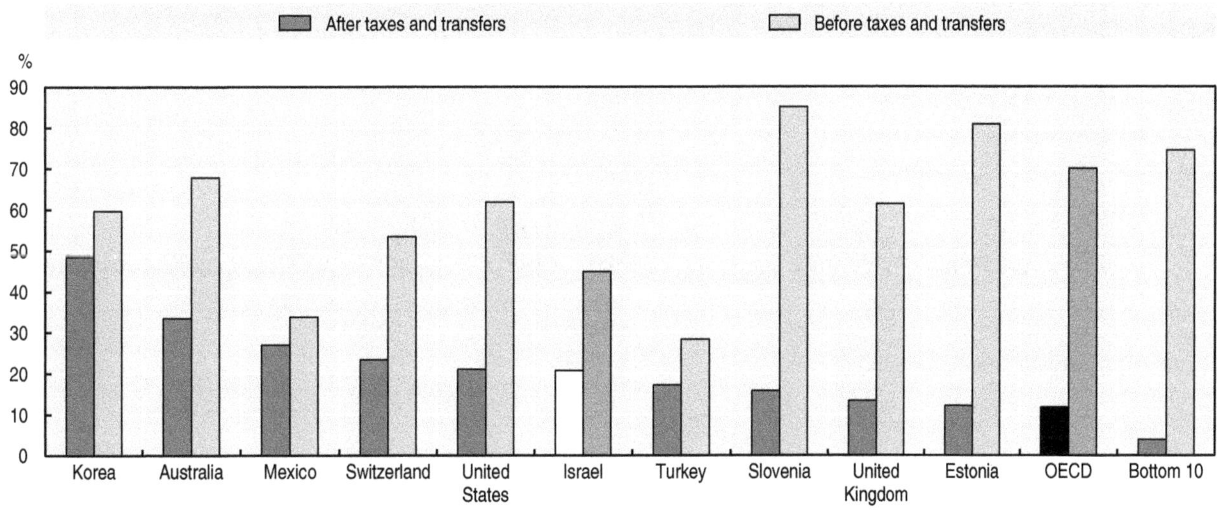

Note: Share of people aged over 65 years with an income below 50% of the respective national median income. No recent data available for Chile or Japan.

Source: OECD Income Distribution (database), http://dx.doi.org/10.1787/socwel-data-en.

StatLink http://dx.doi.org/10.1787/888933293540

Wealth inequalities between population groups

In recent years, the role of wealth (as opposed to income) in creating and sustaining economic inequality in general, and ethnic inequalities in particular, has been increasingly recognised (Conley, 2001; Campbell and Kaufman, 2006; Piketty, 2014). Wealth disparities tend to be much greater than income disparities, as they accumulate over time. People's wealth is also a significant determinant of well-being in older age after leaving the labour market, and plays an important role in reducing economic insecurity. Data on the distribution of household wealth tend to be much less developed than those measuring household income, and Israel is no exception in this regard. However, a recent study by Tel Aviv University researchers provides some indication of wealth inequalities by population group in Israel; these data, however, do not identify the Haredim as a separate group, and are based on a 2005-6 European research survey on ageing that covered only the population aged over 50 (Semyonov and Lewin-Epstein, 2011).[10]

The study focuses on five population groups: Israeli-born Jews, Israeli Arabs, Jews born in either Europe or America, Jews born in either Asia or Africa, and new immigrants arriving from the Former Soviet Union (FSU) after 1989. It finds that the net worth of Arabs is less than a quarter that of Israeli-born Jews, and less than half that of Israeli Jews born in Europe, America, Asia or Africa (Figure 2.35). The most wealth-deprived group identified by the study is that of the newest group of immigrants from the FSU, with less than one-twentieth of the net worth of Israeli-born Jews. These findings highlight that while ethnicity is an important determinant of wealth inequalities in Israel, immigration also plays a role as some immigrants tend to arrive in the country with very little wealth.

Figure 2.35. **Distribution of household net worth in Israel, by selected population group, 2005-06**

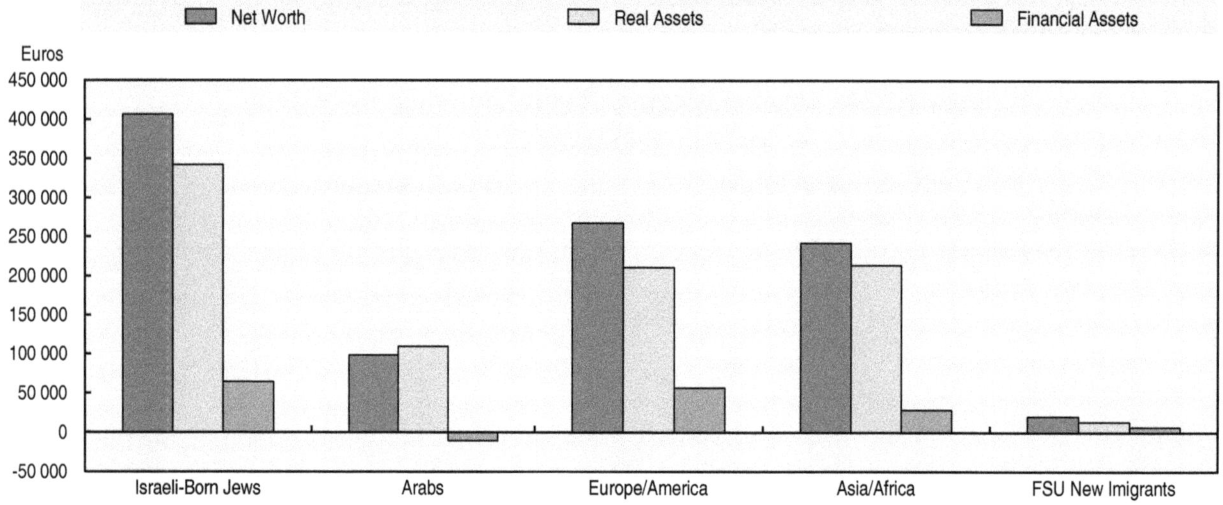

Source: Semyonov and Lewin-Epstein (2011).

StatLink http://dx.doi.org/10.1787/888933293553

While Israeli Jews born in Europe, America, Africa and Asia, arriving in earlier waves of immigration had several decades to establish themselves in the country, it is clear that those arriving more recently from the Former Soviet Union have found it harder to accumulate wealth. One reason for this is that immigrants are much less likely to have benefitted from inheritance: 35% of Israeli-born Jewish households received an inheritance (compared to 24% of European-Americans, 19% of Asian-Africans, 19% of Arabs, and only 2% of new Former Soviet Union immigrants); also, the value of that inheritance was almost ten times larger than that of new FSU immigrants, more than twice that received by Arabs and Asian-Africans and 1.3 times larger than that received by European-Americans; (Semyonov and Lewin-Epstein, 2011).

Real assets (the bulk of which for most households is made up of housing) account for most net worth for all population groups. For Arabs, the value for financial assets is actually negative; indicating that debts and financial obligations exceed non-financial holdings. Home ownership rates tend to be much higher among Israeli Arabs than among Israeli Jews, and while the value of Arab housing is much lower, it plays a more significant role in wealth accumulation in Arab households.

Economic insecurity

Economic security is broader than income and wealth, but it is a closely-related issue and should therefore be considered in addition to measures of income poverty, as insecurity impacts on well-being above and beyond a person's current standard of living.

Job insecurity, as measured by the share of people who fear to lose their jobs, has declined slightly over the last decade for all population groups (Figure 2.36). Despite this, pessimism regarding their future economic situation increased slightly for both Arabs and the non-Haredi Jewish population over the most recent five-year period. While the Arab population is characterised by relatively high levels of economic insecurity, the Haredi population report lower levels of insecurity than other Jews. This is consistent with the relative disengagement from the labour market and high level of dependence on the welfare state characteristic of the Haredi population. Although Haredim people have low levels of income, they are less exposed to economic shocks than other groups of Israeli society.

Figure 2.36. **Trends in perceived economic insecurity in Israel, by population group**

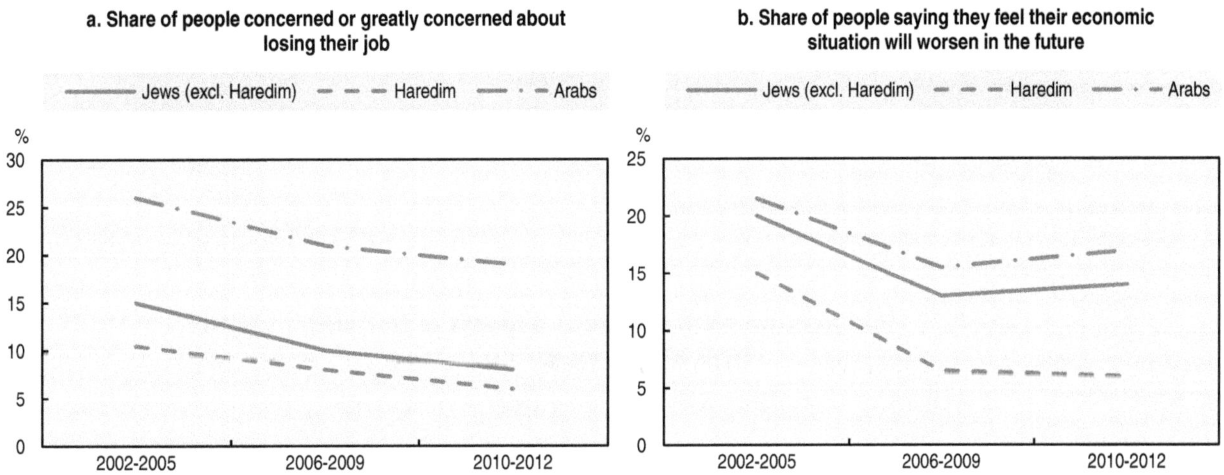

Source: Israeli General Social Survey, Central Bureau of Statistics.

StatLink http://dx.doi.org/10.1787/888933293565

Given the importance of economic insecurity to people's well-being, it would be important to compare the degree of economic insecurity in Israel to that existing in other OECD countries. However, no established measures currently exist in this field.

Housing

There are significant differences between population groups in terms of housing quality. Housing density is almost twice as high in Arab households compared to non-Orthodox Jewish households, with an average of 0.8 rooms per person in the former group, compared with 1.5 rooms per person in the latter (Figure 2.37). Housing density is also high among Haredi households, with an average of 0.9 rooms per person. Housing density is an imperfect substitute for comparing housing size, as individual rooms tend be somewhat larger in Arab households than in Jewish ones (Epstein et al., 2004). However housing density does give a general sense that Arab and Haredi households tend to live in more crowded conditions than is the case for the Jewish non-Haredi population. This is also likely to reflect the much larger family size of Arab and Haredi households. For example, according to the 2012 General Social Survey, 40% of Arab households and 45% of Haredi households consisted of 6 or more people, as compared to only 16% for the Israeli population as a whole.

Another way of comparing differences in housing quality among the population is through subjective measures of housing satisfaction. Figure 2.38 compares the levels of

Figure 2.37. **Housing density in Israel, by population group**

2012

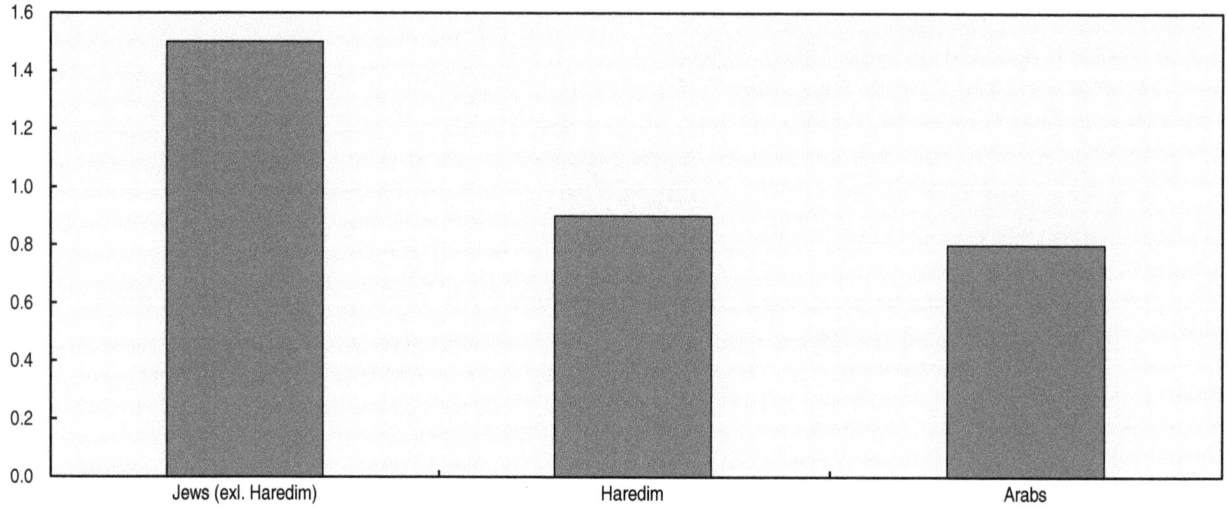

Source: Israeli General Social Survey, Central Bureau of Statistics.

StatLink http://dx.doi.org/10.1787/888933293573

Figure 2.38. **Satisfaction with different aspects of housing in Israel, by population group**

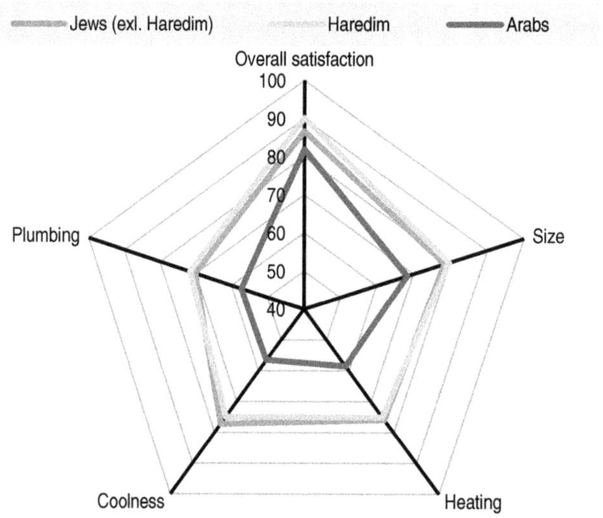

Note: Data for overall satisfaction of dwelling from 2012, all other data from 2006.
Source: Israeli General Social Survey, Central Bureau of Statistics.

StatLink http://dx.doi.org/10.1787/888933293581

satisfaction by different population group with a number of aspects of housing, such as the heating, coolness and size of the dwelling, as well as the condition of plumbing and overall housing satisfaction. Overall, these measure highlight little difference between Haredi and non-Haredi Jews; Arabs, however, report much lower satisfaction than both of those groups in all areas of housing covered.

Beyond issues pertaining to the quality of the dwelling itself, its location can also have an important impact on people's well-being. Access to education, employment opportunities and public services is highly dependent on location in Israel, with people living in the North and the South of the country tending to be at a greater disadvantage than those in the geographic centre (see Box 2.2).

Box 2.2. **The OECD Regional Well-being Index**

The OECD Regional Well-being Index gives some insight into how well-being outcomes differ across regions within Israel (Figure 2.39). The Index measures performance in OECD sub-national regions across a number of well-being dimensions, which are similar but not identical to those presented in the *How's Life?* framework, assigning a score from 10 to 0, where 10 is the best score across OECD regions and 0 is the worst. Tel Aviv scores highest in terms of housing, accessibility to services, jobs, income and (jointly with the Central district) education. The Jerusalem district scores very high for safety, but very low for housing, jobs and accessibility to services. The Northern and Southern districts tend to have lower scores, particularly for health, safety, jobs and housing. While the Index is a crude measure, it highlights a high degree of variability across Israeli regions on these well-being outcomes.

Figure 2.39. **OECD Regional Well-being Index among Israeli regions**

2014 or latest year available

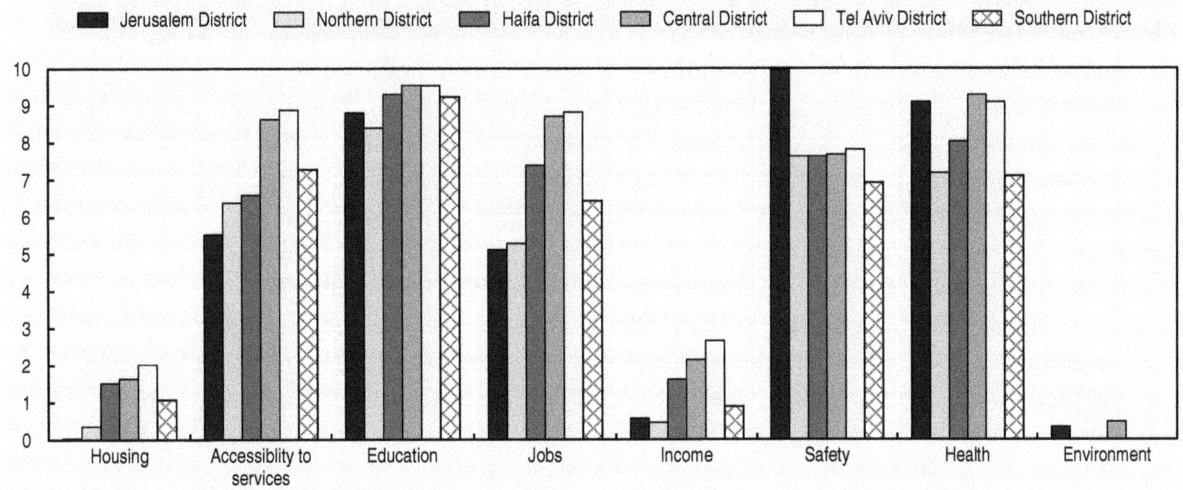

Source: OECD Regional Well-being Database, http://dx.doi.org/10.1787/region-data-en.

StatLink http://dx.doi.org/10.1787/888933293595

The way people feel about their local area is also important. Figure 2.40 shows a selection of indicators of satisfaction with the local area by population group. Haredi Jews are the most satisfied with their neighbourhood at 92%, followed by non-Haredi Jews at 85% and Arabs with only 75%. In all cases – satisfaction with neighbourhood, satisfaction with cleanliness of neighbourhood, and satisfaction with public green space – Arabs show the lowest levels of satisfaction, with a particularly large gap in the area of cleanliness and green space, with only 39% and 19% of Arabs saying they are satisfied, respectively, compared with 68% and 61% of non-Haredi Jews. Across all regions, Israeli performance is worst in the domains of the environment, housing and income.

Figure 2.40. **Indicators of satisfaction with local area in Israel, by population group, 2012**

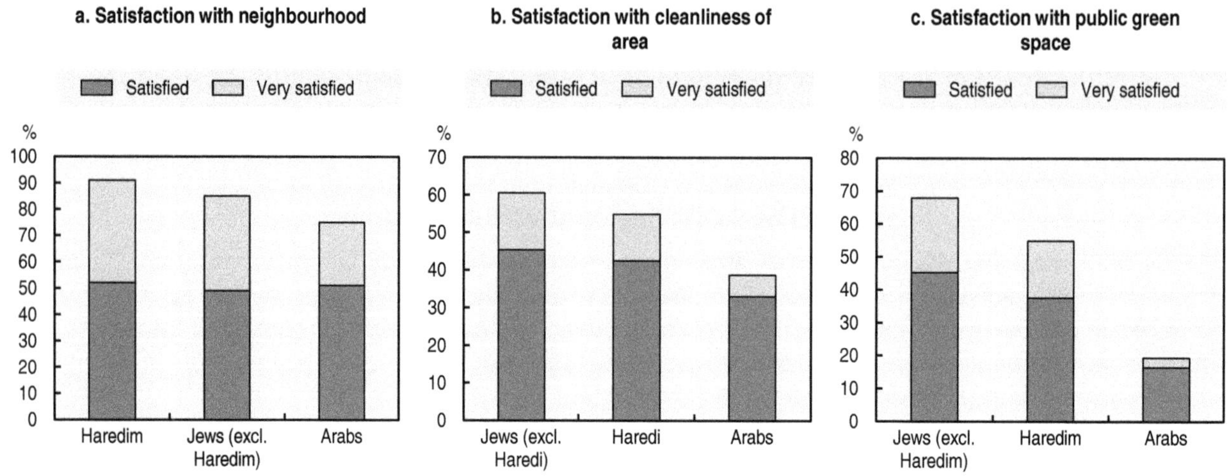

Source: Israeli General Social Survey, Central Bureau of Statistics.

StatLink http://dx.doi.org/10.1787/888933293602

Health

Despite an overall strong performance in the area of health, as with other dimensions of well-being, inequalities exist. Arabs have significantly lower life expectancy (3 years less in the case of men, 3.4 years less in the case of women in 2013 according to CBS data) and higher rates of respiratory disease, diabetes, heart disease, and cancer, as well as having higher rates of child and infant mortality than Jews (OECD, 2012). These differences reflect socio-economic and cultural differences between communities. For example, variations in mortality between Arab and Jewish localities have been found to be largely accounted for by socio-economic differences between localities (Chernichovsky and Anson, 2005).

Summary of differences in well-being outcomes by population group

Figure 2.41 shows outcomes for a selection of headline indicators related to well-being for the Haredi and Arab populations as a ratio of outcomes for the non-Haredi Jewish population. All indicators have been presented so that the higher the ratio the better the outcome in relation to non-Haredi Jews. What is striking about the chart is that while Arabs show a clear pattern of poor well-being outcomes in relation to non-Haredi Jews across all measures, the picture is much more mixed for Haredi Jews. Labour force participation and tertiary educational study are the only areas where outcomes are unambiguously worse for both Arabs and Haredim. As discussed earlier in this chapter, improving access to education and employment for minority groups is a key concern for Israel, for both current and future well-being.

Conversely, Haredim report better health outcomes (in terms of both health satisfaction and freedom from disability) and higher levels of perceived safety, life satisfaction, and satisfaction with their economic situation, than both Arabs and non-Haredi Jews. Little research is available to explain why health outcomes are generally better amongst this group. It is hard to obtain reliable data about Haredi behaviour as these communities may be insular and mistrusting or even hostile towards external interference, leading to a much lower response rate in surveys or research studies (Rier et al., 2008). Ultra-Orthodoxy emerged in the late 19th and early 20th centuries as a rejection of the Western liberal tradition, putting a higher value on spiritualism and religious study than material

Figure 2.41. **Headline well-being indicators in Israel, by population group**

Well-being outcomes for Haredim and Arabs, benchmarked against outcomes for non-Haredi Jews

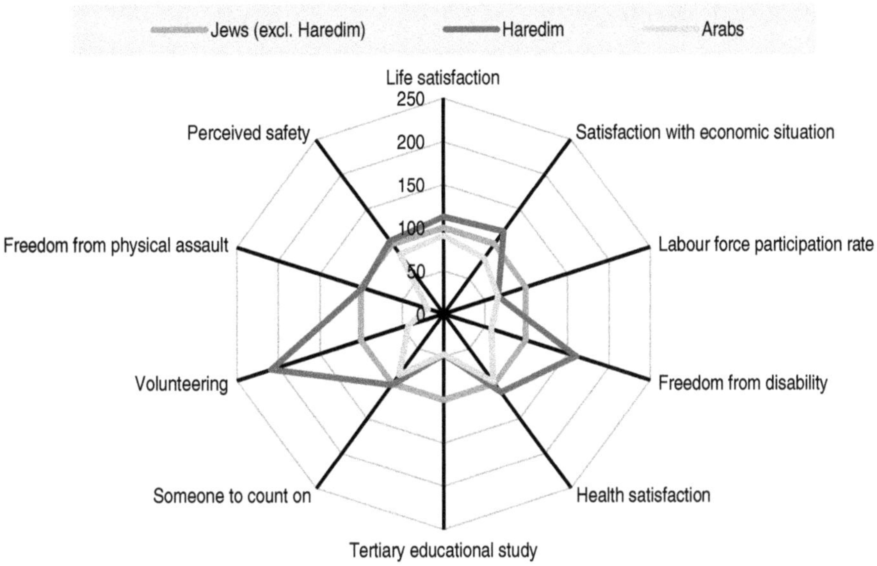

Source: Israeli General Social Survey 2012.

StatLink http://dx.doi.org/10.1787/888933293617

well-being (Berman, 2000). As a result, Haredi values and lifestyles are radically different from those of other groups in Israeli society (see Chapter 4). This may go some way towards explaining why they score higher in these areas despite having generally lower incomes and rates of employment and education.

Well-being outcomes for men and women also vary by population group. Figure 2.42 shows outcomes for men and women in four areas: labour force participation, tertiary educational study, self-reported health status and life satisfaction.

Gender inequalities by population group in labour force participation and educational attainment were discussed earlier in this chapter: while gender gaps for non-Haredi Jews in these areas tend to be relatively small, the impact of gender has quite divergent effects on the Haredi and Arab populations, with Haredi men being much less likely to work or study at the tertiary level than Haredi women, and Arab women having much lower labour force participation rates than Arab men. According to General Social Survey data, while rates of tertiary educational study are much lower for Arabs overall, the gender gap for Arabs at this level of education is almost non-existent. Regarding self-reported health status, while men report better health status than women for all population groups, the gender gap is largest for non-Haredi Jews at 5 percentage points, and smallest for Haredim at only 1 percentage point. Finally, the gender gap in life satisfaction is completely different for the three population groups: non-Haredi Jewish women report lower levels of life satisfaction than non-Haredi men, Haredi women report slightly higher levels than Haredi men, and Arab men and women report the exact same levels of life satisfaction.

However, with the exception of labour force participation rates among the Arab and the Haredim, and tertiary education study among the Haredim, in general, differences between groups are more important than gender differences within groups.

Figure 2.42. **Gender differences in selected well-being outcomes in Israel, by population group**
Share of population %, 2013 or latest available year

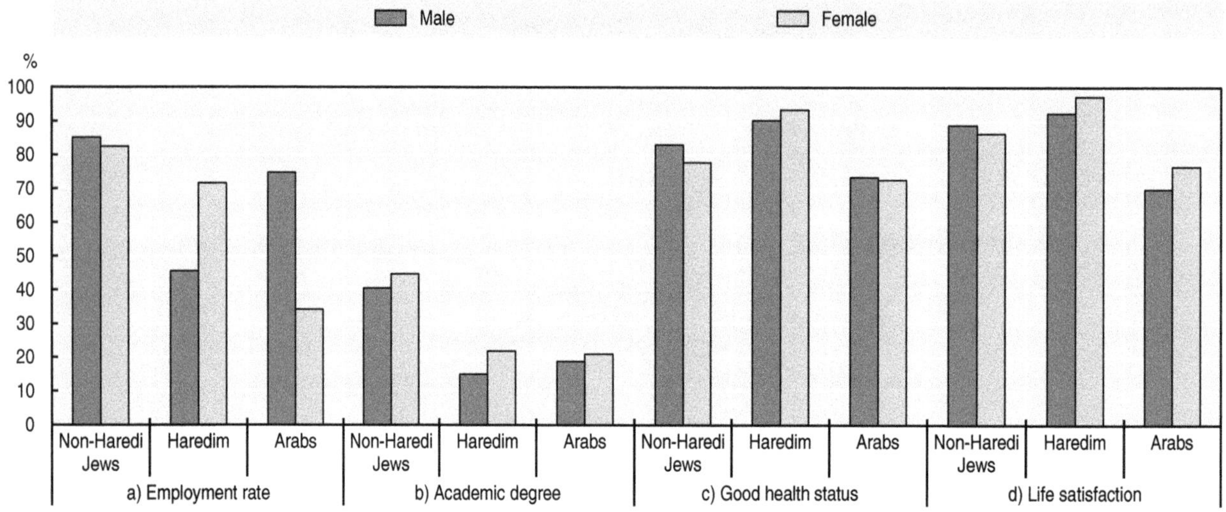

Note: Chart shows the share of people in each population group, and by gender who, a) are employed, b) have studied in a learning institution towards an academic degree; c) report that their health is "good", "very good" or "excellent", and d) say that they are "satisfied" or "very satisfied" with their life. Employment rate data are from 2014, and represent the share of the working-age population, defined as 25-66 years for men and 25-61 years for women. All other data are from 2013, and represent the share of the total population group.
Source: Israeli Labour Force Survey and Israeli General Social Survey, Central Bureau of Statistics.

StatLink http://dx.doi.org/10.1787/888933293626

Conclusion

Israel is a complex, and in many ways, unique country, given its history, geo-political situation and demographic make-up. Reflecting this complexity, well-being outcomes vary significantly depending on the measure selected, and the sub-group considered. While on some aggregate measures, the country performs well – and is among the best in the OECD, particularly in terms of life satisfaction, health status and educational attainment – Israel also presents some of the poorest outcomes in the OECD in areas such as income poverty, housing and air quality. Some paradoxes are also present within individual well-being domains, such as in education, where high upper secondary and tertiary educational attainment rates contrast with comparatively low learning outcomes of students, as measured by PISA scores.

However, the main message of this chapter is that average measures alone do not give a complete picture of well-being conditions: it is simply impossible to understand well-being outcomes in Israel without an in-depth examination of the distribution of outcomes and the differences between population groups. For the three population groups covered here – non-Haredi Jews, Haredim, and Arabs – well-being outcomes differ significantly. Among these three groups, Israeli Arabs are unambiguously disadvantaged across all dimensions for which measures are available, experiencing higher rates of poverty, and lower levels of labour force participation, educational attainment and health status. These multiple disadvantages are likely to be mutually reinforcing, with low educational attainment leading to unfavourable labour market outcomes, for example.

The picture is slightly different for the Haredim. While Haredi Jews also experience higher levels of income poverty and lower levels of labour force participation and educational attainment, they tend to report much higher levels of satisfaction with their life, economic situation, housing, and health. These differences may well reflect fundamental differences in values among the Haredi population, which themselves constitute barriers to convergence in well-being outcomes between the Haredi and the rest of Israeli society (see Chapter 4). In other words, Haredi disadvantage is strongly influenced by cultural preferences that prevail within the group, while Arab disadvantage – although undoubtedly also reflecting some cultural attitudes and values (e.g. family size, female labour force participation) – is strongly influenced by broader factors. Inequalities also exist that go beyond the three broad groups here, and which cut across all population groups, such as the high levels of income poverty among children. While Arab Israelis and Haredi Jews face the highest risk of income poverty, a third of all Israelis in poverty belong to neither of these groups.

Notes

1. According to the latest estimations available from the Central Bureau of Statistics, approximately 222 400 Bedouin were living in the southern district in Beer Sheva sub-district in 2013, and a further 51 000 in the northern district.
2. Air quality guidelines from the World Health Organisation (WHO) recommend a $PM_{2.5}$ concentration standard of not more than 10 micrograms per cubic metre for average annual exposure (WHO, 2006). A European Union Air Quality Directive places an obligation on countries to limit the population's annual $PM_{2.5}$ concentration exposure to 20 micrograms per cubic metre, based on a three-year average period (European Commission, 2015).
3. Deaths by assault and homicide rates are similar, but not identical indicators. Deaths by assault figures are obtained from administrative data on cause of death, whereas homicide rates depend on police crime records. The *How Life?* framework uses deaths by assault as the more accurate indicator for the 2015 edition. However, the date here, while not directly comparable nonetheless give a meaningful picture of violent deaths, and the contribution of terrorist violence in Israel.
4. Survey questions pertaining directly to the impact of political violence on subjective well-being are not available, and so it is currently difficult to directly evaluate this important aspect of Israeli personal security. Romanov et al. (2012) use life satisfaction data to explore this issue in Israel and found that terrorism had practically no immediate or delayed effect on the happiness of Jewish Israelis, but adversely affected the happiness of Israeli Arabs.
5. For example, differences in well-being outcomes exist between Jewish sub-groups of different ethnic/geographic origin, for example between Ashkenazi Jews, of primarily European descent, and Mizrahi Jews, of primarily African and Middle Eastern descent (Haberfeld and Cohen, 2007). The large group of post-Cold War immigrants from the Former Soviet Union (FSU) also show significant differences in well-being outcomes with respect to the rest of the Jewish population (Al-Haj, 2004). While the majority of Israeli Arabs are Muslim, the Arab population also includes Christian and Druze sub-groups. Within the Arab population, the Bedouins tend to be particularly disadvantaged (Abu-Bader and Gottlieb, 2009).
6. Israeli official poverty figures are provided by the National Insurance Institute. While the OECD and National Insurance Institute (NII) both calculate poverty in a similar way (with median disposable income as the relevant indicator of standard of living and the poverty line defined as half of that), the method of translating the number of individuals in a family in consumption units ("weighting scale") is different. See the Annual Reports of the NII (NII 2007-12) for more information.
7. At the time of writing, the most recent NII report was from 2013. However, problems with the data for population breakdowns mean that only the aggregate data from 2013 is presented in this chapter, with 2012 being the most recent data available for population breakdowns between Jews, Haredim and Arabs.
8. And as NIII calculations for the Jewish population include the Ultra-Orthodox, the actual rates for non-Haredi Jews are lower still.
9. *www.oecd.org/els/soc/CO2_2_ChildPoverty_Jan2014.pdf.*
10. These researchers reason that the focus on people aged 50 or older allows examining households that have had the opportunity to accumulate wealth.

References

Abu-Bader, S. and D. Gottlieb (2009), "Poverty, Education and Employment in the Arab-Bedouin Society: A Comparative View", *National Insurance Institute Working Papers* No. 98, *www.btl.gov.il/Publications/research/Documents/mechkar_98.pdf*.

Al-Haj, M. (2004), *Immigration and Ethnic Formation in a Deeply Divided Society: The Case of the 1990s Immigrants from the Former Soviet Union in Israel*, Brill, Boston.

Andrews, D. and A. Caldera Sanchez (2011), "The Evolution of Homeownership Rates in Selected OECD Countries: Demographic and Public Policy Influences", *OECD Journal: Economic Studies*, Vol. 2011/1, *http://dx.doi.org/10.1787/eco_studies-2011-5kg0vswqpmg2*.

Bank of Israel (2012), *Annual Report 2011*, *www.boi.org.il/en/NewsAndPublications/RegularPublications/Pages/eng_doch11e.aspx*.

Bank of Israel (2015), *Annual Report 2014* (extract), *www.boi.org.il/en/NewsAndPublications/PressReleases/Pages/18-03-2015-LevelOfInfrastructure.aspx*.

Ben-David, D. (2012), "The Start-Up Nation's Threat from Within", in Ben-David, D. (ed), *State of the Nation Report 2011-12: Society, Economy and Policy in Israel*, Taub Center for Social Policy Studies in Israel, *http://taubcenter.org.il/tauborgilwp/wp-content/uploads/State-of-the-Nation-Report-2011-2012-21.pdf*.

Ben-David, D. and H. Bleikh (2013), "Poverty and Inequality Over Time: in Israel and the OECD", *State of the Nation Report 2013: Society, Economy and Policy in Israel*, Taub Center for Social Policy Studies in Israel, *http://taubcenter.org.il/index.php/featured-publication/state-of-the-nation-2013/lang/en/*.

Berman, E. (2000), "Sect, subsidy and sacrifice: an economist's view of Ultra-Orthodox Jews", *Quarterly Journal of Economics*, August 2000, pp. 905-953.

Brezzi, M. and D. Sanchez-Serra (2014), "Breathing the Same Air? Measuring Air Pollution in Cities and Regions", *OECD Regional Development Working Papers*, No. 2014/11, OECD Publishing, Paris, *http://dx.doi.org/10.1787/5jxrb7rkxf21-en*.

Campbell, L. and R. Kaufman (2006), "Racial Differences in Household Wealth: Beyond Black and White", *Research in Social Stratification and Mobility*, 24:131-152.

CBS Central Bureau of Statistics Israel (2012), "Long-Range Population Projections for Israel: 2009-59", Central Bureau of Statistics, Demography and Census Department, Israel, *www.cbs.gov.il/publications/tec27.pdf*.

CBS Central Bureau of Statistics Israel (2014), *Israel in Figures 2014*, *www1.cbs.gov.il/publications/isr_in_n14e.pdf*.

Chernichovsky, D. and J. Anson (2005), "The Jewish-Arab Divide in Life Expectancy in Israel", *Economics & Human Biology*, 3:1, pp. 123-137.

Conley, D. (2001), "Decomposing the Black-White Wealth Gap: the Role of Parental Resources, Inheritance and Investment Dynamics", *Sociological Inquiry*, 71:1, pp. 39-66.

European Commission (2015), Air Quality Standards, *http://ec.europa.eu/environment/air/quality/standards.htm* (accessed on 5 July 2015).

EEA European Environment Agency (2014), *Horizon 2020 Mediterranean report Annex 3: Israel*, EEA Technical Report 6/2014, *www.sviva.gov.il/English/env_topics/InternationalCooperation/European-Union/Documents/SEIS-Israel-Country-Report-June2014.pdf*.

ESS European Social Survey database (2002-12), *www.europeansocialsurvey.org/*.

Gallup World Poll, *www.gallup.com/strategicconsulting/en-us/worldpoll/aspx*.

Gottlieb D. and L. Kushnir, 2009, "Social Policy Targeting and Binary Information Transfer between Surveys", *Economics: The Open-Access, Open-Assessment E-Journal*, Vol.3, 2009-30.

Gruber, N. (2014), "The Israeli Housing Market", in *State of the Nation Report 2014*, Taub Center for Social Policy Studies in Israel, *http://taubcenter.org.il/the-singer-series-state-of-the-nation-report-2014/*.

Haberfeld, Y. and Y. Cohen, "Gender, ethnic, and national earnings gaps in Israel: The role of rising inequality", *Social Science Research*, 36:2, pp. 654-672.

Kahneman, D. and A. Krueger (2006), "Developments in the Measurement of Subjective Well-Being", *The Journal of Economic Perspectives*, 20:1, pp. 3-24.

Lewin-Epstein, N., I. Adler and M. Semyenov (2004), "Home ownership and social inequality in Israel" in Grusky, D. and P. England (eds.), *Home Ownership and Social Inequality in Comparative Perspective*, Stanford University Press, Stanford, California.

NII National Insurance Institute (2007-12), *Poverty and Social Gaps Annual Reports 2007-12*, *www.btl.gov.il/English%20Homepage/Publications/Poverty_Report/Pages/default.aspx*.

OECD (2009), *OECD Economic Survey: Israel*, OECD publishing, Paris, *http://dx.doi.org/10.1787/eco_surveys-isr-2009-en*.

OECD (2011a), *How's Life? Measuring Well-being*, OECD Publishing, Paris, *http://dx.doi.org/10.1787/9789264121164-en*.

OECD (2011b), *OECD Environmental Performance Reviews: Israel*, OECD Publishing, Paris, *http://dx.doi.org/10.1787/9789264117563-en*.

OECD (2012), *OECD Reviews of Healthcare Quality: Israel*, OECD Publishing, Paris, *http://dx.doi.org/10.1787/18151973*.

OECD (2013a), *How's Life 2013? Measuring Well-Being*, OECD Publishing, Paris, *http://dx.doi.org/10.1787/23089679*.

OECD (2013b), *OECD Economic Surveys: Israel*, OECD Publishing, Paris, *http://dx.doi.org/10.1787/22251847*.

OECD (2013c), *Review of Recent Developments and Progress in Labour Market and Social Policy in Israel*, OECD Publishing, Paris, *http://dx.doi.org/10.1787/9789264200401-en*.

OECD (2013d), *Education at a Glance 2013: OECD Indicators*, OECD Publishing, Paris, *http://dx.doi.org/10.1787/19991487*.

OECD (2013e), *Health at a Glance 2013: OECD Indicators*, OECD Publishing, Paris, *http://dx.doi.org/10.1787/19991312*.

OECD (2013f), *Government at a Glance 2013*, OECD Publishing, Paris, *http://dx.doi.org/10.1787/22214399*.

OECD (2014a), *OECD Science, Technology and Industry Outlook 2014*, OECD Publishing, Paris, *http://dx.doi.org/10.1787/19991428*.

OECD (2014b), *Society at a Glance 2014: OECD Social Indicators*, OECD Publishing, Paris, *http://dx.doi.org/10.1787/19991290*.

OECD (2014c), *Green Growth Indicators 2014*, OECD Green Growth Studies, OECD Publishing, Paris, *http://dx.doi.org/10.1787/9789264202030-en*.

OECD (2015), *How's Life?: 2015 Measuring Well-being*, OECD Publishing, Paris, *http://dx.doi.org/10.1787/how_life-2015-en*.

OECD (2016), *OECD Economic Surveys: Israel*, OECD Publishing, Paris.

Piketty, T. (2014), *Capital in the Twenty-First Century*, Belknap Press of the Harvard University Press, Cambridge, Massachusetts.

Rier, D., A. Schwartzbaum and C. Heller (2008), "Methodological Issues in Studying an Insular, Traditional Population: A Women's Health Survey Among Israeli Haredi (Ultra-Orthodox) Jews", *Women & Health*, 48:4, pp. 363-381.

Rosenhek, Z. and M. Shalev (2014), "The political economy of Israel's "social justice" protests: A class and generational analysis", *Contemporary Social Science*, 9:1.

Romanov, D., A. Zussman and N. Zussman (2012), "Does Terrorism Demoralize? Evidence from Israel", *Economica*, 79: 183-198.

Scrivens, K. and C. Smith (2013), "Four Interpretations of Social Capital: An Agenda for Measurement", *OECD Statistics Directorate Working Paper* STD/DOC(2013)6, *www.oecd.org/std/social-capital-project-and-question-databank.htm*.

Semyonov, M. and N. Lewin-Epstein (2011), "Wealth Inequality: Ethnic Disparities in Israeli Society", *Social Forces*, 89: 3, pp. 935-960.

Senor, D. and S. Singer (2011), *Start-up nation: The story of Israel's economic miracle*, Random House, LLC.

Shalev, M. (2012), "The Economic Background of the Social Protest of Summer 2011", in Ben-David, D. (ed), *State of the Nation Report 2011-12: Society, Economy and Policy in Israel*, Taub Center for Social Policy Studies in Israel, *http://taubcenter.org.il/tauborgilwp/wp-content/uploads/State-of-the-Nation-Report-2011-2012-21.pdf*.

Startup Genome (2012), *The Startup Ecosystem Report 2012*, *http://blog.startupcompass.co/pages/entrepreneurship-ecosystem-report*.

World Health Organisation (WHO) (2006), *World Health Organization: Air Quality Guidelines for Particulate Matter, Ozone, Nitrogen Dioxide and Sulfur Dioxide*, Global Update 2005, *www.who.int/phe/health_topics/outdoorair/outdoorair_aqg/en/*.

World Health Organisation (WHO) (2014), *Ambient (outdoor) Air Pollution in Cities 2014* (database), *www.who.int/phe/health_topics/outdoorair/databases/cities/en/*.

Chapter 3

How sustainable is well-being over time in Israel?

Will future generations in Israel enjoy the same standards of well-being as the generation living today? This is the central question addressed by this chapter, which focuses on the sustainability of well-being over time in Israel. Assessing the sustainability of well-being over time is challenging, since many of the things that will affect people's well-being in the future are either difficult to measure or they simply cannot be known in the present. However, it is possible to make an initial assessment of the sustainability of well-being in Israel by looking at the capital stocks that underpin future well-being outcomes. The indicators presented in this chapter do not allow drawing a definitive picture with respect to the sustainability of well-being in Israel, although they show some improvements in stocks of produced capital and suggest that Israel needs to boost its human capital. Beyond this the picture is more mixed, and there are significant measurement gaps in the area of natural and social capital.

The statistical data for Israel are supplied by and under the responsibility of the relevant Israeli authorities. The use of such data by the OECD is without prejudice to the status of the Golan heights, East Jerusalem and Israeli settlements in the West Bank under the terms of international law.

Introduction

Will future generations in Israel enjoy the same standards of well-being as the generation living today? This is the central question addressed by this chapter, which focuses on the sustainability of well-being over time in Israel. Assessing the sustainability of well-being over time is challenging, since many of the things that will affect people's well-being in the future are either difficult to measure or they simply cannot be known in the present. For example, the changing tastes, needs and wants of future generations as well as the technology available to them will have a significant impact on future well-being, but cannot be predicted now. It is, however, possible to look at the stocks of resources that are available today, and which will be used to produce well-being tomorrow, and to evaluate whether these stocks are increasing over time, being depleted, or will remain largely unchanged. This is at the heart of the *capital approach* to measuring sustainability, which provides the framework for this chapter.

What is sustainability?

Sustainability is concerned with the issue of whether future generations will be able to enjoy the same levels of well-being that people enjoy today. This was reflected in the definition of sustainable development adopted by the United Nations World Commission on Environment and Development in 1987: "Sustainable development is the kind of development that meets the needs of the present without compromising the ability of future generations to meet their own needs". At the heart of the concept of sustainability is the idea of a potential trade-off between current and future well-being. If people deplete the resources that will sustain future well-being in pursuing better outcomes now, then those resources will not be available in the future.

It is important to note that sustainability is primarily focused on thinking inter-temporally (i.e. about change over time), rather than being specifically focused on environmental concerns. Although the natural environment comprises one set of resources that are essential to future well-being, economic, human, and social resources also need to be preserved or developed for the future.

Why measure sustainability?

The *How's Life?* well-being framework (see Chapter 1) was developed to inform better policy-making. A narrow focus on the economic outcomes of policy creates a risk that economic gains are offset by losses to other unmeasured dimensions of well-being, such as environmental quality, work/life balance, or personal and economic security. Measuring well-being makes these losses transparent, and allows policy makers to build a better picture of the overall impact of key decisions. However, measuring the current well-being of the population is not sufficient. In particular, focusing on the well-being of the current generation runs the risk that policy decisions maximise current well-being at the expense of running down the resources that underpin future well-being. A robust well-being framework needs to incorporate measures of sustainability as well as of the current state of the population.

While a significant level of consensus has emerged over the last decade on how to measure current well-being (Boarini, Kolev and McGregor, 2014), it has taken much longer for a similar body of knowledge to build up on the best way to measure sustainability. A number of different models and frameworks have been proposed over the years (e.g. triple bottom line, pressure-state response). Today, however, a consensus has emerged around monitoring sustainability via a "capital stocks" framework. This approach has several advantages. It is relatively simple, and has solid theoretical foundations (Stiglitz et al., 2009). Further, the data requirements for measuring the relevant capital stocks, while significant, are less extensive than those associated to some other proposed approaches to monitoring sustainability, and can make use of much data already collected for other purposes.

Measuring sustainability: the capital approach

The *capital approach* to measuring sustainability followed here reflects the recommendations on measuring sustainable development endorsed in 2014 by the Conference of European Statisticians, which in turn build on the work of a UNECE/Eurostat/ OECD *Task Force for Measuring Sustainable Development* (TFSD), and are ultimately grounded in the Brundtland definition of sustainable development as "development that meets the needs of the present without compromising the ability of future generations to meet their own needs" (UN, 1987).[1] As outlined in *How's Life? 2013*, sustaining well-being outcomes over time requires preserving four types of resources, or capital stocks, for future generations: i) economic capital, ii) natural capital, iii) human capital, and iv) social capital. In broad terms, these capital stocks represent the tangible and intangible assets that, together, contribute to the production of well-being outcomes in the future, and that are affected by decisions taken today. Economic capital consists of both produced capital – such as roads or machinery – and financial capital. Natural capital includes natural resources that enter economic production (such as land and water) but also non-market resources (such as biodiversity) whose services are critical to the health of human and eco-systems. Human capital covers the knowledge, skills and health conditions of future generations of workers. Finally, social capital comprises a range of factors related to the capacity for people to cooperate in society, including trust and social norms.

While certain capital stocks may have a bigger impact on some dimensions of well-being than on others, each of the four capital stocks contributes in one way or another to outcomes in all dimensions of well-being. Natural capital, for example, clearly has a direct and strong impact on environmental quality. But it would be a mistake to assume that natural capital is the only capital stock that matters for environmental quality, or that environmental quality is the only outcome that natural capital affects. Environmental quality is also affected by economic capital (e.g. the transport infrastructure, water treatment facilities), social capital (e.g. people's willingness to adhere to environmental regulations) and human capital (e.g. the skills of environmental planners). Similarly, natural capital encompasses the natural resources used to generate income and wealth, as well as the ecosystem services that underpin human health and survival.

An important element of the capital stocks model is the distinction between fixed and renewable capitals. Fixed capital stocks – such as mineral resources or oil – are depleted when they are used in production, while renewable capital stocks – such as human capital – can be used without diminishing the size of the initial capital stock. A key implication of this is that when fixed capital stocks are used, they can be converted into another form of capital rather than used to support current well-being. For example, revenues from oil could be used to finance investment in physical infrastructure such as roads, or to finance human capital via investment in schools. In this way, the depletion of the fixed capital stock does not diminish the country's total stock of capital assets, and future generations may share in the benefits of using available oil reserves.

Box 3.1. The OECD and Israeli approaches to measuring sustainability

Both the OECD and the Israeli authorities have adopted the capital stock framework for measuring sustainability. It is useful, therefore, to compare the two approaches in more detail. In each case the general approach taken is very similar, with some minor differences in how developed the measurement framework is.

Consistent with the recommendations of the Conference of European Statisticians on Measuring Sustainable Development (UNECE, 2014) and the Stiglitz, Sen and Fitoussi Report (2009), the OECD *How's Life?* framework for measuring well-being measures the stocks of the four capitals (natural, economic, human, and social) to understand whether current well-being can be maintained over time (OECD, 2013b, Chapter 6). Two key processes affect the evolution of these four capital stocks over time (Figure 3.1). These are the use of the stocks to produce well-being, and the changes to the levels of the stocks through flows and management of resources. The key flows that drive the levels of capital stocks in the OECD model are investment, depreciation or depletion, and emissions or waste. Investment in a capital stock increases the level of that stock, while the use of a capital stock to produce well-being will decrease the level of the stock through depletion or depreciation. Emissions and waste also have a negative impact on capital stocks, and capture the spill-overs from the use of one capital stock onto others.

Figure 3.1. **The OECD capital stocks framework**

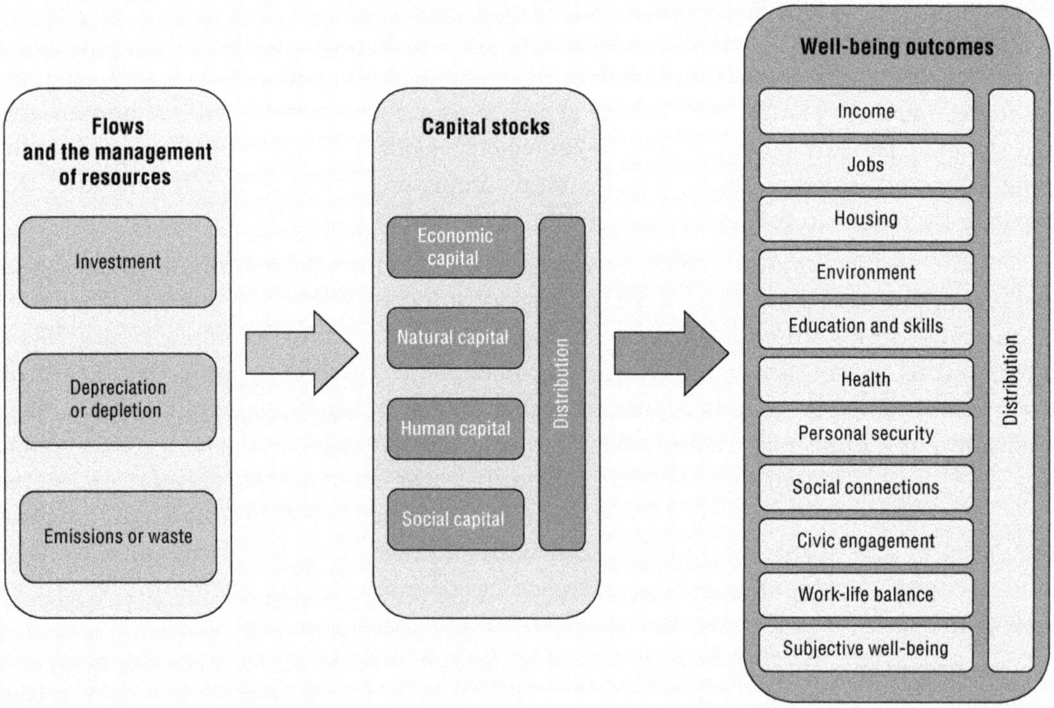

Box 3.1. **The OECD and Israeli approaches to measuring sustainability** *(cont.)*

Although the OECD framework for measuring sustainability is reasonably well-developed, the same cannot be said with respect to indicators of sustainability. Some indicators for each of the capital stocks are discussed in *How's Life 2013* (OECD, 2013b). These are listed below in Table 3.1. *How's Life? 2015* (OECD, 2015) has taken this approach one step further by providing a comparison across OECD countries for those indicators that are available. However, data shortages mean that for some capital stocks – particularly natural capital – the list of available indicators is much more limited than in an "ideal" set.

Table 3.1. **Suggested measurement themes and indicators for sustainability, *How's Life? 2013***

Capital	Measurement theme	Example indicators
Natural	Environmental assets *SEEA Central Framework classifications*	Mineral and energy resources Land Soil resources Timber resources Aquatic resources Other biological resources Water resources
	Ecosystems, biodiversity *Sub-themes and indicators to be developed, in line with SEEA Experimental Ecosystem Accounts. May include:* • Atmosphere • Oceans • Forests • Biodiversity	Atmospheric CO_2 concentrations (World Meteorological Organisation) State of the ozone layer (concentration of stratospheric ozone) Land use (FAO; *OECD Environmental Outlook*), including forest cover Species abundance (*OECD Environmental Outlook*); threatened species (OECD Environment data)
	Conditions determining the environmental quality of life	Urban exposure to particulate matter (*OECD Environmental Outlook*) Water quality Availability of recreational and green space
Human	Economic value of human capital	Lifetime Income Approach estimates for select OECD countries (Liu, 2011)
	Education	Highest educational level attained (OECD Education statistics) PISA student skills (OECD) and PIAAC adult skills (OECD, forthcoming)
	Health	Life expectancy at birth (OECD Health data); Healthy life years (Eurostat)
Social	Trust	Trust in others (European Social Survey; Gallup World Poll)
	Institutions/governance	The quality of institutions and processes to engage citizens (OECD, *to be further developed*)
	Co-operative norms	Shared values and expectations that underpin societal functioning and enable mutually beneficial co-operation – e.g. tolerance and reciprocity (*to be developed*)
Economic	Produced assets	Produced assets, including knowledge capital (OECD National Accounts data)
	Financial capital (part of non-produced assets)	Assets minus liabilities (OECD National Accounts data)

Note: Themes and indicators are a subset of the TFSD well-being "later" measurement themes, adapted here as follows:
i) Measures of natural capital have been reconfigured to reflect the SEEA classifications for environmental assets.
ii) The theme "climate" has been understood as atmosphere, which is included in the broader category of "ecosystems".
iii) The themes "air quality" and "water quality" have been grouped under a new theme: "conditions determining environmental quality of life", to which the availability of recreational and green space has been added.
iv) "Co-operative norms" have been added to social capital, following Scrivens and Smith (2013).
v) "Knowledge capital" has been included under "produced assets", consistent with the SNA.
vi) Some OECD-specific data sources are also included under the "example indicators" column.

The framework for measuring sustainability proposed in the Israeli project is very similar to that of the OECD. As discussed in Chapter 1, the well-being domains used in the OECD and Israeli frameworks are similar, and the same capital stocks are identified. In fact, the Israeli capital stocks framework (Figure 3.2) is substantially the same as the OECD well-being framework in almost all elements of its general outline (see Chapter 1). There are, however, a few minor differences that are worth highlighting. First, the Israeli framework specifically identifies one of the key issues associated with the capital stocks model that is only

Box 3.1. The OECD and Israeli approaches to measuring sustainability *(cont.)*

Figure 3.2. Israel's proposed capital stocks framework

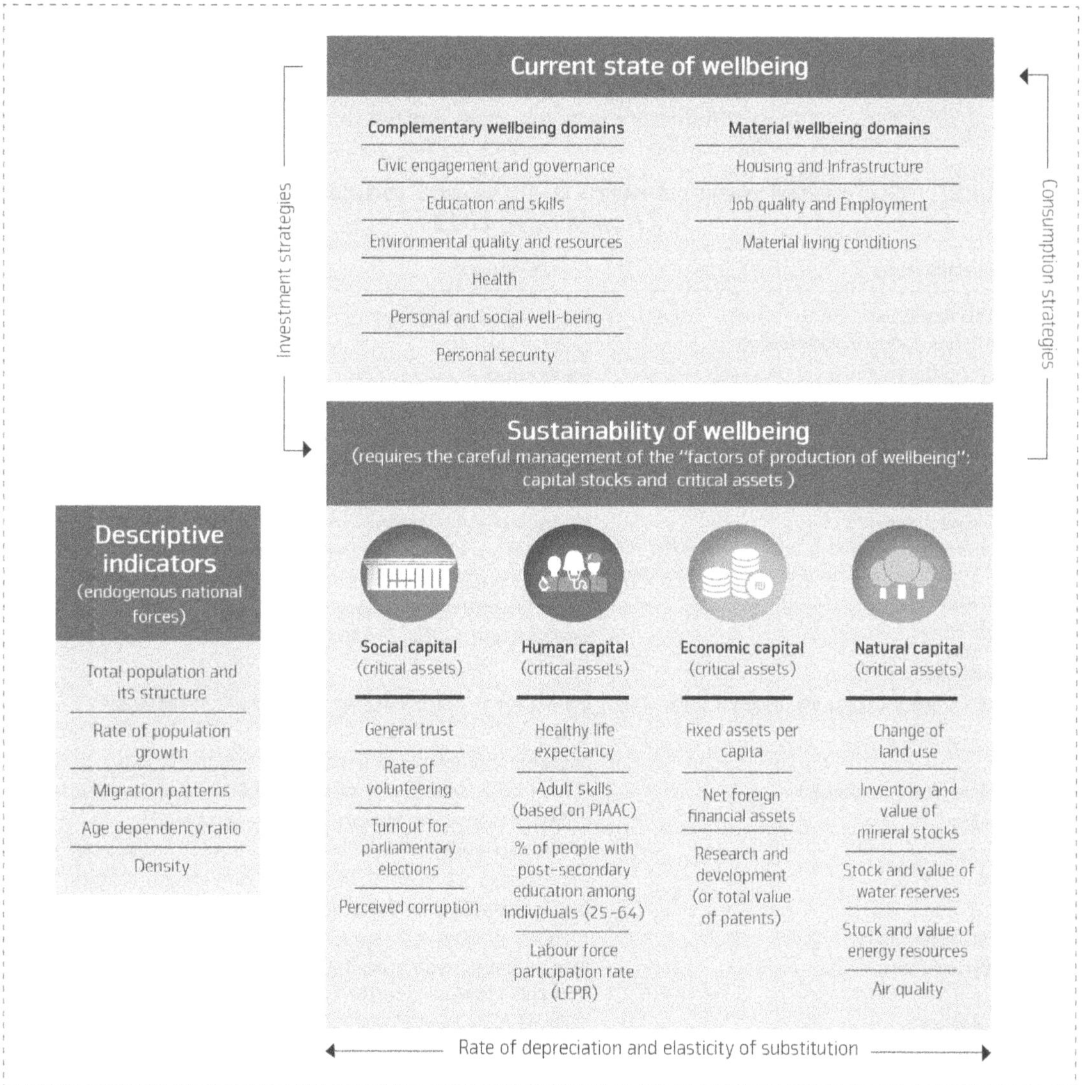

Source: Tzachor, Asaf (2015): Report on the Measurement of Sustainability, State of Israel, the Ministry of Environmental Protection, Jerusalem.

implicit in the OECD model. This is the issue of the elasticity of substitution between capital stocks. If all types of capital are perfect substitutes for each other, then what matters for sustainability is the total value across all of the four capital stocks. If, however, there is no substitutability between types of capital, then the sustainability of well-being over time is constrained by the lowest of the four capital stocks. While reality is likely to fall somewhere between the two extremes of perfect substitutability and no substitutability, it is not obvious exactly where. By highlighting this issue, the Israeli framework draws attention to one of the key issues in the measurement of sustainability. Furthermore, the Israeli framework opens up a discussion into the less-explored areas of the assets that together comprise Israel's natural, economic, human and social capital stock. The framework includes a preliminary outline of these assets.

While the capital approach is intellectually appealing, there are a number of conceptual and practical difficulties in implementing it in a country setting. First, the concepts of economic, natural, human and social capital are hard to measure, due to the difficulty of quantifying and valuing all relevant aspects. Second, the four types of capital are themselves heterogeneous: while in some cases (e.g. economic capital), its various components can be aggregated through a common metric (i.e. money prices), in other cases this is not possible, as individual components lack a common unit of measurement; as a result, while indicators exist for selected aspects of natural and social capital, it is difficult to use these to form an overall picture of the stock of capital that they represent. Third, data scarcity in some areas, especially in relation to the environment, precludes a fully-fledged description of trends in sustainability across all dimensions.

This chapter follows a pragmatic approach to implementing the capital approach in the case of Israel. It presents a dashboard of indicators of the total levels of capital stocks where these are available, and of investment in or depreciation of these stocks where adequate stock measures are lacking. Each capital stock is treated in sequence, and indicators are selected that best capture underlying trends in the level and distribution of the stock. The choice of indicators is grounded in the same criteria used to select the indicators of current well-being in Chapter 2. However, the data gaps with respect to the indicators of sustainability are more significant. For this reason, the indicators used here represent a trade-off between presenting the best information currently available (whatever its limitations) and the ideal indicators.

An overview of capital stocks in Israel

Economic capital

Economic capital is the capital stock that is the easiest to measure. Market prices provide a convenient metric for aggregating different stocks of capital, and the totals are systematically measured and reported as part of the system of national accounts. There are two main aspects of economic capital: i) produced capital (sometimes described as "man-made capital"), and ii) financial capital. Produced capital consists of tangible assets such as roads, railways, buildings, and machinery (i.e. fixed assets), as well as inventories of final and intermediate goods, and knowledge assets such as intellectual property or computer software. Financial capital includes assets such as currency and deposits, stocks and bonds, derivatives, accounts receivable, private pension funds, and insurance reserves. In a closed economy, financial capital is zero sum (i.e. for every asset there is a liability of equal value), but in an open economy financial assets can exceed liabilities or vice versa. Even in a closed economy, the distribution of financial assets among the different sectors (households, general government, corporations,) as well as within them can affect the sustainability of the economic system and of well-being more generally.

Four indicators are used here to measure Israel's levels of economic capital. These are fixed assets per capita, financial net worth per capita, gross government debt as a proportion of GDP and the financial net worth of government as a proportion of GDP.

Fixed assets

Fixed assets are the most direct measure of the value of the produced capital stock of a country, and provide an indication of the physical resources available to enter the production process. Israel has experienced a steady increase in the stock of fixed assets per capita over the last decade and a half, albeit at a slower rate compared to other OECD countries (Figure 3.3, Panel B). While the pace of accumulation of fixed assets in Israel was unaffected by the financial crisis of 2008, in sharp contrast to some other OECD countries such as the United Kingdom or Finland, the stock of fixed assets per capita in Israel is the second lowest among OECD countries for which data is available (Panel A), and below countries that have lower per capita GDP than Israel such as Slovenia and Hungary.

Figure 3.3. **Fixed assets per capita in Israel and in selected OECD countries**

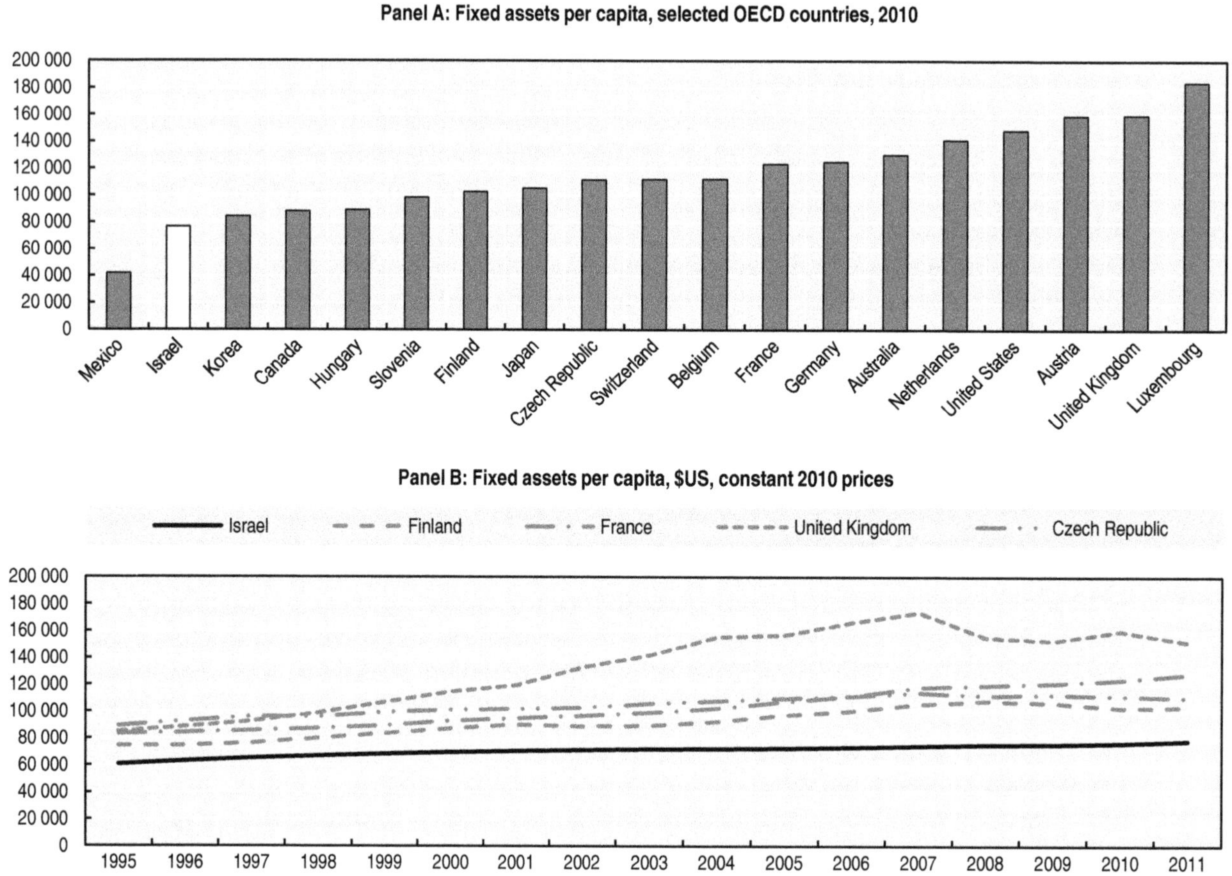

Source: OECD (2014).

StatLink http://dx.doi.org/10.1787/888933293637

Financial net worth

While Israel has relatively low levels of produced capital (as measured by fixed assets), it has much higher levels of financial capital. Israel is one of 7 OECD countries with a positive financial net worth, implying that the stock of its financial claims on the rest of the world is well in in excess of its liabilities (Figure 3.4, Panel A). The two OECD countries with the highest levels of financial net worth per capita are Norway and the Netherlands, both of which have benefited from well-managed oil revenues whose proceeds have, to a significant extent, fuelled the build-up of funds that will support the well-being of future generations. This suggests that Israel's financial net worth has the potential to improve significantly in the future if revenues from the offshore gas fields that started coming on-stream from 2013 are not entirely used to support current consumption. Israel's financial

Figure 3.4. **Financial net worth per capita in in Israel and in selected OECD countries**

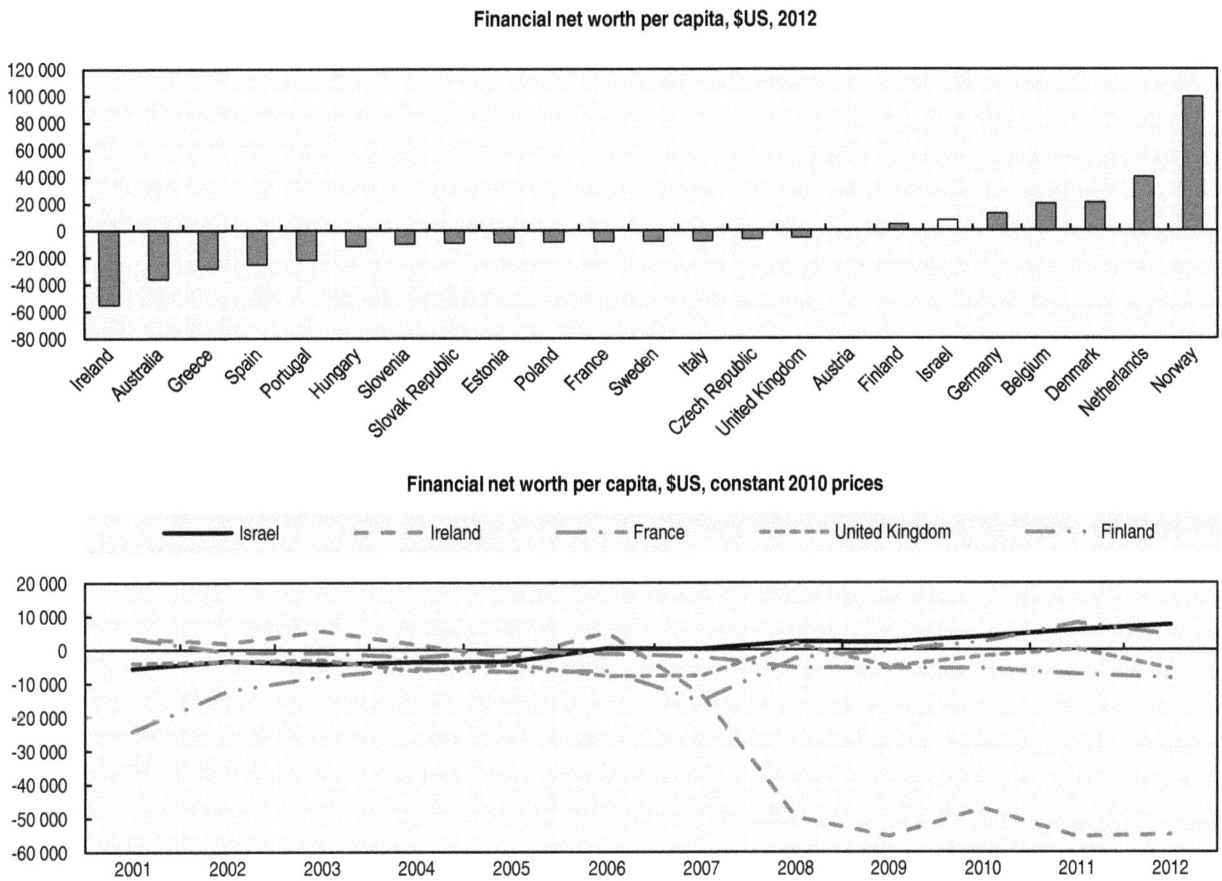

Source: OECD (2014).

StatLink http://dx.doi.org/10.1787/888933293640

net worth has been improving steadily over the last decade as a result of current account surpluses averaging 1.4% of GDP over the last 14 years, and suffered no negative consequences from the global financial crisis of 2008. This is in sharp contrast to other small OECD countries at similar income levels such as Ireland or, less dramatically, Finland.

Government debt

While the stock of fixed assets and the financial net worth describe the overall level of Israel's economic capital, the vulnerability of different sectors of the Israeli economy is also relevant for its economic sustainability. In particular, the general government debt positions is relevant to sustainability: while a large government deficit can support economic activity and the building up of economic capital, it can also have a significant impact on economic sustainability if the need to reduce government debt were to lead to large, rapid cuts in public expenditure.

Weak revenue growth and high spending pressures have led to large and persistent public deficits in Israel over the past twenty years. In 2012, the public deficit was equal to 5% of GDP, well above the OECD average of 3.5%. Although a significant proportion of the government deficit (29%) is accounted for by gross fixed capital formation, these outlays

Figure 3.5. **Government gross debt and financial net worth in Israel and in selected OECD countries**

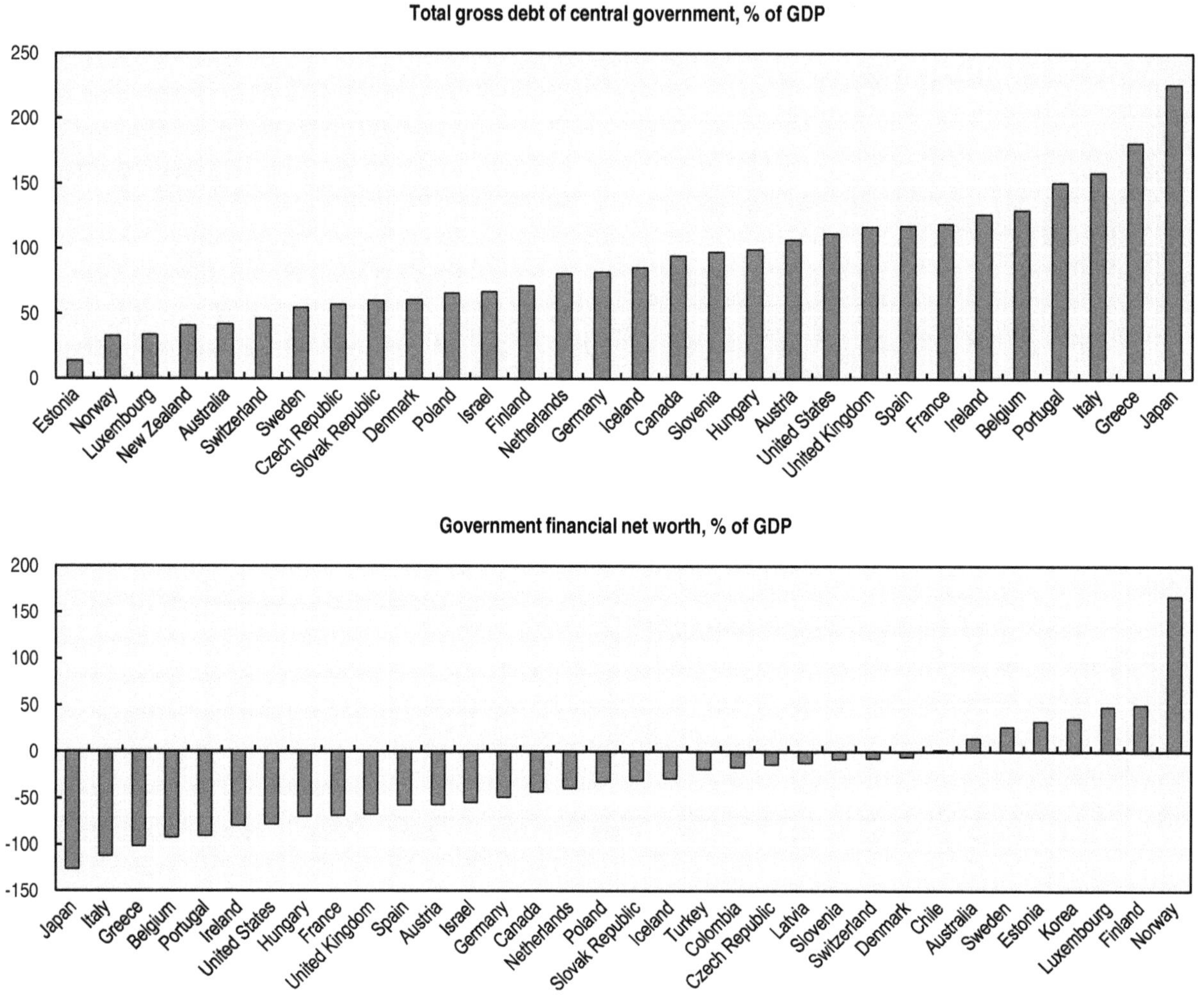

Source: OECD (2014).

StatLink http://dx.doi.org/10.1787/888933293653

still represents an increase in government gross liabilities. Over the past two decades, strong economic growth triggered a sustained reduction in gross public debt as a share of GDP, from 100% in 1995 to 67% in 2014 (OECD, 2013a). As long as economic growth remains strong, public debt levels will remain manageable, but a significant decline in the rate of economic growth represents a potential threat to public finances and economic sustainability.

Although the ratio of gross debt to GDP is the most frequently-used measure of government indebtedness, and the one that is easier to compare across countries, the net worth of general government would give a more complete picture of the government role in supporting (or undermining) economic sustainability. Unfortunately, data on the stock of real economic assets held by the government sector are not easily available. Data on the financial assets held by the government indicate that the ratio of net government debt to GDP (at 55%) is lower than that of gross debt (65%), although Israel's position relative to other OECD countries is very similar whether gross or net debt is considered.

Human capital

Human capital is usually understood as comprising the knowledge, skills, competencies, and health of individuals that contribute to the production of well-being. It thus has both a quantitative dimension (the amount of labour input that a person is able to provide) and a qualitative dimension (the skills and knowledge of those people). Although much research on human capital focuses on the contribution of skills and knowledge to economic output, human capital (as with other capital stocks) is also a fundamental input in the production of other dimensions of well-being. For example, higher levels of education and skills are associated with better health status, greater political participation at the individual level, lower criminality, stronger social cohesion, and greater political stability at the societal level (OECD, 2013b). A systematic review of the human capital literature concluded that the social and non-market returns to human capital are of the same order of magnitude as the market returns (Wolfe and Haveman, 2002).

Like many of the other capital stocks underpinning sustainability, human capital is difficult to measure. There are a number of different approaches to aggregating indicators of people's skills and education into a "stock" of human capital. One approach is to estimate the lifetime income associated with different levels of education (Jorgensen and Fraumeni, 1989). This approach is appealing, in that it produces a single monetary measure of the stock of human capital, and has been estimated for Israel and other OECD countries (Liu, 2011). However, this approach omits the social returns to human capital, is limited to people who are currently living, and rests on the assumption that the earnings of younger generations upon reaching adult age will be the same as those of people who are currently adult. Further, the extensive data requirements of this approach mean that estimates for Israel are only available for a few years (2002-07), making the information less useful for assessing the sustainability of well-being over time.[2]

For this chapter, four indicators of Israel's stock of human capital are used. Civilian employment as a share of the working-age population is an indicator of the quantity of human capital that is currently available, while average years of schooling[3] is used as an indicator of the quality of human capital. Data from the OECD Programme for International Student Assessment (PISA) are also used to provide more detailed information on the skills and competencies of Israeli 15 years-old students. Finally, total human capital is measured by the number of "effective" units of labour available in the country (i.e. the quantity of labour adjusted for quality, as measured by years of schooling). This is a synthetic measure that brings together information on both the quantity and quality of human capital to produce a single over-arching measure.

Civilian employment

The low employment rate is Israel is the key driver of the relatively low levels of human capital in the country, when compared with the OECD average. As shown in Figure 3.6, the civilian employment rate (as a share of the population aged 15-64 years) in 2011 was 5.5 percentage points lower in Israel than in the OECD average (OECD, 2014a), ranking 26th out of the 37 countries shown in the figure. Compared to the OECD countries with the highest levels of labour force participation, such as Switzerland, Norway, the Netherlands, or New Zealand, the employment gap is even larger, while Israel compares favourably to most southern European countries (Portugal, Spain, Greece, Italy, as well as Turkey).

Figure 3.6. **Civilian employment in OECD countries, 2011**

Civilian employment as a share of the population of working age

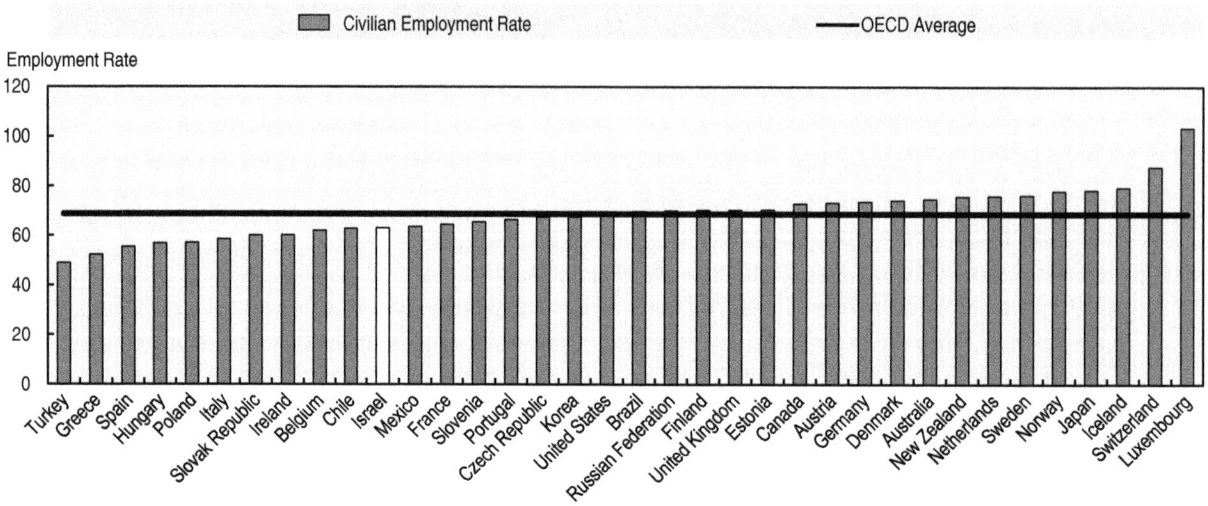

Source: OECD calculations based on Analytical Database (OECD, 2014a) and OECD (2012).

StatLink http://dx.doi.org/10.1787/888933293666

Average years of schooling

In terms of quality, the average years of schooling of the Israeli adult population is close to the OECD average (Figure 3.7). However, there are significant gaps between Israeli performance and the best-performing countries. With an average of 11.4 years of schooling among the population aged 25 to 64 years, Israel is about 2 years behind the best-performing countries in the OECD (the United Kingdom, Switzerland, Japan and Canada).

Figure 3.7. **Average years of schooling among the adult population in OECD countries, 2011**

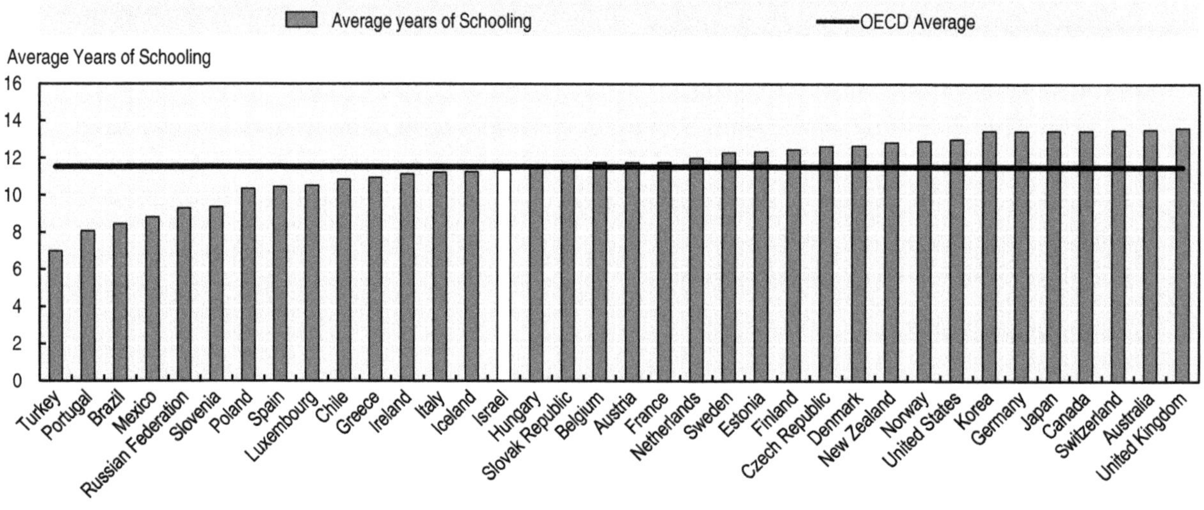

Source: OECD Education Database.

StatLink http://dx.doi.org/10.1787/888933293676

These estimates of average years of schooling hide stark differences across population groups. Mean years of schooling were equal to 10.3 years among Haredi Jews in 2010, 9 years among Arab-Israelis and 12 years among other Jews. Despite a modest catching-up of Arab-Israelis and Haredi Jews relative to other Jews among younger generations (i.e. the population aged 25-29), these differences in education among adult population groups are going to persist for many decades due to the inherent inertia in the process of generational replacement.

PISA results

Years of schooling are limited as a measure of the quality of human capital. Ideally, it would be important to look at the actual stock of skills and competencies of the Israeli workforce. Unfortunately, Israel is not currently among the countries participating in the OECD Programme for the International Assessment of Adult Competencies (PIAAC), which provides this type of information. However, high-quality, internationally-comparable information on the skills and competencies of Israeli students at age 15 is available through the OECD Programme for International Student Assessment (PISA). While this information relates to a cohort that has not yet entered the labour market, it provides a proxy measure of the competences of adults to the extent that the characteristics of the school system that shape these educational outcomes are relatively persistent over time. As shown in Table 3.2, the average level of achievement of Israeli students at age 15 is significantly below OECD average, mostly due to a higher share of low performers. These low performers are likely to be concentrated among the Arab Israeli and Haredi populations. Several reforms have been engaged over the past six years to raise the quality of education among Arab-Israeli and Haredim (OECD, 2013a), which may have contributed to the progress in PISA outcomes observed over the period 2008 12 (Table 3.2).

Table 3.2. **Skills and competencies of 15-year-old students, 2012 in Israel and the OECD average**

	Mathematics				Reading		Science	
	Mean score	Share of low achievers	Share of top performers	Annualised change in score points	Mean score	Annualised change in score points	Mean score	Annualised change in score points
Israel	466	33.5	9.4	4.2	486	3.7	470	2.8
OECD average	494	23.1	12.6	-0.3	496	0.3	501	0.5

Source: PISA.

StatLink http://dx.doi.org/10.1787/888933293819

Effective units of labour

This measure takes into account both the quantity and quality dimensions of human capital, and looks at the size and composition of the workforce, as well as its skill level.[4] The total stock of human capital is reported as effective units of labour relative to the size of the workforce; since the impact of human capital is to increase the productivity of labour, the stock of human capital measured in effective units of labour will obviously exceed the labour force (measured in terms of headcounts) of the country considered.

Israel's total stock of human capital, measured in effective units of labour, is around twice the size of the working-age population, a value that places Israel in the middle rank of OECD countries and 12% below the OECD average (Figure 3.8). Based on this measure, Israel has a similar stock of human capital to Ireland, Chile, Belgium and France, but significantly lower than the majority of northern European, English-speaking, and East-Asian OECD countries, where the human capital stock ranges from 2.5 times the size of the working-age population (Korea, Denmark, Sweden) up to 3 or more times (Japan, Switzerland).

Figure 3.8. **A summary measure of total human capital across OECD countries, 2011**

Effective units of labour relative to the size of the labour force

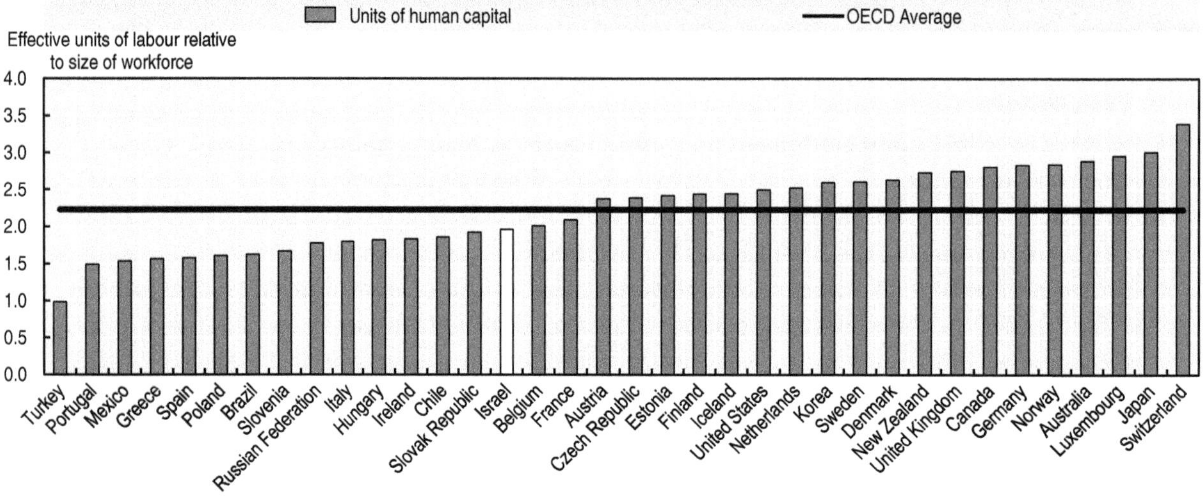

Note: Effective units of labour are defined as the product of the quality of labour and the employment rate, expressed as a share of working-age population. Quality of labour is measured as a function of the average years of schooling in various countries, while the rate of return to schooling is assumed to be the same in all countries (at 10%).

Source: OECD (2012) and Morrisson and Murtin (2009) Education Database.

StatLink http://dx.doi.org/10.1787/888933293687

Natural capital

Natural capital comprises both renewable and non-renewable environmental assets including mineral and energy resources, land and soil, water, and biological resources such as timber or animal stocks. As a small, densely populated and desert country, Israel's stock of natural capital per capita is likely to be small compared to many other OECD countries, and will come under increasing pressure as the population increases. Key pressures on stocks of natural capital include water use, land use, and air pollution, all of which are positively associated with a growing population.

The OECD's *How's Life? 2015* report identifies seven indicators relating to different aspects of environmental capital. These include air quality ($PM_{2.5}$ exposure), concentration of carbon dioxide in the atmosphere, forest cover per capita, freshwater resources per capita, greenhouse gas emissions per capita, freshwater abstractions per capita, and threatened species. These indicators represent a balance between what information is available across OECD countries and the need to capture the different elements of natural capital. Unfortunately, this set of indicators is poorly adapted to Israel. Data for Israel are only available for a sub-set of the indicators and for some of the indicators, even when data are available, the measure is inappropriate for other reasons. In particular, as a desert country, forest cover is a poor indicator of the state of land use in Israel and provides relatively little information on the integrity of the natural environment. Surprisingly, currently available data on fresh water resources per capita are also of little use with respect to Israel. While Israel faced significant water pressure in its recent past, it has significantly reduced reliance on groundwater sources and now makes extensive use of desalination plants to support freshwater needs.

Given these constraints, only two indicators are available for which there is both good data for Israel and the OECD, and for which comparisons are relevant. Greenhouse gas emissions per capita provide a "flow" indicator that complements information about the atmospheric stock of greenhouse gases. The second indicator focuses on threatened species, which provide one indication of the pressure on biodiversity. Biodiversity is intrinsically valuable to people, and biological resources also provide important ecosystem services that support human well-being. Risks to biodiversity include changes in land use and land cover, chemical contamination and pollution, invasive alien species, climate change and pollution (OECD, 2014f).

Figure 3.9 provides information on greenhouse gas emissions from domestic production expressed in thousands of kilograms per capita. In the OECD area in 2012, annual greenhouse gas emissions from activities located in each country were highest in Canada, the United States, Luxembourg and Australia (at 20 000 kilograms per capita or greater), and lowest in Mexico, Sweden, Turkey and Chile (at around 6 000 kilograms per capita). Israel, by way of comparison, ranks 18th out of 34 OECD countries in terms of these per capita emissions; at approximately 10 000 kilograms per capita, Israeli emissions from domestic production are well below the OECD average of about 13 000 kilograms per capita. In most OECD countries, per capita greenhouse gas emissions from their domestic economic production declined between 2000 and 2012, with the largest falls in Ireland, Denmark, Belgium, United Kingdom, Spain, Sweden, Italy and Portugal. The fall in emissions per capita was smaller than this in Israel, but still significant at 12%.

Figure 3.9. **Greenhouse gas emissions from domestic production**

Kilograms of CO_2 equivalent per capita, in thousands

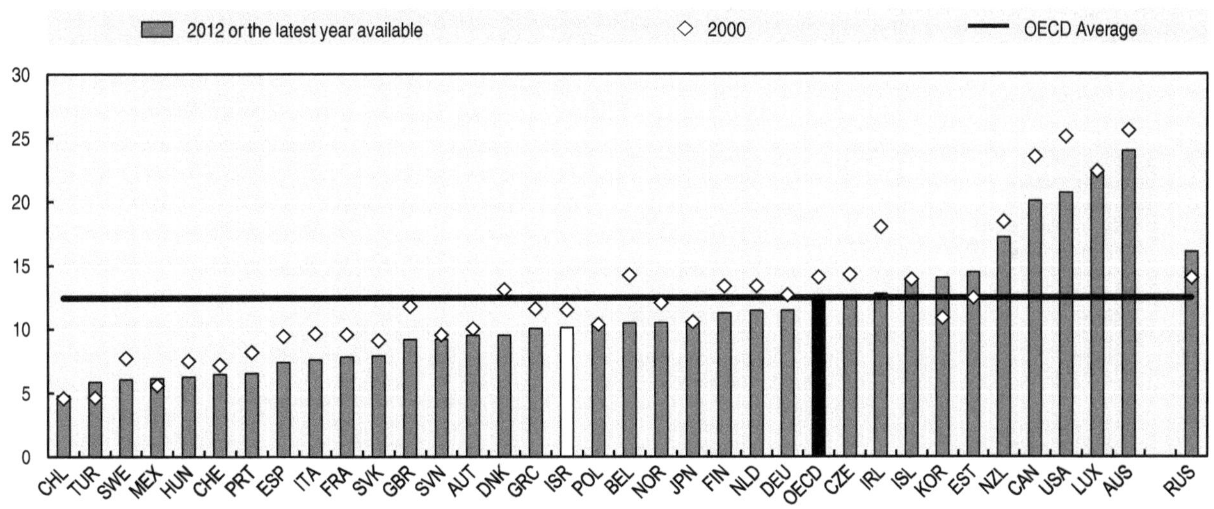

Note: The latest available year is 2011 for Israel and Korea; 2010 for Mexico; and 2006 for Chile. The OECD average is population-weighted.

Source: "Greenhouse gas emissions by source", *OECD Environment Statistics (database), http://dx.doi.org/10.1787/data-00594-en.*

StatLink http://dx.doi.org/10.1787/888933293695

Expressing carbon emissions on a per capita basis means that, in the context of rising populations, a country's total emissions can increase even as per capita levels fall. A further consideration is that, wherever carbon emissions take place, their impacts are inherently trans-boundary: they contribute to higher concentrations of greenhouse gases in the atmosphere regardless of where they are emitted, while the effects of climate change will be felt hardest in some of the countries that contributed the least to global emissions.

The picture for threatened species in Israel is varied. Figure 3.10 shows the proportion of threatened species by country, broken down into mammals, birds, and vascular plants.

Figure 3.10. **Threatened species in OECD countries**

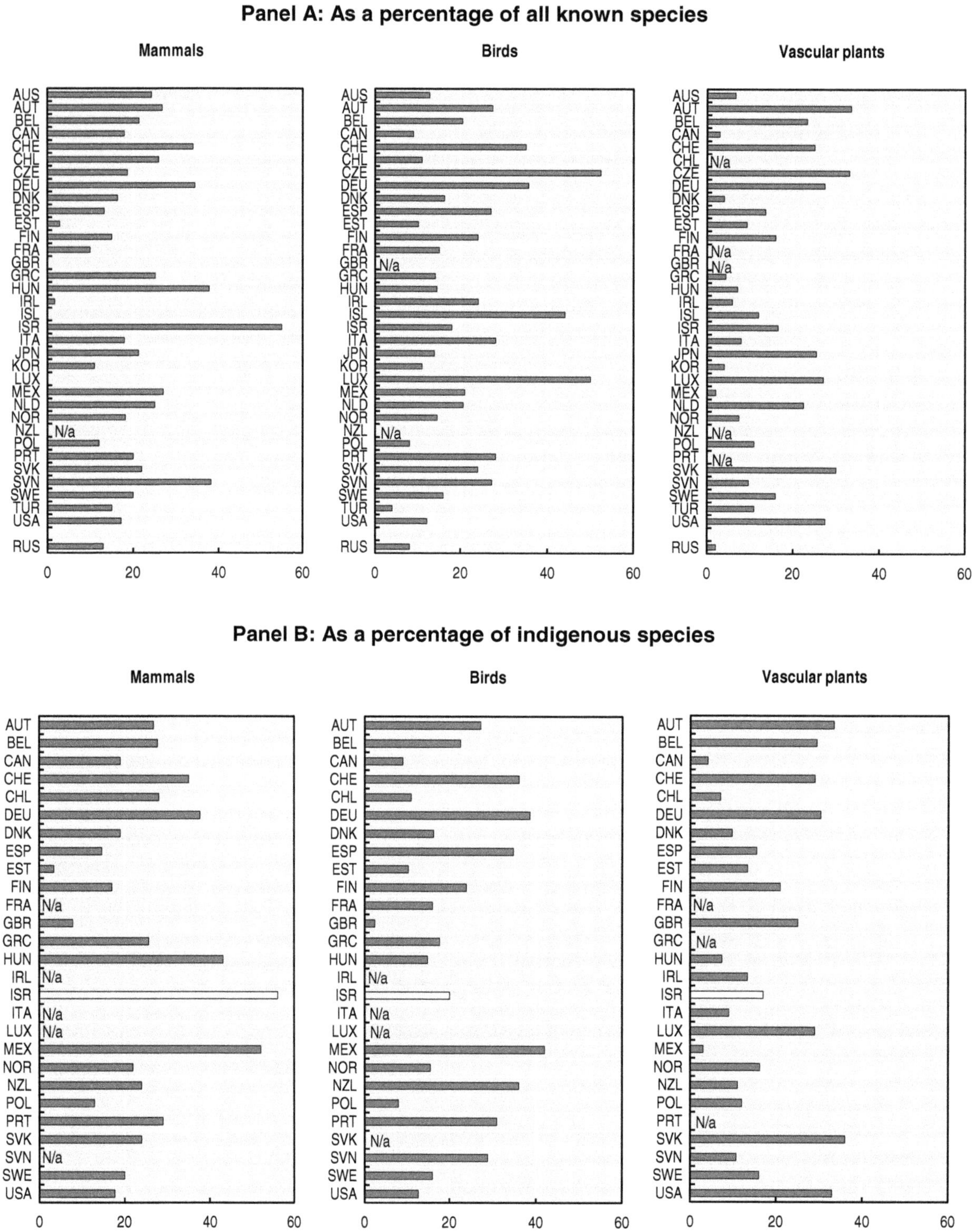

Note: "Threatened" refers to "endangered", "critically endangered" and "vulnerable" species, i.e. species in danger of extinction and species soon likely to be in danger of extinction. The data presented here refer to the latest year available, which corresponds to the late 2000s for most countries.

Source: "Threatened species", *OECD Environment Statistics (database). http://dx.doi.org/10.1787/data-00605-en*; data for Israel were supplied by the Israel Nature and Parks Authority.

StatLink http://dx.doi.org/10.1787/888933293706

Compared to other OECD countries, Israel stands out for a very high proportion of threatened mammal species. In fact, in the dataset used here all indigenous mammal species in Israel are threatened, along with over half of all known mammal species. Mexico and Luxembourg are the only other OECD countries that even come close to these rates. The picture is, however, very different with respect to birds and vascular plants, where the rate is less than 20% for both known bird species and known vascular plant species. In both cases, these levels put Israel amongst the better performing OECD countries with respect to biodiversity. To a large degree, the biodiversity picture for Israel reflects the relatively small size and densely settled nature of the country, which places more pressure on mammal species requiring a larger habitat than on birds or plants, which can develop even on small areas.

Ideally, a full set of natural capital indicators would include measures of non-renewable environmental assets such as mineral, energy and land resources. Unfortunately, internationally comparable data on these resources does not currently exist, and this remains the one of the largest gaps in the measurement of Israel's stock of natural capital.

Although internationally comparable measures are not available for Israel's stocks of non-renewable resources, it is worth noting that exploitation of the natural gas fields recently developed in Israel will have a large impact on how these stocks evolve. Offshore gas fields came on stream in 2013 and had a positive impact on economic growth by replacing fuel imports. However, as offshore gas deposits represent a fixed stock that will be depleted as it is used, the substantial additional revenues from the gas field would need to be invested in other forms of capital so that the depletion of the gas fields does not represent a decline in Israel's total capital stocks. In 2013, Israel established a sovereign wealth fund to manage natural gas export revenues similar to those that exist in other countries who are producers of fossil fuels, with the ambition of avoiding the appreciation of the shekel and a loss in competitiveness. This fund represents an important step in the long-term management of natural gas resources. In a sustainability perspective, the fund should be used to support investment in economic, human, social, and environmental capital.

Social capital

Social capital is a major determinant of economic prosperity and societal progress, yet it is neither well understood nor well measured. While social capital is a multi-dimensional construct (Scrivens and Smith, 2013), generalised trust (i.e. trust in others)[5] has gained prominence as the single, most useful indicator of social capital. Research has identified several positive correlations between generalised trust and different outcomes relevant to well-being (e.g. total factor productivity, firms' R&D, lower income inequalities and higher life satisfaction). Using time variation to identify the effect of trust on economic performance, Algan and Cahuc (2010) argued that causality runs from higher generalized trust to higher incomes rather than in the opposite direction.

In the Israeli context, it is not possible to measure generalised trust from the Household Social Survey, which constitutes an important limitation to the analysis of social capital presented here, especially in a country marked by ethnic and religious cleavages. Data on generalised trust are, however, available for Israel and European countries from the European Social Survey (ESS), and this is the primary measure used in this section to assess social capital in Israel. Two additional indicators are also used in order to provide a more detailed picture of some of the channels through which social capital impacts other outcomes.

Confidence in national governments and in the judicial system captures one important channel whereby a lack of trust affects the functioning of government institutions. Similarly, the perception that corruption is widespread in government says something important about the trustworthiness of institutions – an essential component of social capital.

Levels of generalised trust are relatively high in Israel, with a mean score of 5 on a scale of 0 to 10, as opposed to an average across European OECD countries of about 4.5 (Figure 3.11). Within the broader context of countries participating in the ESS, Israel is well below the group of high social capital countries including the Netherlands and the Nordic countries (Sweden, Finland, Denmark, Norway), all of which report mean scores of 6 or more. However, Israel has much higher levels of generalised trust than is the case for the worst performing countries in the ESS, i.e. Turkey, Portugal, Slovakia and Greece which all report mean scores of 4 or below. Israel's performance in this field is more striking given the diversity of Israeli society and the wide range of different values and beliefs held by different Israeli communities. It is also interesting to note that levels of generalised trust have increased marginally in Israel since 2002.

Figure 3.11. **Trust in others in Israel and European countries, 2002-12**

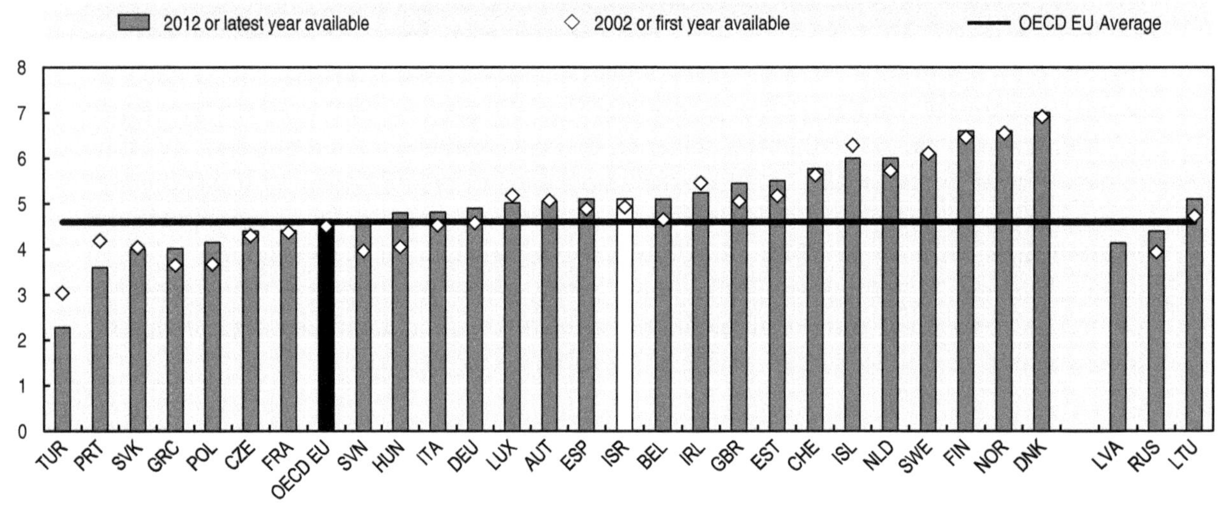

Note: The latest available year is 2010 for Greece; 2008 for Turkey; 2006 for Austria; and 2004 for Luxembourg. The first available year is 2004 for Estonia, Iceland, the Slovak Republic, and Turkey; and 2006 for the Russian Federation.
Source: European Social Survey (ESS), *www.europeansocialsurvey.org*.

StatLink http://dx.doi.org/10.1787/888933293717

Figure 3.12 moves from generalised trust to confidence in national governments and judicial systems. It can be seen that there is a clear relationship between the two indicators, with countries that have a higher degree of confidence in the national government also showing a higher degree of confidence in the judiciary. The group of countries doing well in both dimensions of trust in institutions is similar to the group of countries with high levels of generalised trust. The Nordic countries, the Netherlands, and Switzerland all have high levels of confidence in institutions, as do New Zealand, Canada, and Germany. At the bottom end of the spectrum, the picture is more different. Slovenia, Portugal, Poland, and Spain do poorly on both aspects of institutional trust, while Chile shows low levels of confidence in the judiciary but somewhat higher levels of confidence in the national government.

Figure 3.12. **Confidence in national governments and in judicial systems**

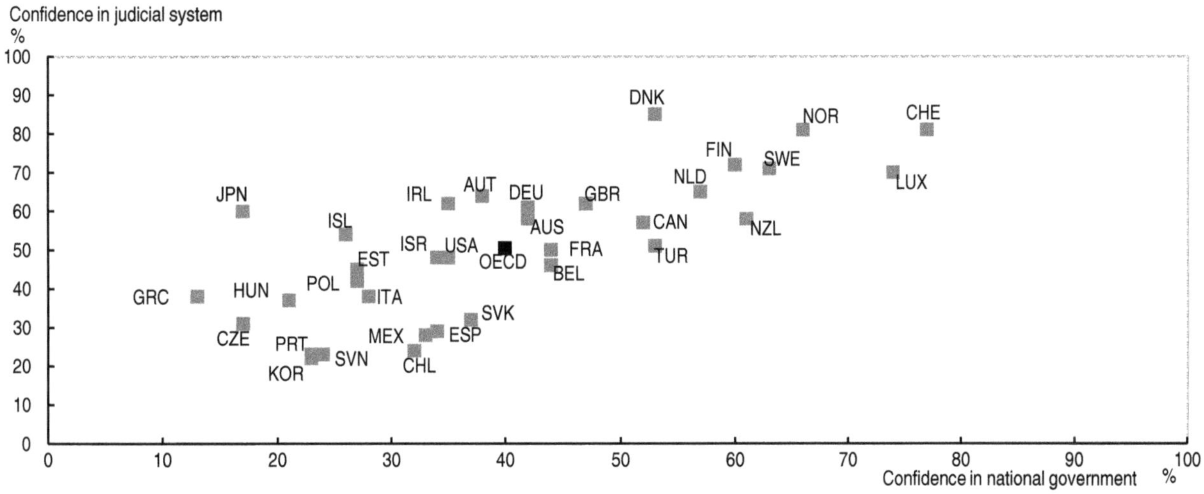

Note: Data refer to 2013 for Iceland. Share of people reporting trust in national government (y-axis), and in the judicial system and courts (x-axis).
Source: Gallup World Poll.

StatLink http://dx.doi.org/10.1787/888933293728

The picture for Israel shows that around 60% of the population express confidence in the judiciary, but less than 50% confidence in the national government. This puts Israel among those countries with a relatively high confidence in institutions, but towards the bottom of this group along with Australia, Great Britain, and Japan.

The final indicator of social capital used here – the perception that corruption is widespread in government – is where Israel performs least well (Figure 3.13). Israel is one of the OECD countries where corruption is perceived to be widespread by over 80% of the population. In Greece, Poland, Portugal, Slovakia, the Czech Republic, Hungary, and Slovenia more than 90% of the population perceives corruption to be widespread or indicate that they don't know.[6] Conversely, in the Nordic countries, Switzerland, New Zealand and Luxembourg, the rate is less than 40%.

Figure 3.13. **Perceptions that corruption is widespread in government, OECD countries in 2014**

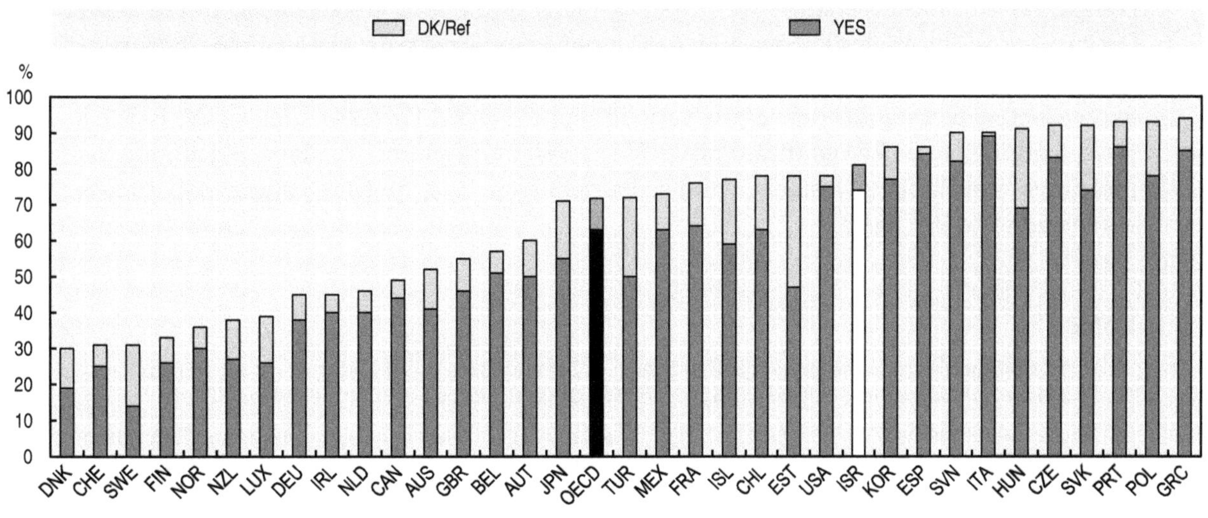

StatLink http://dx.doi.org/10.1787/888933293732

Conclusion

Although Israel has relatively low per capita levels of produced capital compared to other OECD countries, this stock has been steadily increasing over time. Unlike many OECD countries, the 2008 financial crisis had relatively little impact on either the stock of produced capital or its rate of growth. In terms of its net financial position relative to the rest of the world Israel ranks 6th among the 23 OECD countries for which data are available. If revenues from off-shore gas are well-managed, Israel has the potential to further improve its net financial position in the future.

Israel needs to boost its human capital, which is significantly below OECD average, mostly due to low labour market participation among Arab-Israelis and Haredi Jews. This requires enhancing the entry of young male Haredi Jews and young female Arab-Israelis into the labour force, and delaying the exit of older Arab-Israelis from the labour market. While the average years of schooling among the adult population is close to the OECD average, it is widely unequal across population groups, and this affects the average level of skills attained as measured by PISA for students.

It is difficult to draw a clear overall picture of the state of natural capital in Israel and how this compares with other countries given the limited set of internationally comparable information available. Within the limited range of information available, however, Israel fares relatively well. As a small, densely settled country, carbon dioxide emissions from domestic production per capita are relatively low compared to other OECD countries, and decreasing. Although a high proportion of mammal species are threatened, the rate is much lower for both birds and vascular plants.

The picture with regards to social capital in Israel is mixed. Levels of generalised trust are relatively high, and Israel does similarly well when measures of confidence in government are considered. Although not one of the group of very high social capital countries from northern Europe, Israel is solidly within the next group of countries down, and outperforms close to the OECD average. However, perceived corruption in Israel is high, which is a cause for concern and is in contrast to confidence in the national government.

The indicators presented in this chapter do not allow drawing a definitive picture with respect to the sustainability of well-being in Israel. In particular there are significant measurement gaps in the area of natural capital, and it is difficult to make international comparisons or look at change over time for many of the indicators relating to the other capital stocks. The analysis above provides a brief overview of what the available indicators suggest, but the key conclusion from this chapter is the critical importance of developing and collecting better indicators of the various capital stocks. This is an area where Israel is well positioned to make significant progress if relevant measures are identified among the indicators of well-being, resilience and sustainability and is the Israeli statistical office is resourced to collect them.

Notes

1. A similar approach has been adopted in the New Zealand Treasury's Living Standards Framework (2011) and by Harper and Prince (2011) for the UK Government's Social Impacts Task Force.
2. The estimates provided by Liu (2011) suggest that Israel is the only country (among the 12 countries included in the study) where the total stock of human capital does not consistently increase over the period examined, and where human capital per capita is lower at the end of the period than the start.

3. Based on Labour Force Surveys data between 1995 and 2011, the highest grades attained are transformed into the number of years of schooling for each cohort of age, gender and population group. This methodology was preferred to the use of the 'years of schooling' variable, as available in national reports, which counts religious study among Haredi Jews of school age as equivalent to other study.
4. More specifically, human capital (HC) is defined as the product of the quality of labour (h) and the employment rate (L), expressed as a share of working-age population. As described by Hall and Jones (1999), the quality of labour is in turn proxied by a Mincer human capital equation, which is a function of years of schooling, so that:

$$HC_i = h_i.L_i$$
$$h_i = e^{r.S_i}$$

where r denotes the return to schooling and S the number of years of schooling among the population aged between 25 and 64 years in country i. By convenience, the analysis in this section ignores cross-country differences in the return to schooling, and an average return of 10% is assumed (Morrisson and Murtin, 2013). Similarly, the simple measure of human capital shown in this section ignores information on the quality of schooling. The education data is drawn from OECD (2013) and on the Morrisson and Murtin (2009) education database.
5. This variable is traditionally measured as the percentage of people answering that "Most people can be trusted" to the survey question: "Generally speaking, would you say that most people can be trusted or that you need to be very careful in dealing with people?" In the case of the ESS, this question is slightly different, and the response is given on a 0 to 10 scale.
6. "Don't know" responses are added to "yes" responses in this analysis because, in many of the countries where corruption might be perceived to be most widespread, confidence in the anonymity of survey responses will also be low. This may bias overall estimates of corruption up a little, but has an important impact on reporting in a number of countries (e.g. Estonia, Turkey).

References

Alesina, A. and E. La Ferrara (2002), "Who trust others?", *Journal of Public Economics,* Vol. 85(2), pp. 207-234.

Alesina, A. and E. La Ferrara (2000), "Participation in heterogeneous communities", *Quarterly Journal of Economics,* Vol. 115 (3), pp. 847-904.

Algan, Y. and P. Cahuc (2014), "Trust, Growth and Well-being", Chapter in *Handbook of Economic Growth,* Eds. P. Aghion and S. Durlauf, Elsevier.

Algan, Y. and P. Cahuc (2010), "Inherited trust and growth", *American Economic Review,* Vol. 100, pp. 2060-92.

Boarini, R., A. Kolev and A. McGregor (2014), "Measuring Well-being and Progress in Countries at Different Stages of Development: Towards a More Universal Conceptual Framework", *OECD Development Centre Working Papers,* No. 325, OECD Publishing, Paris, *http://dx.doi.org/10.1787/5jxss4hv2d8n-en.*

Boarini, R., M. Comola, C. Smith, R. Manchin and F. de Keulenaer (2012), "What Makes for a Better Life?: The Determinants of Subjective Well-Being in OECD Countries – Evidence from the Gallup World Poll", *OECD Statistics Working Papers,* 2012/03, OECD Publishing, *http://dx.doi.org/10.1787/5k9b9ltjm937-en.*

CBS Central Bureau of Statistics Israel (2012), "Long-Range Population Projections for Israel: 2009-59", Central Bureau of Statistics, Demography and Census Department, Israel, *www.cbs.gov.il/publications/tec27.pdf.*

De Serres, A. and F. Murtin (2014), "Unemployment at Risk: The Policy Determinants of Labour Market Exposure", *Economic Policy* Vol. 29 (80), pp 603-637.

Elsby, M., B. Hobijn and A. Sahin (2013), "Unemployment Dynamics in the OECD", *Review of Economics and Statistics,* Vol. 95(2), pp.530-48.

Fujita, S., and G. Ramey (2009): "The Cyclicality of Separation and Job Finding Rates", *International Economic Review,* 50(2), pp. 415-430.

Hall, R. and C. Jones (1999), "Why Do Some Countries Produce So Much More Output than Others?", *Quarterly Journal of Economics,* Vol. 114, No. 1, pp. 83-116.

Hamilton, K. and G. Liu (2013), "Human Capital, Tangible Wealth, and the Intangible Capital Residual", *OECD Statistics Working Papers,* No. 2013/02, OECD Publishing, Paris, *http://dx.doi.org/10.1787/5k4840h633f7-en.*

Jorgenson, D.W. and B.M. Fraumeni (1989), "The Accumulation of Human and Non-Human Capital, 1948-1984", in R.E. Lipsey and H.S. Tice (eds.), *The Measurement of Savings, Investment, and Wealth*, The University of Chicago Press, Chicago.

Jung, P. and M. Kuhn (2014), "Labour Market Institutions and Worker Flows: Comparing Germany and the U.S.", forthcoming *Economic Journal.*

Li, H., J. Zhang and J. Zhang (2007), "Effects of Longevity and Dependency Rates on Saving and Growth: Evidence from a Panel of Cross Countries", *Journal of Development Economics*, Vol. 84, No. 1, pp. 138-154.

Liu, G. (2011), "Measuring the Stock of Human Capital for Comparative Analysis: An Application of the Lifetime Income Approach to Selected Countries", *OECD Statistics Working Papers*, No. 2011/06, OECD Publishing, Paris, *http://dx.doi.org/10.1787/5kg3h0jnn9r5-en.*

Miaari, S., A. Zussman and N. Zussman (2012), "Ethnic conflict and job separations", *Journal of Population Economics*, Springer, Vol. 25(2), pp. 419-437.

Morrisson C. and F. Murtin (2009), "The Century of Education", *Journal of Human Capital*, Vol. 3(1), pp.1-42.

Morrisson, C. and F. Murtin (2013), "The Kuznets Curve of Education: A Global Perspective on Education Inequalities", *Journal of Economic Inequality*, Vol. 11(3), pp 283-301.

Johansson, Å. et al. (2013), "Long-Term Growth Scenarios", *OECD Economics Department Working Papers*, No. 1000, OECD Publishing, Paris, *http://dx.doi.org/10.1787/5k4ddxpr2fmr-en.*

OECD (2014), "How good is your job? Measuring and assessing job quality", in OECD, *OECD Employment Outlook 2014*, OECD Publishing, Paris, *http://dx.doi.org/10.1787/empl_outlook-2014-6-en.*

OECD (2013a), *OECD Economic Surveys: Israel 2013*, OECD Publishing, Paris, *http://dx.doi.org/10.1787/eco_surveys-isr-2013-en.*

OECD (2013b), *How's Life 2013? Measuring Well-Being*, OECD Publishing, Paris, *http://dx.doi.org/10.1787/9789264201392-en.*

OECD (2013c), *Education at a Glance 2013: OECD Indicators*, OECD Publishing, Paris, *http://dx.doi.org/10.1787/eag-2013-en.*

Rothstein, B. and E.M. Uslaner (2005), "All for One: Equality, Corruption, and Social Trust", *World Politics*, Vol. 58 (1), pp.41-72.

Shimer, R. (2007), "Reassessing the Ins and Outs of Unemployment," *Working paper 13421*, National Bureau of Economic Research.

Tzachor, Asaf (2015): *Report on the Measurement of Sustainability*, State of Israel, the Ministry of Environmental Protection, Jerusalem

Uslaner, E.M. (2012), *Segregation and Mistrust: Diversity, Isolation and Social Cohesion*, Cambridge University Press.

Wolfe, B. and R. Haveman (2002), "Social and nonmarket benefits from education in an advanced economy", in *Education in the 21st Century*, Federal Reserve Bank of Boston.

World Commission on Environment and Development (1987), *Our common future,* Oxford University Press, Oxford.

Zussman, A. (2013), "Ethnic Discrimination: Lessons from the Israeli Online Market for Used Cars", *Economic Journal*, Vol. 123(11), pp. F433-F468.

UNECE (2014), *Conference of European Statisticians Recommendations on Measuring Sustainable Development*, United Nations, New York and Geneva, *www.unece.org/fileadmin/DAM/stats/publications/2013/CES_SD_web.pdf.*

UNECE, OECD, and Eurostat (2009), *Measuring Sustainable Development*, United Nations, Geneva, *www.unece.org/fileadmin/DAM/stats/publications/Measuring_sustainable_development.pdf.*

Chapter 4

Well-being in Israel: Putting the pieces together

Understanding what well-being means to Israeli citizens, and in particular how the importance of different outcome domains varies across the population, has important implications for informing policy decisions. This chapter puts all the pieces presented in the previous chapters together to examine what well-being means to Israeli citizens and illustrates how information on well-being in multiple domains can be brought together to provide a picture of overall well-being in Israel. An analysis based on the Israeli Social Survey suggests that the level and distribution of income is of crucial importance to the well-being of Israeli citizens as are social connections, environmental quality and health. A particular tension here is that the well-being of the Haredi population appears to be only marginally affected by income, jobs, or the secular aspects of education. In contrast, Arab Israeli preferences mirror those of mainstream Jews relatively closely, suggesting that if the social and economic causes of poor Arab outcomes are addressed, there is scope for relatively rapid convergence.

The statistical data for Israel are supplied by and under the responsibility of the relevant Israeli authorities. The use of such data by the OECD is without prejudice to the status of the Golan heights, East Jerusalem and Israeli settlements in the West Bank under the terms of international law.

Introduction

Understanding what well-being means to Israeli citizens, and in particular how the importance of different outcome domains varies across the population, has important implications for informing policy decisions. This information is essential to the validity of the frameworks used to measure well-being (as discussed in Chapter 1) and can help policy makers in prioritizing different areas of policy focus and understanding trade-offs. This chapter puts all the pieces presented in the previous chapters together. It examines what well-being means to Israeli citizens and illustrates how information on well-being in multiple domains can be brought together to provide a picture of overall well-being in Israel.

The first part of the chapter focuses on quantifying the importance of the different dimensions of well-being to Israeli citizens. Although the notion of quantifying people's preferences might seem far-fetched, information about the relative importance of different outcome areas to people is fundamental to any policy decisions involving trade-offs between different outcomes. Beyond this, looking at the relative importance of different outcome domains can help to understand the degree to which Israeli citizens have a relatively similar set of priorities. As earlier described, Israel is a diverse society, and it is therefore important to understand how different groups value different outcomes.

The second part of this chapter aims to present information on the multiple outcome domains that comprise well-being in a manner that can inform decision-making, as well as the general public. This is important, as a dashboard of many different well-being indicators does not provide a simple picture, making it difficult to identify the key messages for policy-making. Two approaches are used to illustrate how well-being measures can be used to highlight potentially policy relevant information. The first builds on the information on preferences developed in the first part of the chapter, while the second focuses on regional variations in well-being.

What does well-being mean to Israeli citizens?

As discussed in Chapter 1, consultation with citizens by the Israeli government in the process of developing the indicators of well-being, resilience, and sustainability indicates the same broad set of elements constituting the "good life" as in the rest of the world: adequate and secure material living conditions, access to quality jobs, housing, good health, social contact, a clean environment, good governance, and security from personal victimization. However, while consultations are important to identify the outcome domains that constitute well-being, they provide little information on how much these things matter to people (i.e. on their relative importance).

Information on people's preferences is at the core of policy-making since policy decisions inevitably involve trade-offs between different outcomes. For example, a decision to fund an active labour market programme to assist job-seekers into paid work comes at the expense of alternative uses for the same funds such as early childhood education or primary health care. Ultimately, a democratically elected and accountable government should ensure that policy decisions involving trade-offs between different outcome domains are made effectively and in ways that reflect people's preferences. However, to inform the decision-makers involved, it is essential to have information on the relative impact that different outcomes will have on people's overall well-being.

One way to get a sense of how much different outcome domains matter to people is to look at surveys where people are asked about their preferences directly. This technique has been used recently in Austria (OECD, 2013b), as well as in Italy and the United Kingdom: being based on large samples, answers to these surveys have a strong claim to be taken as representatives of the true preferences of the resident population. In Israel, such surveys have not yet been conducted, although the public consultation that was part of the process of selecting indicators provided some information on these preferences, as the public was asked to rate the domains on a scale of 1 to 5. Some useful, albeit limited, information on people's preferences is provided by the OECD's Better Life Index (Box 4.1).

Box 4.1. **The OECD Better Life Index**

The *OECD Better Life Index* (BLI) provides information on the overall well-being performance of OECD countries in terms of the 11 dimensions of the *How's Life?* report (refer to Chapter 1). On the website, users provide their own weights to the 11 *How's Life?* outcome domains in an interactive manner, which allows them to see how this affects a single summary measure of overall well-being. Users also have the option to share indices they have created with friends, and to let the OECD store information on the weights that they have assigned to different dimensions. Through this tool, the OECD has accumulated a database of over 50 000 weightings provided by people from all around the world, of which only about 250 are from Israel. Although this sample is far from representative,[1] it is possible to look at how the weights provided by residents of Israel compare to those shared by users from all OECD countries (Figure 4.1).

Figure 4.1. **Average BLI weights for Israel and the OECD**

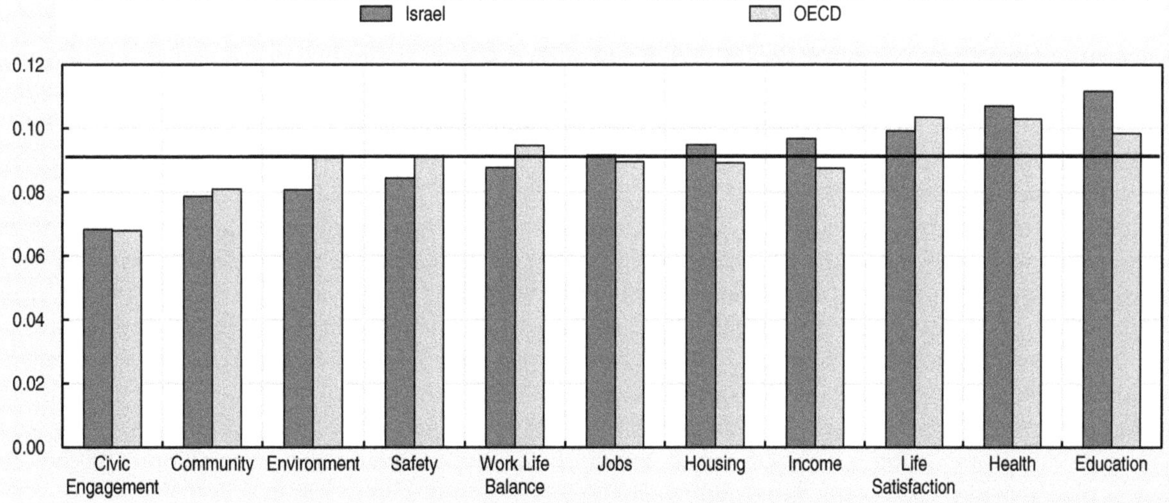

Note: The vertical axis of this chart shows the weighting applied to the domain. As there are 11 domains, an equal weighting applied to each domain would results in each domain receiving a weighting of approximately 0.091 (indicated by the horizontal black line) Sample sizes are: Israel 261; OECD 52 377.

Source: OECD Database on BLI user-weights, 2014.

StatLink http://dx.doi.org/10.1787/888933293745

Box 4.1. **The OECD Better Life Index** *(cont.)*

Figure 4.1 highlights a number of key points. First, all domains receive significant weight from Israeli's users – i.e. no dimensions of the *How's Life?* framework is deemed by users as irrelevant. Second, there is some significant variation in the importance attached to different outcome areas by Israeli users relative to those in other countries: in particular, education and health are ranked very highly, with weights roughly 50% greater than the lowest ranked outcome, i.e. civic engagement (the other dimensions with the lowest weights are community, environment, and safety). In addition to health and education, life satisfaction, income, housing, and jobs are seen as relatively important.

Compared to BLI-users for the OECD as a whole, education, housing, and income are ranked as particularly important by Israeli respondents, while the environment, safety, and work/life balance have a lower weight.

In the absence of a full-fledged survey asking about people's preferences, it is possible to elicit information on people's preferences from measures of subjective well-being. Because measures of life evaluation capture people's overall assessment of their life circumstances, examining the determinants of life satisfaction provides information on what matters the most for how people evaluate their lives. Box 4.2 discusses the application of this approach to Israel.

Box 4.2. **Assessing people's preferences using measures of subjective well-being**

Although economists and statisticians have traditionally been cautious about using measures of subjective well-being, interest in these measures has increased exponentially over the last 15 years. This reflects increasingly strong evidence that measures of subjective well-being provide valid information on issues where more traditional measures are unable to help, and that they are influenced by several aspects of well-being.

Subjective well-being can be understood as encompassing three distinct elements: i) life evaluations, i.e. a reflective assessment on a person's life or some specific aspect of it; ii) affect, i.e. a person's feelings or emotional states, typically measured with reference to a particular point in time; and iii), eudaimonia, which is typically understood as having a sense of meaning or purpose in life.

The available evidence strongly supports the view that measures of life evaluation and affect provide valid information (OECD, 2013c), while evidence is still limited for measures of eudemonia. Survey measures of these items have low item-specific non-response rates and respondents take a low time to reply, implying that they find the questions very easy to answer. Measures of life evaluations and affect correlate with ratings made by friends, relatives and interviewers, by smiling and by a range of bio-physical measures of the person being interviewed. They also predict subsequent behaviour of respondents (e.g. employees providing a lower evaluation of their job are more likely to quit). Finally, measures of subjective well-being display the expected relationship with other objective variables (OECD, 2013c). In addition, there is also good evidence that subjective evaluations of specific outcomes such as jobs (Clark, Georgellis and Sanfey, 1998), air and water quality (Silva and Brown, 2013), and material welfare (Ravallion, 2012) match closely objective measures of the same outcomes.

A subjective well-being approach to looking at people's preferences has been applied in a number of countries, including Russia (Fleurbaey et al., 2009), New Zealand (Brown, Smith, and Woolf, 2012), and the OECD as a whole (Boarini et al., 2012). The data available through the General Social Survey of the Israeli Central Bureau of Statistics, which captures information on people's overall life evaluations and a wide range of other aspects included in the OECD well-being framework, allow applying the same approach to

Box 4.2. **Assessing people's preferences using measures of subjective well-being** *(cont.)*

the case of Israel. This approach has several advantages. First, because it relies on the observed relationship between different outcomes and how people evaluate their lives overall, rather than asking people directly what they think is important, results are less likely to be driven by stereotypes about what is important or by the social acceptability of different responses.[2] Also, analysis of life evaluations allows estimating the relative size of the implicit weights associated with each well-being outcome based on a common unit.

Table 4.1 reports the results of a series of regressions of different well-being indicators against life satisfaction using data from the General Social Survey of Israel (2007-12). The dependent variable is life satisfaction, while the independent variables include basic demographic controls and a range of indicators corresponding to the different dimensions of well-being in the *How's Life?* framework. With a few exceptions (income, education, unemployment), drivers of life evaluations are measured by synthetic indices constructed from questions in the General Social Survey relating to each outcome area. Each driver consists of responses to several questions relating to the objective circumstances of the respondent in a specific dimension (e.g. physical limitations for health; specific aspects of housing quality), weighted based on the results of a regression against satisfaction with the outcome domain in question (e.g. satisfaction with housing). In the case of unemployment, security, and health status, an increase in the variable is associated with worse outcomes, hence the negative sign on the coefficient.

Table 4.1. **Life satisfaction regressions: General Social Survey**

	Baseline	Full model	Full model + population group
Male	0.018**	-0.007	-0.017*
Age	-0.064***	-0.118***	-0.116***
Age2	0.002***	0.008***	0.009***
Equivalised HH income (log2)	0.121***	0.046***	0.067***
Secondary Education	0.063***	-0.013	0.015
Tertiary education	0.065***	-0.042***	-0.011
Job quality		0.054***	0.054***
Unemployed		-0.137***	-0.115***
Housing		0.060***	0.055***
Social connections		0.162***	0.150***
Security		-0.027***	-0.024***
Environmental Quality		0.045***	0.047***
Health status		-0.130***	-0.125***
Working long hours		-0.053***	-0.042***
Arab			0.092***
Haredi			0.341***
N	36,960	34,009	34,009
R^2	0.091	0.202	0.204

Notes: * indicates that values are significant at the 10% confidence level; ** indicates that values are significant at the 5% confidence level; *** indicates that values are significant at the 1% confidence level. The regression reported is using OLS with year and regional (sub-district) fixed effects. An ordered probit run for all models produces qualitatively similar results.

StatLink http://dx.doi.org/10.1787/888933293824

The analysis in Box 4.2 largely confirms the choice of the well-being dimensions in the *How's Life?* framework and in the framework used for the Israeli indicators of well-being, resilience, and sustainability in that the indicators for each domain are highly significant and show the expected sign. Both people's income and their level of education are important to their subjective well-being. Doubling (equivalised) household income increases subjective well-being by roughly twice the amount of having a secondary education as opposed to only elementary education (Table 4.1, column 1). Job quality, access to employment, housing quality, social connections, personal security, environmental quality, health status, and work/life balance all also matter to people's life-evaluation, and this is independent of the higher income that may be associated to them (Table 4.1, column 2). Health status, social connections, and unemployment have the largest impacts on life satisfaction while, conversely, job quality, work/life balance, and environmental quality seem to have smaller impacts. These results are broadly consistent with the experience of other countries (Dolan, Peasgood, and White, 2008; Boarini et al., 2012).

One interesting fact highlighted by the analysis in Box 4.2 is that education appears to be of primarily instrumental value (i.e. after controlling for other dimensions of well-being such as income and health, the correlation between life satisfaction and education is no longer significant). This suggests that Israelis value education because of what it can bring to them in other domains of life (higher incomes, better jobs, better health) rather than as an end in itself, a pattern that is consistent with what has been found for other countries (Helliwell, 2003).

Two further patterns from the analysis should be highlighted. First, the significant impact of the population-group variables in the analysis above (Table 4.1, column 3) suggests that the drivers of life-evaluations vary significantly across the different population groups. In particular, the life satisfaction for Haredim and, to a lesser degree the Arab population, differs significantly from that implied by well-being weights for Israel as a whole. Second, it would be of interest to use the results to look at the relative importance of different outcome domains. Where Table 4.1 looks at the direct contribution of each outcome area to well-being at the individual level, a natural extension of the analysis would be to include both the independent effect of each outcome domain and the instrumental impact via other outcome domains. The next section addresses both these issues.

Quantifying preferences: how important is each outcome domain?

Figure 4.2 presents evidence on the relative importance of different outcome domains to the subjective well-being of Jews (excluding the Haredim), Haredi Jews, and Arab Israelis.[3] The analysis captures both the direct effect of each outcome domain on subjective well-being (e.g. the contribution of health to subjective well-being) as well as the indirect effect (e.g. the contribution of health to subjective well-being via its impact on jobs, social connections, etc.). Intuitively, the size of the bars in Figure 4.2 can be thought of as capturing the impact on a person's life satisfaction of a change in their personal circumstances in each domain equivalent to moving from the average for the median sub-district in Israel to the average for the top three sub-districts in Israel with respect to that domain. As such, these estimates provide an empirical basis for thinking about the "weight" that each outcome area has in contributing to well-being as a whole.

Generally speaking, the relative importance of the different domains for the life-satisfaction of the mainstream Jewish population is similar to that observed in other countries. Income and related economic outcomes are important, along with health and social contact. The importance attached to environmental quality and low weight attached to education are a little more surprising. While the size of the impact of environmental quality can be traced to the large variation in environmental conditions across sub-districts, it is less clear what could account for the weak weight attached to education, one possibility being the relatively crude nature of the measures of education used here (graduation from secondary school and receiving a tertiary education).

Figure 4.2. **Relative well-being weights based on determinants of life satisfaction, by population group**

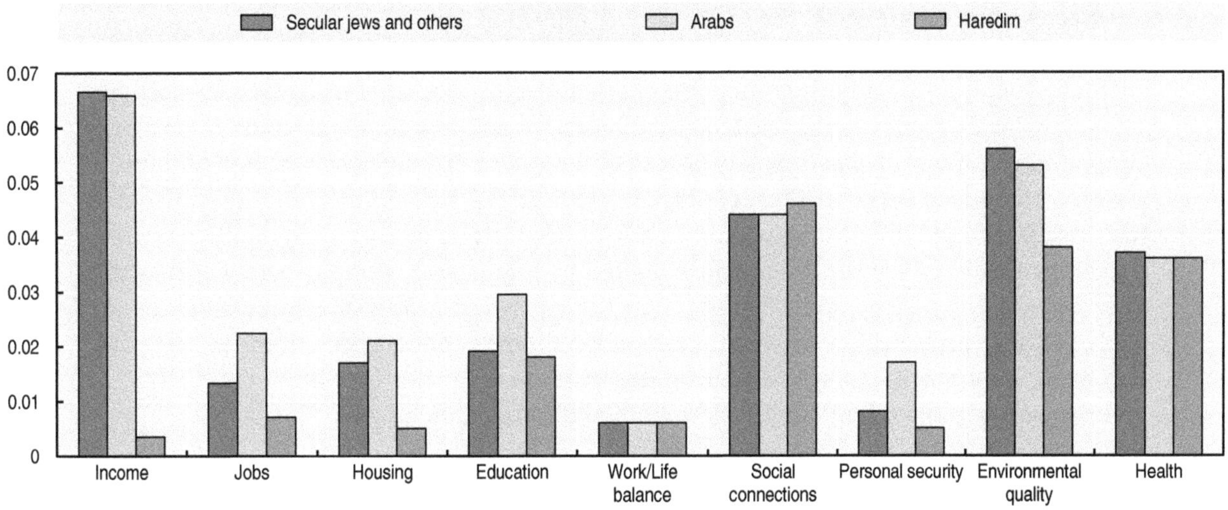

Note: All values for secular Jews and others are significant at p = 1%; all values for Arabs are significant at p = 1% except work/life balance which is not significant; education, social connections, environmental quality and health status are significant for Haredim at p = 1% and jobs is significant at p = 5%.

Source: OECD analysis based on data from the General Social Survey of Israel.

StatLink http://dx.doi.org/10.1787/888933293750

The most important features highlighted by Figure 4.2 are the differences in the relative importance of various aspects between sub-groups of the Israeli population. In general, the effects for the Arab Israelis are very similar to those for the mainstream Jewish population. With respect to the domains with the largest weights (income, social connections, environmental quality, and health) there is essentially no difference between the two groups. Education, jobs, housing, and personal security are all more important to Arab Israelis than to other parts of Israeli society. This is consistent with findings from other countries (Helliwell, 2008) that poorer groups generally place greater weight on economic outcomes.

The Haredi community is, however, quite different. They are similar to other Jews with respect to the importance attached to education, social connections, and health. Environmental quality is relatively a little less important, while economic factors (jobs, housing, and income) have little to no impact on the life satisfaction of Haredi Jews. This is a striking finding. Generally the literature on well-being finds only weak differences in the determinants of life satisfaction between different cultural groups (Fleche, Smith, and Sorsa, 2012), and both income and jobs are always found to have an important impact on life satisfaction. However, it is also a plausible finding in the case of Israel: ultra-orthodox Judaism is associated with a strongly held set of aspirations and values that differ substantially from those common in other communities. In particular, there is a strong focus on non-material goals and the priority of religious over secular outcomes.

The implications of the marked difference in the weights attached to different aspects of well-being by the Haredi community relative to the rest of Israeli society are twofold. First, this heterogeneity of values is likely to be more of an issue in forming a well-being centred policy agenda in Israel than is the case for other OECD countries. Where other OECD countries have a high degree of commonality on the relevance of economic outcomes across cultural lines, this is not the case in Israel.[4] Pursuing a policy focused on reducing poverty and increasing engagement in the labour market within the Haredi community is deemed to confront significant challenges (OECD, 2013d).

Second, the difference in the factors driving life satisfaction between the Arab Israelis and the Haredim highlights a key difference with respect to the causes of disadvantage in each community. While both groups are characterized by relatively high income poverty rates, low levels of attainment in tertiary education, and low levels of paid employment compared to the rest of Israeli society (OECD, 2013d), the analysis presented here reinforces the view that much of Haredi disadvantage is a side effect of the priority that they attribute to non-material goals; conversely, Arab disadvantage reflects mainly an inability to achieve outcomes that are very similar to those valued by mainstream Israeli society. While this does not provide additional information on the causes of Arab disadvantage, which are likely to be diverse and potentially include a wide range of historical, cultural, religious, and environmental factors, the finding does underscore that fundamentally different mechanisms are at work in determining Arab and Haredi outcomes.

Assessing well-being across multiple outcome domains

Measuring and assessing well-being in Israel, consistently with the Israel's Well-being, Resilience, and Sustainability indicators, takes a multi-dimensional approach to measuring well-being. However, the use of multiple dimensions makes it challenging to present an overall picture of well-being in Israel. When 11 dimensions of well-being are considered, it is much more challenging to identify key policy priorities than is the case when the focus is on two or three key indicators. While policy decisions in Israel should clearly be grounded in the Well-being, Resilience, and Sustainability indicators, which have a clear political and public mandate, it is possible to illustrate how a multi-dimensional approach to measuring well-being can be used to inform policy with the OECD indicators used here.

The approach taken here is to present a framework for thinking about how policy priorities might be identified in a multi-dimensional context. The chapter does not go so far as to identify specific priorities, as these will depend, not just on the level of outcomes, but also on the ability of government to change them and the cost of doing so. Nonetheless, looking at well-being outcomes and preferences does provide a useful starting point for discussing policy priorities and illustrates how information on well-being can potentially be used to inform policy-making.

Figure 4.3 combines information on people's preferences across outcome domains for Israeli society as a whole (derived in the previous section from measures of subjective well-being,[5] on the vertical axis) with data on the performance of Israel in each outcome domain compared to the OECD average (on the horizontal axis). Nine[6] of the eleven OECD outcome domains are plotted on Figure 4.3, showing the position of each domain with respect to Israel's performance relative to the OECD, and the weight of that domain in affecting the life satisfaction of Israeli citizens from the regression results reported in Figure 4.2.

Outcomes in the top right quadrant have a large impact on the well-being of Israeli citizens and are areas where Israel performs relatively well. The bottom right quadrant captures areas where Israel performs relatively well, but which have a smaller impact on the well-being of Israelis. In the bottom left quadrant are outcomes with a low importance to Israelis and relatively poor performance compared to other OECD countries. Finally, the top left quadrant

Figure 4.3. **Relative performance and weights of average well-being outcomes in Israel**

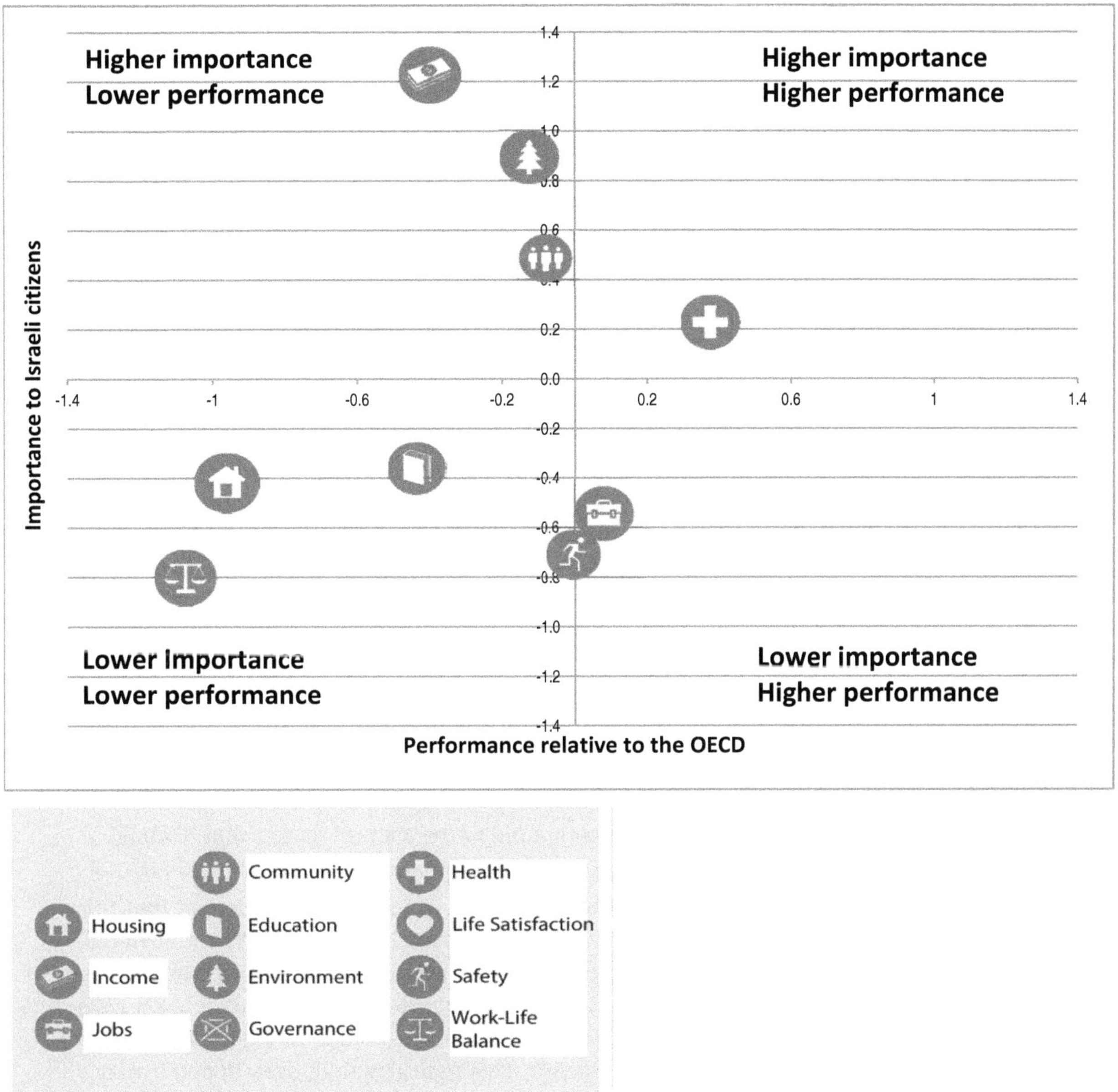

Source: OECD analysis based on data in the General Social Survey of Israel.

StatLink http://dx.doi.org/10.1787/888933293766

captures those areas of high importance to Israelis but where Israel performs relatively poorly. These are the outcomes for which there is a prima facie case for policies to focus on.

Based on Figure 4.3, outcomes for work/life balance, education, health, and housing are aligned with their relative importance to Israelis (i.e. higher performance is associated with higher importance, and lower performance occurs for those outcomes with lower importance to Israeli citizens). Israel performs relatively well in the areas of jobs and personal security compared to the impact they have on people's current well-being. However, incomes, environmental quality, and social contact are all areas that matter for people's well-being, but where performance is relatively poor.

Raising incomes is an obvious implication of Figure 4.3, but it is important to note that the income measure used (the logarithm of income) implies that an increase in income at the bottom of the distribution has a larger impact on well-being than an equivalent change at the top. This suggests that Israel's large degree of income inequality, noted in Chapter 2, is a significant drag on average well-being. The policy significance of the high importance and poor performance with respect to social connectedness is less clear cut given the lack of direct policy levers in this area. However, as discussed in Chapter 3, low levels of "bridging" social capital between population groups are potentially a significant issue in Israel, suggesting that a better understanding of the drivers and consequences of social connectedness in Israel would bring significant benefits. Similarly, it would be of value to better identify what aspects of environmental quality account for the large impact on well-being, as some of the measures used to measure environmental quality in Figure 4.3 are potentially policy amenable (e.g. air quality, noise). Chapter 5 discusses some of the information needs associated with improving knowledge in both of these areas.

It is also important to note that Figure 4.3 only captures the impact of the different outcome domains on *current* well-being. Several of the outcomes that are assigned a relatively low importance in Figure 4.3 have significant implications for future well-being. As discussed in Chapter 3, education and jobs underpin good future performance in a number of other domains despite having a low importance in terms of current well-being. This highlights the importance for well-being centred policy analysis to focus not just on the static relationships between different outcomes, but also how they evolve over time.

Well-being outcomes for different population groups

The same approach applied in Figure 4.3 to Israel as a whole can be used to look at outcomes for specific population groups within society. Figures 4.4, 4.5 and 4.6 apply the group-specific weights estimated earlier in this chapter (Figure 4.2) to the average outcomes for non-Haredi Jews, Haredim, and Arabs compared to the average for Israel as a whole.

Figure 4.4 shows that the outcomes for non-Haredi Jews across all of the 9 outcome areas considered here are very close to the average for Israel, reflecting the fact that this population group accounts for roughly 70% of the total Israeli population. The non-Haredi Jewish population has slightly higher incomes than the average for Israel and is also better educated and has more favourable labour market outcomes. Work/life balance is a little below the average. One key feature to note is that the outcomes in Figure 4.4 make a diagonal line sloping downwards and to the left. This indicates that, overall, performance in the different outcome domains for this population group is reasonably well aligned with their relative importance.

Figure 4.5 shows that the Haredi population attains relatively good well-being outcomes in those domains that are important to them. Social contact, health, and environmental quality are all at or above the Israeli average. In contrast, the domains where the Haredim do less well – income and education – are those that have little value to them, on average, in terms of how they value their life overall. When looking at jobs, housing, and personal security, the Haredi community does relatively well compared to Israel as a whole, even though these outcomes are not of particularly high importance to them. The most extreme manifestation of this pattern is work/life balance, where the incidence of long working hours is so low among the Haredi community that the work/life balance indicator does not even appear on the chart (it is off to the right of the low importance/high performance box).

Figure 4.4. **Relative performance and weights of average well-being outcomes in Israel for non-Haredi Jews**

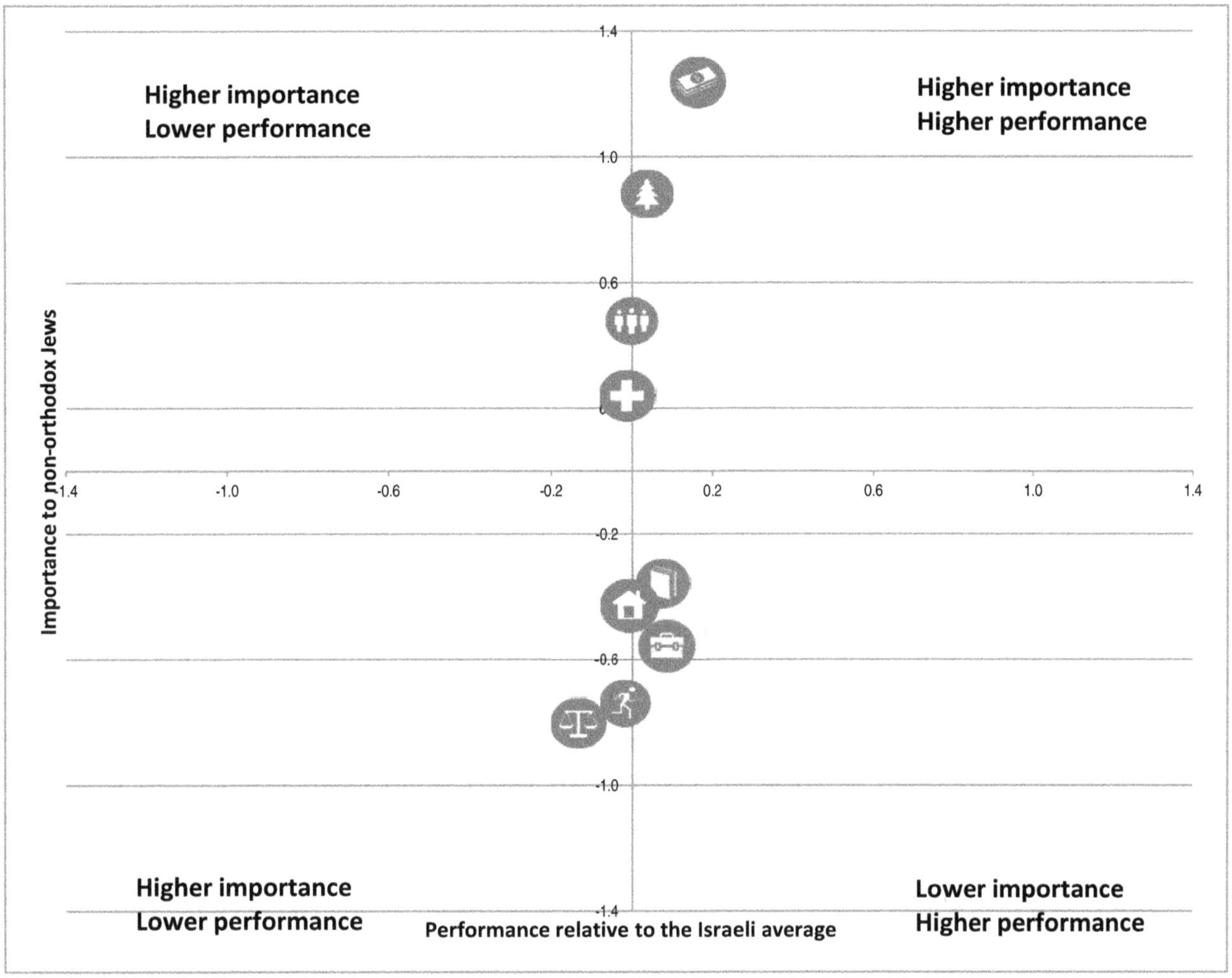

Source: OECD analysis based on data in the General Social Survey of Israel.

StatLink http://dx.doi.org/10.1787/888933293777

The picture that emerges from Figure 4.5 suggests a tension between the need to raise Haredi educational attainment and labour market participation, which was highlighted in Chapter 3, and the (low) importance of these dimensions as drivers of the subjective well-being of the Haredi population. The factors driving poor Haredi outcomes in these areas are not limited to the nature of the educational system, but also reflect a strong focus on the part of many Haredim on non-material priorities. This will be a significant challenge to overcome over the next 45 years, as Haredi increase as a share of the Israeli population from 10% currently to approximately 30% by 2059. It is important to note, however, that this analysis is static. It is quite possible that a change in economic outcomes for the Haredi community would also lead to a change in their *preferences* over time.

Figure 4.6 shows, overall, an inverse correlation between the importance of the different domains for life-evaluations of the Arab Israelis and average outcomes for the Arab Israeli population. In contrast to the Haredi population, Arab Israelis perform worst in those domains that are most important to them, and do better in domains that have a smaller impact on their current well-being. In particular, the high importance attached to

Figure 4.5. **Relative performance and weights of average well-being outcomes in Israel for Haredi Jews**

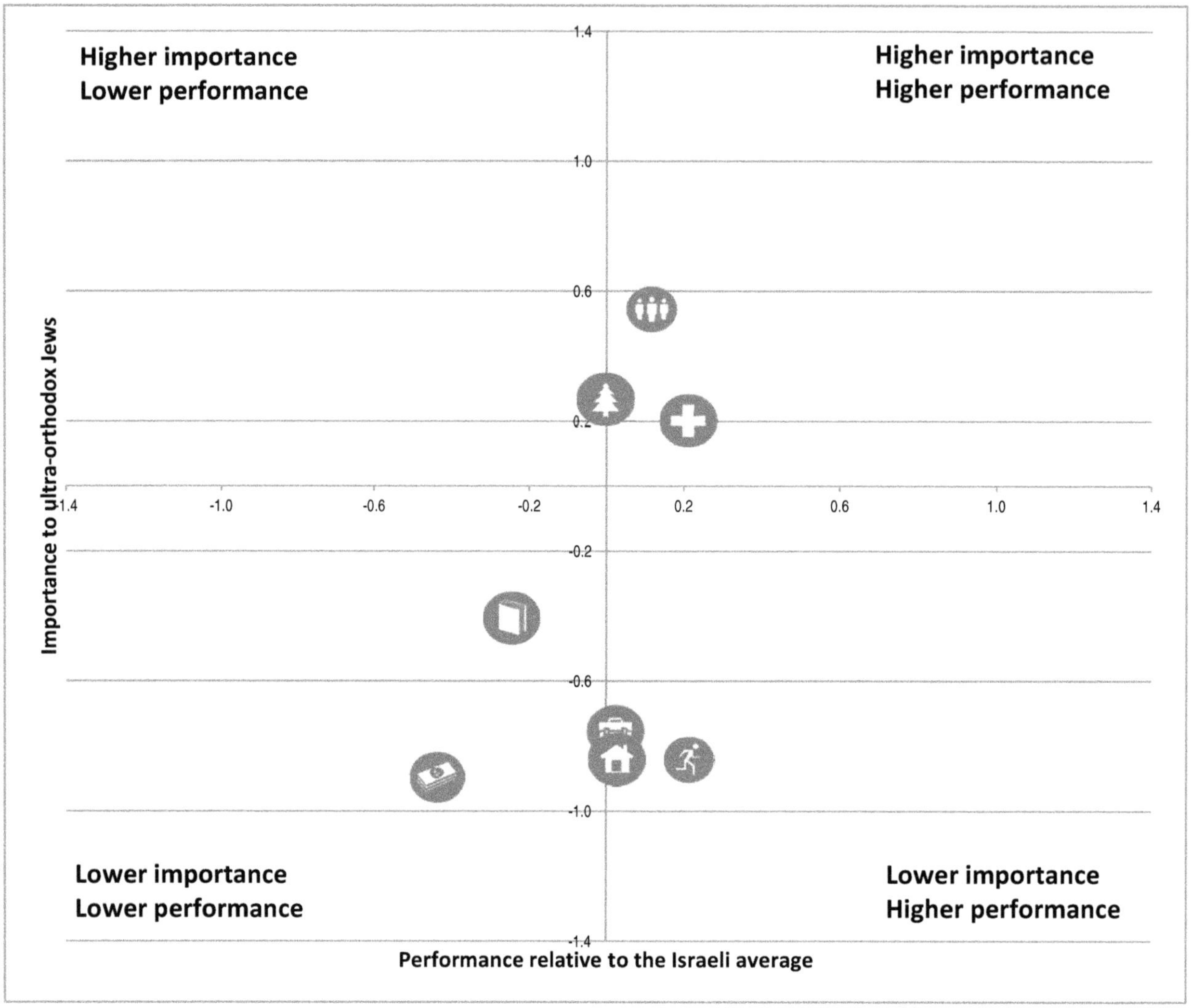

Source: OECD analysis based on data in the General Social Survey of Israel.

StatLink http://dx.doi.org/10.1787/888933293780

income suggests that it is not a lack of desire to do well in the economy that holds back Arab-Israelis. Similarly, both education and jobs are very important as drivers of life-evaluation among the Arab Israelis, while achievements in these dimensions among the Arab Israelis is much lower than on average among all Israeli citizens. The strong alignment between the areas important to Arab-Israelis and the key areas identified in Chapter 3 as needing improvement if Israel is to maintain its stocks of human capital suggest a potential win/win situation in improving the quality of Arab-Israeli education and labour market access.

One of the well-being domains where Arab Israelis do relatively well compared to the Israeli population as a whole is housing. The relatively high achievement of the Arab-Israeli population in this field mainly reflects their relatively high rates of home ownership. This pattern of high home ownership, combined with poor economic, educational,

Figure 4.6. **Relative performance and weights of average well-being outcomes in Israel for the Arab population**

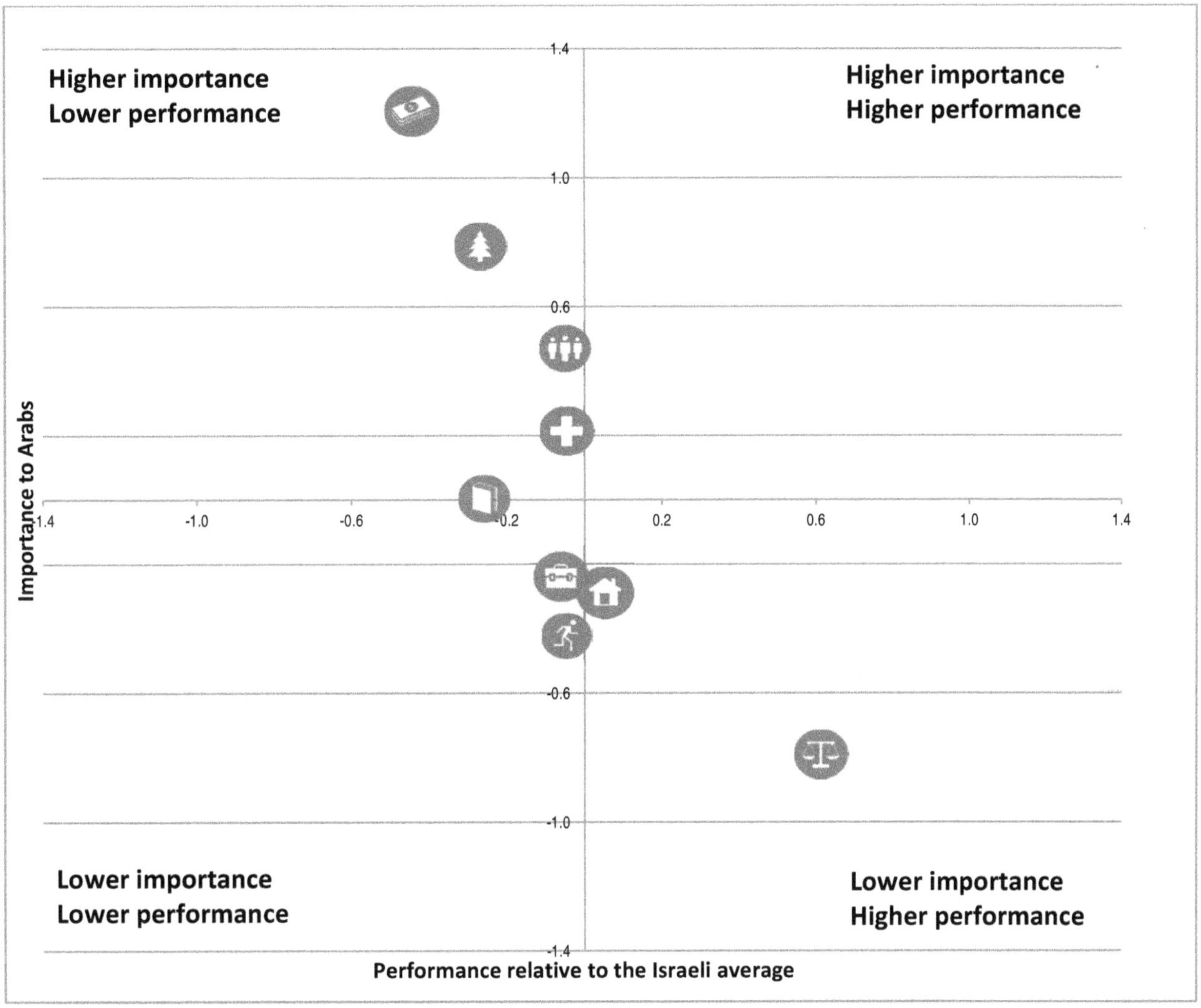

Source: OECD analysis based on data in the General Social Survey of Israel.

StatLink http://dx.doi.org/10.1787/888933293792

environmental and labour market outcomes, is consistent with a picture where Arab Israeli disadvantage has a strong geographic component to it (see Chapter 2).

The geographical distribution of well-being in Israel

Another way of looking at well-being data is to examine the geographical distribution of well-being across Israel. The geographical spread of outcomes is of interest for a number of reasons. First, it provides a concrete example of the range of outcomes achievable within Israel, and thus gives a sense of the scope for improvements in well-being that is not provided by international comparisons. Second, information about how good and bad outcomes cluster in specific areas can provide information about where to target scares resources, and on the contribution of geographical factors to differences in well-being in Israeli society.

Figure 4.7 presents information on the performance of different regions of Israel across 20 well-being outcome indicators for the period 2010 to 2012. Data are drawn from

Figure 4.7. **Well-being outcomes in Israel across sub-districts**

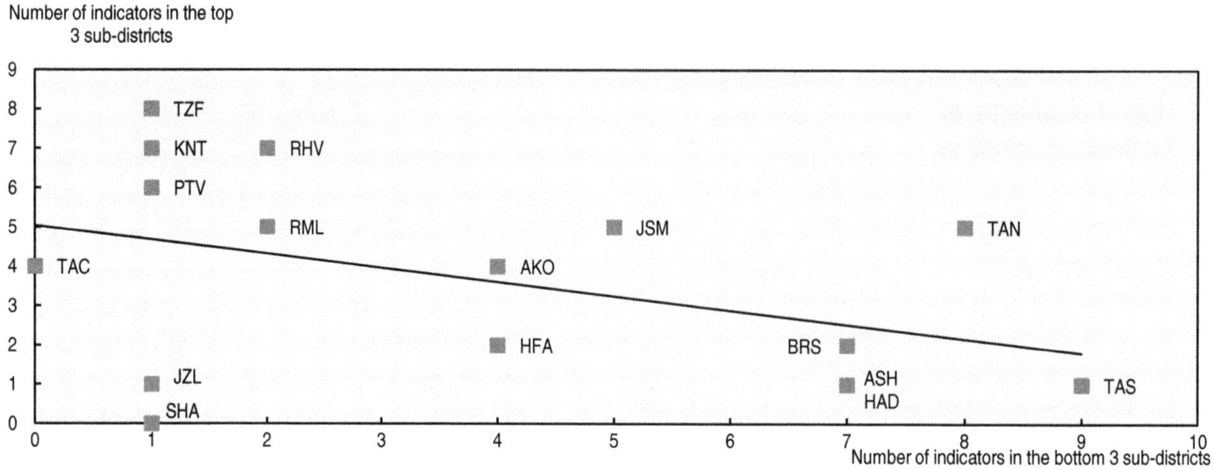

Source: CBS Social Survey, OECD calculations.

StatLink http://dx.doi.org/10.1787/888933293806

the General Social Survey of Israel covering 10 of the 11 outcome domains in the OECD *How's Life?* framework. The governance domain is excluded as no governance measures at the local level are available in the General Social Survey, and as features of national governance are presumed to affect in similar ways across sub-national regions. The unit of analysis available in the Israeli General Social Survey is generally the sub-district. However, several sub-districts with small populations are excluded from Figure 4.7 as, even after averaging data over the period 2010-12, the sample size remains too small to support statistical analysis. In addition, the data for the Tel-Aviv sub-district are broken down in Figure 4.7 into three smaller areas (north, central, and south). In Figure 4.7, each area is classified by the number of outcome measures for which it is one of the top 3 areas in Israel, and by the number of outcome measures for which it is one of the 3 areas in Israel with the worst outcomes.

Several points stand out from Figure 4.7. First, no single region performs better or worse than all of the others. Even the best performing sub-districts overall (Tsfat, Kinneret) are among the worst performing areas with respect to one indicator. Likewise, the worst performing sub-districts overall (southern Tel Aviv, Beersheva, Hadera, Ashkelon) are among the best performing regions with respect to at least one outcome indicator. This highlights the problems with composite indices that reduce well-being to a single dimension.

Despite variation across regions, there is a clear pattern to the distribution of well-being outcomes provided by Figure 4.7. Most regions cluster along a line from good performance (top left) to poor performance (bottom right). Also, a distinct geographical dimension to this pattern is evident, with northern (Tzfat, Kinneret) and central (Rehavit, Peah Tikva, Ramla) districts doing relatively well and southern (Beersheva, Ashkelon) and the north-western coastal districts (Hadera, Haifa) doing less well. Jezreel and Sharon are outliers to this general pattern.

A second pattern that emerges from Figure 4.7 is the large diversity of outcomes among the major metropolitan sub-districts (Tel Aviv and Jerusalem). Where most of the sub-districts are concentrated towards the two ends of the spectrum in terms of outcomes, the major urban regions are much more diverse. In particular, Jerusalem and northern Tel Aviv combine high levels of performance in some indicators with very low levels in others.

Conclusion

Forming a coherent overall picture across eleven domains of well-being means looking not just at how Israel is doing, but also how much different outcome domains contribute to well-being and for whom. Putting such a picture together for Israel is challenging, not least because Israel is a diverse society and different outcome domains are important to different parts of the population. Nonetheless, using the indicators from this report, several key themes can be identified.

An analysis based on the Israeli Social Survey suggests that the level and distribution of income is of crucial importance to the well-being of Israeli citizens. This is an area where Israel generally under-performs the OECD average, and which has a large impact on how Israelis feel about their lives as measured by life satisfaction. Jobs and education, by way of contrast, appear to have a relatively smaller direct effect on well-being. However, as discussed in Chapter 3, they are crucially important drivers of future outcomes. A particular tension here is that the well-being of the Haredi population appears to be only marginally affected by income, jobs, or the secular aspects of education – even though the Haredim will form an increasing part of the Israeli population over the next few decades. Both social contact and environmental outcomes are areas where Israel performs poorly compared to the OECD area as a whole using the indicators measured here, but which have a large impact in terms of current well-being. This is potentially important, because social contact and environmental quality are closely associated with levels of social and environmental capital respectively, and thus drive future well-being in Israel as well. While some caution is needed here – particularly for the environmental domain given the limited range of indicators on environmental quality available in the Israeli General Social Survey – the implication is that improvements in either social contact or environmental quality have the potential to yield gains in well-being both now and into the future. By way of contrast, in other outcome areas, performance relative to the OECD appears to align well with the estimated preferences of Israeli citizens. For example, health outcomes are both above the OECD average, and also of higher importance to Israelis.

The large differences in the drivers of subjective well-being for Haredi Jews and the rest of Israeli society also have important implications. In particular, it underscores the degree to which Haredi outcomes reflect differences in preferences, and thus suggests that bringing outcomes for this population group in terms of income, education and jobs, up to the level of Israeli society as a whole will be challenging. In contrast, Arab Israeli preferences mirror those of mainstream Jews relatively closely, suggesting that if the social and economic causes of poor Arab outcomes are addressed, there is scope for relatively rapid convergence.

Finally, there is a distinct geographical component to the distribution of outcomes in Israel. In particular, the southern and north western regions do poorly on many outcome dimensions compared to the northern and central regions. This is certainly driven strongly by the population make-up of these regions, as areas with a large Arab population tend to do worse than other regions. This suggests that a policy that addresses inequalities in well-being across different population groups will also have a large impact on regional inequalities.

The picture of overall well-being in Israel and the associated policy implications presented here are illustrative rather than definitive. Experience from initiatives to measure well-being for policy purposes from other parts of the world, such as the recent British initiative, has established that it is essential that the measures of well-being used have a clear political and public mandate. Ultimately, it is the indicators of Israel's well-being, resilience, and sustainability developed within the country that should guide policy making for Israel. However, the analysis here highlights how a coherent picture of different policy issues can be developed from a multi-dimensional approach to measuring well-being.

Notes

1. People who choose to look at the BLI on the OECD website and share their indices are not a representative sample of the Israeli population, and only a relatively small number of responses are available. Re-weighting the responses to make them better reflect the make-up of Israeli society on the basis of age group and sex (all which is possible with BLI data) has little impact on the overall data, although education assumes a slightly higher degree of importance relative to other outcomes.
2. For example, if people are asked whether the environment matters to their well-being, some people might respond not on the basis of whether the environment matters to them, but on what is seen as the socially acceptable thing to say on environmental matters. By using measures of subjective well-being, it is possible to analyse whether the life satisfaction of people living in areas of good environmental quality is higher than those living in areas with lower environmental quality, after taking other factors into account, thus circumventing this risk.
3. The weights are the coefficients from a series of regressions (one for each population group) including the outcome indicator in question, and controls for demographic variables, sub-district, year, and income. They thus capture the direct effect of the outcome on life satisfaction, as well as any indirect effect via the impact on other outcomes (except for income). All of the outcome measures have been standardized so that a one unit change in the outcome measure is equivalent one standard deviation in the average level of the outcome across Israel's 16 sub-districts.
4. Generally speaking there is a high degree of commonality with respect to what dimensions are important for well-being across countries (Alkire, 2002). However, research has highlighted some differences between cultural groups in the relative importance of social and spiritual values (Durie, 2006).
5. The approach presented here builds on the importance weights estimated from life satisfaction data. However, it is not tied specifically to this approach to identifying the relative importance of different outcome domains. The same conceptual approach could by applied using weights developed from the public consultation process in Israel, a survey of stated preferences, or any other methodology.
6. Governance and life satisfaction are excluded, as it is not possible to estimate importance weights for them with the methodology used here. Governance is largely the same across Israel, while life satisfaction is used as the metric to assign weights.

References

Alkire, S. (2002), "Dimensions of Human Development", *World Development* 30 (2), pp 181-205.

Boarini, R., Comola, M., Smith, C., Manchin, R. and F. de Keulenaer (2012), "What Makes for a Better Life?: The Determinants of Subjective Well-Being in OECD Countries – Evidence from the Gallup World Poll", *OECD Statistics Working Papers*, 2012/03, OECD Publishing, *http://dx.doi.org/10.1787/5k9b9ltjm937-en*.

Brown, D., J. Woolf and C. Smith (2012), "An empirical investigation into the determinants of life satisfaction in New Zealand", *New Zealand Economic Papers* 01/2012.

Clark, A., Y. Georgellis and P. Sanfey (1998), "Job Satisfaction, Wage Changes and Quits: Evidence From Germany", *Research in Labour Economics* Vol. 17.

Dolan, P., T. Peasgood and M. White (2008), "Do we really know what makes us happy? A review of the economic literature on the factors associated with subjective well-being", *Journal of Economic Psychology* 29(1).

Durie, M. (2006), "Measuring Maori Wellbeing", *New Zealand Treasury Guest Lecture Series*, Wellington, *www.treasury.govt.nz/publications/media-speeches/guestlectures/pdfs/tgls-durie.pdf/view*.

Fleche, S., C. Smith and P. Sorsa (2012), "Exploring Determinants of Subjective Wellbeing in OECD Countries: Evidence from the World Value Survey", *OECD Statistics Working Papers*, No. 2012/01, OECD Publishing, Paris, *http://dx.doi.org/10.1787/5k9ffc6p1rvb-en.*

Fleurbaey, M., E. Schokkaert and K. Decanq (2009), "What Good is Happiness?", *CORE Discussion Papers* No. 2009017, Université catholique de Louvain.

Helliwell, J. (2008), "Life Satisfaction and Quality of Development", *NBER Working Paper* 14507, NBER.

Helliwell, J. (2003), "How's Life? Combining individual and national variables to explain subjective well-being", *Economic Modelling* Vol. 20(2).

OECD (2013a), *How's Life 2013? Measuring Well-Being*, OECD Publishing, Paris, *http://dx.doi.org/10.1787/9789264201392-en.*

OECD (2013b), *OECD Economic Surveys: Austria 2013*, OECD Publishing, Paris, *http://dx.doi.org/10.1787/eco_surveys-aut-2013-en.*

OECD (2013c), *OECD Guidelines on Measuring Subjective Well-being*, OECD Publishing, Paris, *http://dx.doi.org/10.1787/9789264191655-en.*

OECD (2013d), *Review of Recent Developments and Progress in Labour Market and Social Policy in Israel: Slow Progress Towards a More Inclusive Society*, OECD Publishing, Paris, *http://dx.doi.org/10.1787/9789264200401-en.*

OECD (2011), *How's Life?*, OECD Publishing, Paris, *http://dx.doi.org/10.1787/9789264121164-en.*

Ravallion, M. (2012), "Poor or Just Felling Poor? On Using Subjective Data in Measuring Poverty", *World Bank Policy Research Working Paper* No. 5968.

Silva, J. and Z. Brown (2013), "More than the Sum of their Parts: Valuing Environmental Quality by Combining Life Satisfaction Surveys and GIS Data", *OECD Statistics Working Papers*, No. 2013/01, OECD Publishing, Paris, *http://dx.doi.org/10.1787/5k4840hfpwkb-en.*

Chapter 5

Measuring well-being in Israel: The statistical agenda ahead

This chapter draws together the information gathered during the preparation of Measuring Well-being in Israel *to identify key gaps in Israel's statistical system and to suggest some priorities for statistical development. In addition, this chapter briefly reviews the progress made by the Central Bureau of Statistics in addressing issues related to the geographical coverage of Israeli statistics raised during the process of Israel's accession to the OECD. Recommendations to improve Israeli statistics in order to better measure well-being fall into two groups. The first focuses on the structure of the Israeli statistical system including the make-up of the survey programme, the harmonization across surveys, the timing and frequency of data collection, and changes to the population coverage. This is supplemented by a second set of recommendations focused on the content of existing surveys and other statistical collections.*

The statistical data for Israel are supplied by and under the responsibility of the relevant Israeli authorities. The use of such data by the OECD is without prejudice to the status of the Golan heights, East Jerusalem and Israeli settlements in the West Bank under the terms of international law.

Introduction

This report has analysed the important effort on well-being indicators recently undertaken by the Israeli authorities, and has also taken stock of the quality and comprehensiveness of Israeli statistics to measure well-being and sustainability. This chapter draws together the information gathered during the preparation of *Measuring and assessing well-being in Israel* to identify key gaps in Israel's statistical system and to suggest some priorities for statistical development. In addition, this chapter briefly reviews the progress made by the Central Bureau of Statistics in addressing issues related to the geographical coverage of Israeli statistics raised during the process of Israel's accession to the OECD.

The Israeli statistical system

Israel has a sound base of statistical information for measuring well-being. This information is grounded in a strong official statistical system collecting information on a broad array of relevant dimensions. The Central Bureau of Statistics (CBS) collects a wide range of data relevant to measuring well-being, and much of this is published in a format very close to that required for effectively monitoring well-being either directly by the CBS itself (e.g. *Society in Israel*) or by non-governmental organizations (e.g. *Israel: A Social Report* by the Adva Center).

Information for measuring well-being and sustainability is drawn from all parts of the Israeli statistical system – national accounts, health statistics, population statistics, environmental statistics, and household surveys. The household survey programme is of particular importance with respect to measuring well-being, as it provides the primary source of data for many of the dimensions of people's life. Although administrative statistics can provide information on some aspects of well-being (e.g. income, education, health status), they do not provide information on other key outcomes (e.g. social contact, work/life balance, subjective well-being), and are often affected by limitation in population coverage and in the range of background information on individuals and households. Beyond this, survey data are crucial because they provide information on the characteristics of individuals and households, which is not captured by aggregate statistics such as the system of national accounts.

The Israeli Household Survey Programme

Both the Israeli Household Economic Survey and the Household Labour Force Survey provide high quality information on outcomes related to the material conditions in which people live, their jobs, and their educational qualifications. However, from the perspective of measuring well-being, the Israeli General Social Survey is particularly important. Israel is one of few OECD countries with a dedicated General Social Survey (others include Australia, Canada, Japan, Korea, New Zealand, and Poland), and is one of even fewer where the survey is run on an annual basis.

General Social Surveys are particularly valuable to the measurement of well-being for two key reasons. First, they are a key vehicle – indeed, often, the only vehicle – for collecting measures of outcomes not captured elsewhere in the statistical system. The General Social Survey of Israel is the main source of high quality data on outcomes relating to job quality, social contact, victimization, and subjective well-being. In addition, General Social Surveys are generally the only data source that collects information on a wide range of well-being for the same individuals, and are thus fundamental when looking at the joint distribution of outcomes across the population. For example, while there are alternative sources of information on health status in Israel, the General Social Survey is the only vehicle that enables analysis of relationship between household income, health status, and social contact at the individual level. For this reason, a large proportion of the recommendations from this review focus on the Israeli General Social Survey.

Recommendations

The Israeli Statistical System is not static, and a number of improvements are proposed as part of the Government Resolution enabling the production of Well-being, Sustainability and National Resilience Indicators (Government Resolution No. 2494 of 29 April 2015). The recommendations below identify areas where the Israeli statistical system could be improved from the perspective of measuring well-being and sustainability, and make note of key decisions from the government resolution. These improvements fall into two broad categories:

1. Structure of the statistical system, including the make-up of the survey programme, the harmonization across surveys, the timing and frequency of data collection, and changes to the population coverage; and
2. Content of existing surveys and other statistical collections, including the variables collected and alignment of survey questions with international standards.

Structure

From a well-being perspective, the ideal statistical system would include a broad-based annual Social Survey gathering limited information on *all* the domains of well-being, supplemented by a series of more specialised surveys focused on specific outcome areas that collect information in more detail. In broad terms, this ideal is largely consistent with the strategy envisaged by Eurostat in its programme on the modernisation of social statistics (Reis, 2012) and by other national statistical offices such as Statistics New Zealand in its social statistics strategy (Bycroft, 2011a, 2011b). Israel's statistical infrastructure is exceptionally well-placed in this respect, with an annual general social survey covering a wide range of well-being related topics. However, there are several gaps among the supporting surveys that should be addressed. The Government Resolution on Well-being, Sustainability and National Resilience Indicators indicates that a plan for conducting new surveys should be developed. Areas that could be priorities for further development are discussed below.

Time use survey

Israel currently has no time use survey, meaning that it is impossible to look in detail on the impact of time use (work-life balance, commuting time, time spent with others, unpaid work) on well-being for Israelis as a whole, as well as for different sub-groups of the population. The Government Resolution explicitly notes this gap and directs the CBS to establish a team to look at the methodology for a time allocation study. This is an important and positive step forward for measuring well-being in Israel. For example, the *UNECE Guidelines for Harmonising Time Use Surveys* (UNECE, 2013) emphasise the important role that time use surveys play in measuring well-being, unpaid work, and gender inequality. In the case of Israel, a time use survey would allow measuring leisure time, social contact and commuting. Although measures relevant to some of these areas are currently collected in the General Social Survey, a time use survey provides measures of significantly higher quality and with more detail. Beyond this, the contribution of home production and unpaid work to consumption is of crucial importance for sub-groups of the population with relatively low rates of participation in the formal labour market.

Victimisation survey

Until recently Israeli has had no victimisation survey and, along with a time use survey, this was the most significant gap in Israel's survey programme. While Israel compiles the normal range of criminal justice statistics from police and court records, these data do not provide a clear picture on trends in victimisation over time and across groups. This is because the probability of an incident appearing in statistics compiled from administrative data is affected by the resourcing of the justice system, by policy changes, and by the attitudes of the population to reporting different types of crime. Victimisation surveys play an important role in complementing traditional criminal justice statistics as they are largely immune from these types of bias, and can therefore provide valid information on changes in the risk of victimisation over time. In 2014 the CBS conducted Israel's first victimisation survey, providing a basis for meaningful analysis of the trends in victimisation over time.

Consistency in measuring population groups

A cross-cutting problem with the Israeli statistical system is the inability to consistently identify population groups of policy interest across surveys. While methods currently used to identify ethnicity (Jew, Arab, other) are harmonised across surveys, there is no consistent approach to identifying Haredi Jews as a population group of interest. In the General Social Survey, Haredi Jews are identified by combining the population group variable with a religiosity variable that captures the respondent's self-identified degree of religiosity (Datiut Yehudi). However, the same method cannot be implemented in other surveys such as the Household Labour Force Survey, where the Haredi population is identified through the question on the highest educational institution attended by the head of household. Given the policy importance of the education and labour market outcomes of the Haredi population to Israel's future economic development, consistent treatment of these population groups across survey vehicles should be considered a priority.

Youth outcomes

Currently, the General Social Survey samples the population aged 20 and older. This is in contrast to Social Surveys elsewhere were the population is 18 and older (Australia, Poland) or even 15 and older (Canada, New Zealand). The Central Bureau of Statistics should consider broadening the sample of the Israeli General Social Survey to people 15 and older for several reasons. First, this would increase international comparability (since data for the population 18 and older can be drawn from a survey of those 15 and older if needed). Second, it would cover the same population as the labour force survey, allowing comparisons across surveys within Israel. Finally, the survey would allow better analysis of outcomes for youth (15 to 24 years old), which is currently not possible with the existing General Social Survey.

The Bedouin population

Around a fifth of Muslim Arabs are Bedouin, representing a population of around 270 000 people, mostly living in the Beer Sheva District in the South of the country. Around 40% of Bedouin, who constitute one of the most disadvantaged groups in Israel, are not included in CBS survey sampling as they live in villages that are not officially recognised. Well-being statistics should cover the entire resident population of a country, and particularly groups with poor outcomes that are under-represented statistically. Given the size and extent of poverty amongst this group, it is desirable that CBS include Bedouin from the non-recognised villages in their sampling.

Content

A number of changes to the content of existing statistical collections would significantly improve the ability of the Israeli statistical system to measure well-being. Most of the recommendations that follow relate to the Israeli General Social Survey, as there is currently less international standardisation in social surveys than in economic and labour force surveys.

Comparability of information on household adjusted disposable income

Household net adjusted disposable income was selected as a headline indicator in the *How's Life* framework as it was identified as the best measure of people's economic resources that is available from the national accounts, combining information on a large number of market and non-market resources. However, system of national accounts (SNA) data on adjusted disposable income data for Israel are not internationally comparable, as Israeli SNA data for the household sector also include the business sector, which is not the case for other OECD countries. In order to get a clearer picture of households' actual income, it would be important to obtain SNA data on household income that would allow for international comparisons.

Information on the level and distribution of total household wealth

Aggregate information on the financial net worth of Israeli households is available from the system of national accounts. However, from the perspective of measuring well-being, resilience, and sustainability, this information is limited in two important ways. First, existing data provides only incomplete information on non-financial assets such as land. Given high house prices in Israel and the significant role of land and housing as opposed to financial assets for the Arab Israeli, the picture presented by the currently available data is extremely limited. Second, the aggregate nature of existing data is itself a problem; no survey currently provides information on the distribution of household wealth. Information of wealth distribution is of high interest as wealth tends to be distributed more unequally than income, and as how wealth is distributed has implications for the vulnerability to shocks of the Israeli economy and society.

A priority for better information on the material conditions of households should therefore be to consider developing a household wealth survey to collect better information on the level, composition, and distribution of wealth in Israeli society.

Harmonisation of the general Social Survey and additional content

Although the Israeli General Social Survey was designed with reference to general social surveys conducted elsewhere, such as Canada, it does not directly follow any other Social Survey in either in the topics covered or the specific questions used. This is not unusual, as there are no international standards for the content of general social surveys in the same way that there are for labour force surveys. However, it also represents a missed opportunity, as the social surveys represent an important resource for measuring dimensions of quality of life and well-being. The implication is that data from the survey cannot currently be used to compare outcomes for Israel in an international context.

Several steps could be taken to improve the international comparability of the Israeli General Social Survey. As these would involve changing how some questions are asked, it would be important to implement a transition period where a split sample is used to collect both the new and old questions, in order to estimate the impact of the change in question format and avoid losing valuable time series.

Measurement of subjective well-being in the Israeli General Social Survey is not currently in line with the *OECD Guidelines on Measuring Subjective Well-being* (OECD, 2013). As a result, Israeli measures are not comparable with those produced in national statistical offices elsewhere (currently Australia, Canada, France, Korea, Mexico, New Zealand, the United Kingdom, and the European Union – via EU-SILC – collect measures broadly in line with those in the OECD Guidelines). In particular, the 4 point labelled Likert scale currently in use provides lower quality information than a 0-10 end-labelled scale recommended by the OECD Guidelines. Similar issues also exist with respect to questions on social contact, where the general intent is similar to questions used in other OECD countries, but the precise wording and response scale differ.

In order to understand how well-being outcomes interact with economic status it is also necessary to include adequate measures of income in the Israeli General Social Survey. From this perspective, household disposable income (i.e. net of taxes) is the most important measure to capture accurately, with gross household income and wages and salary of significantly lower priority. While recent waves of the General Social Survey seem to have moved in this direction, this move should be reinforced. Generally speaking, data on net household income should be adjusted for household size via an equivalisation scale, rather than simply reporting household income per capita, which implies that information from all members of the same household should ideally be collected.

Although the General Social Survey currently collects information on a broad range of outcomes, it is currently missing information on governance and related issues. Generalised trust is widely recognised as, perhaps, the best single-question measure of social capital (see Algan and Cahuc, 2010) and is widely used in comparative reporting. Adding a question on generalized trust, as well as on people's trust towards different types of institutions, should be a high priority for the Social Survey. Another important aspect of social capital is experience of discrimination. Measures of discrimination on various grounds are collected in the Australian, Canadian and New Zealand general social surveys, and would address a gap in the content of the existing social survey.

In the absence of a time use survey, the Israeli General Social Survey is currently the main source of information for topics that a time use survey would usually cover. While some aspects of this are relatively well covered (social contact), there are some clear gaps.

In particular, free time is a crucial element of well-being and is currently not captured at all in the Social Survey.

Data on housing quality (as opposed to tenure and housing density) and access to public services and transport are also currently not available through official sources. Given the great importance of these issues to well-being in Israel, especially in terms of the geo-spatial distribution of well-being outcomes, more information is desirable.

Implementing changes to the Social Survey

Given the importance of the Israeli General Social Survey to measuring well-being, it would be important to revisit the content and structure of the survey in light of the indicators of well-being, resilience, and sustainability being developed by the Israeli government. In particular, the survey should cover all eleven outcome domains (i.e. material standard of living; civic engagement and governance; employment and work-leisure balance; personal and social well-being; personal safety; infrastructure and housing; health; environment; leisure, community and culture; information technology; and education) identified by the initiative. At least one subjective measure relating to the outcome domain as a whole and two or more objective measures should be included for each domain as part of the core social survey. The subjective measures for outcome domains should be based on the recommendations in the *OECD Guidelines on Measuring Subjective Well-being* – particularly module E of Annex 2. Additional information going into greater depth on specific topics could be included in rotating content for the survey.

The geographic coverage of Israeli data

When conducting its accession review of Israeli statistics, the OECD Committee on Statistics (CSTAT) expressed the following concern:

Irrespective of what may constitute the economic territory of Israel, there may be an issue relating to the inclusion of economic activity that is measured according to the criterion of nationality and not according to the criterion of residency.

To get a better understanding of this issue, the OECD Statistics Directorate conducted a *Study of the geographic coverage of Israeli data* in consultation with the Israeli Central Bureau of Statistics. While the review found that Israel's macro-economic and population statistics generally complied with international standards, it identified several examples of references to statistics for "the Jewish population" or "Jewish localities" in published metadata. These references seemed to suggest that non-Jewish members of the population were not always included, and that decisions on the scope of measurement instruments were based on nationality, religion, or ethnic origin. Although extensive discussions with CBS staff confirmed that this was not the case, the *Study* recommended that the CBS:

- Review and clarify the place of Israeli settlements in Judea and Samaria (West Bank) in the official geographic hierarchy used for collection and dissemination of statistics.
- Review its metadata on geographic coverage and adopt standard wording and guidelines on when and how to include the relevant references in order to ensure comprehensive and consistent treatment, and transparency for users.
- Review its metadata on entries referring to Jewish localities or Jewish population to ensure that any possible confusion concerning scope by nationality is eliminated.

A comparison of the metadata in the CBS *Statistical Abstract of Israel 2013* confirms that changes have been made to metadata since the OECD review in 2010. While the volume of these metadata precluded a systematic analysis of all parts of the Israeli statistical system in the context of the present review, a comparison of the specific areas of concern addressed in the 2010 review indicates that the metadata for the *Statistical Abstract* have been revised following the OECD study. In particular, the metadata have clarified entries referring to Jewish localities so that it is no longer possible to conclude that non-Jewish members of the population are excluded from measurement.

The issue of coverage of the Bedouin population mentioned above is relevant here also. To the extent that Bedouin living in unrecognised villages are omitted from the CBS sampling frame, while being legally resident in Israel, there is a legitimate question as to the degree to which ethnicity or population group rather than residency is the criterion defining the sample frame.

There have also been changes to the metadata describing Israeli settlements in Judea and Samaria (West Bank). In the *Statistical Abstract of Israel 2013,* these are referred to as "Israeli localities in the Judea and Samaria area". However, while "Jewish", "non-Jewish", and "mixed" localities are defined, no definition is provided for what constitutes an "Israeli" locality within Judea and Samaria (West Bank). There is therefore still scope for further clarification in this area.

References

Bycroft, C. (2011a), *Integrated household surveys: a survey vehicles approach, Statistics New Zealand,* Wellington, *http://thehub.superu.govt.nz/project/integrated-household-surveys-survey-vehicles-approach.*

Bycroft, C. (2011b), *Social and population statistics architecture for New Zealand*, Statistics New Zealand, Wellington, *http://thehub.superu.govt.nz/project/social-and-population-statistics-architecture-new-zealand.*

Central Bureau of Statistics (2010), *Statistical Abstract of Israel 2010*, CBS, Jerusalem, *www.cbs.gov.il/reader/shnaton/shnatone_new.htm?CYear=2010&Vol=61.*

Central Bureau of Statistics (2013), *Statistical Abstract of Israel 2013*, CBS, Jerusalem, *www.cbs.gov.il/reader/shnaton/shnatone_new.htm?CYear=2013&Vol=64.*

Central Bureau of Statistics (2013), *Society in Israel. Report No. 6*, CBS, Jerusalem, *www1.cbs.gov.il/webpub/pub/text_page.html?publ=54&CYear=2011&CMonth=1.*

Horlor, D. and P. Houle (2012), *An Overview of Canada's General Social Survey and Highlights from International Social Surveys*, Social and Aboriginal Statistics Division, Statistics Canada.

NII National Insurance Institute (2007-2012), *Poverty and Social Gaps Annual Reports 2007-2012*, *www.btl.gov.il/English%20Homepage/Publications/Poverty_Report/Pages/default.aspx.*

OECD (2010), *OECD Economic Surveys: Israel 2009*, OECD Publishing, Paris, *http://dx.doi.org/10.1787/eco_surveys-isr-2009-en.*

OECD (2010), *Study on the Geographic Coverage of Israeli Data*, OECD, Paris, *www.oecd.org/els/48442642.pdf.*

OECD (2011), *How's Life?*, OECD publishing, Paris, *http://dx.doi.org/10.1787/9789264121164-en.*

OECD (2011), *OECD Environmental Performance Reviews: Israel 2011*, OECD Publishing, Paris, *http://dx.doi.org/10.1787/9789264117563-en.*

OECD (2013a), *How's Life 2013? Measuring Well-Being*, OECD Publishing, Paris, *http://dx.doi.org/10.1787/23089679.*

OECD (2013b), *OECD Economic Surveys: Israel 2013*, OECD Publishing, Paris, *http://dx.doi.org/10.1787/eco_surveys-isr-2013-en.*

OECD (2013c), *Review of Recent Developments and Progress in Labour Market and Social Policy in Israel: Slow Progress Towards a More Inclusive Society*, OECD Publishing, Paris, *http://dx.doi.org/10.1787/9789264200401-en.*

OECD (2014), *Society at a Glance 2014: OECD Social Indicators*, OECD Publishing, Paris, *http://dx.doi.org/10.1787/soc_glance-2014-en.*

Reis, F (2012), *Modernisation of European social statistics*, ESSnet workshop, Rome, *www.destatis.de/EN/AboutUs/Events/DGINS/Document_PaperEUROSTAT.pdf?__blob=publicationFile*.

Switski, S. and E.K. Attias (2012), *Israel: A Social Report 2012*, Adva Center, Tel Aviv, *http://adva.org/en/post-slug-1736/*.

UNECE (2014), *UNECE Guidelines for Harmonising Time Use Surveys*, UNECE, Geneva, *www.unece.org/index.php?id=34496*.

ANNEX A

Policy uses of well-being indicators: Experiences in other selected OECD countries

Applying multi-dimensional well-being indicators to policy is not straight-forward. This Annex, therefore, focuses on the policy uses of well-being measures. The first part of the annex presents an OECD framework for using well-being measures to inform policy. Three ways in which well-being measurement can contribute to making better policy decisions are identified. These are discussed in light of the Israeli experience with developing indicators of well-being, resilience, and sustainability. The second part of the annex then reviews experiences from other OECD countries in using well-being indicators to inform policy with reference to the United Kingdom (both the national government and the Scottish government), New Zealand, and Austria. In each case, these are countries that either have parliamentary political systems or are of less than 10 million people (or both) and are thus good comparators for Israel.

The statistical data for Israel are supplied by and under the responsibility of the relevant Israeli authorities. The use of such data by the OECD is without prejudice to the status of the Golan heights, East Jerusalem and Israeli settlements in the West Bank under the terms of international law.

Introduction

Measuring well-being is not an end in itself. It is a means, ultimately, to a society in which people are better off. This implies that the benefits of measuring well-being do not accrue just from the fact of measuring it. For well-being indicators to result in a better society, they have to result in better decisions by policy makers and by the general public.

This fact was explicitly recognised by the Israeli government in December 2012 when it adopted a resolution to develop indicators on well-being, sustainability, and resilience. The recommendation states that the purpose of the indicators is to:

Formulate a reliable, comprehensive, and up-to-date picture of the country's social, economic and environmental state, which will serve as a basis for shaping government policy or other decision making, will enable a review of the implications of such policy, and will allow the public to evaluate improvements and changes in its quality of life.

Applying multi-dimensional well-being indicators to policy is, however, not straightforward. As discussed in Chapter 4, the lack of a single clear goal to focus on complicates evaluating the consequences of any given policy. This is not in itself a bad thing. In fact, it is one of the main reasons for measuring well-being. However, it also requires that, to get the most value out of well-being measures, effort is put into thinking about how such measures can be used to better inform policy.

This Annex, therefore, focuses on the policy uses of well-being measures. The first part of the annex presents an OECD framework for using well-being measures to inform policy. This framework is grounded in the policy cycle (i.e. strategy development, policy planning, implementation, and evaluation), and identifies three ways in which well-being measurement can contribute to making better policy decisions. These are discussed in light of the Israeli experience with developing indicators of well-being, resilience, and sustainability. The second part of the annex then reviews experiences from other OECD countries in using well-being indicators to inform policy. As Israel moves to integrate well-being measures into its policy process, it is useful to draw on the experiences of other countries that have applied a well-being framework to policy. Countries covered in the chapter are the United Kingdom (both the national government and the Scottish government), New Zealand, and Austria. In each case, these are countries that either have parliamentary political systems or are of less than 10 million people (or both) and are thus good comparators for Israel.

A policy framework for well-being measures

As well-being statistics and indicators improve and become more internationally comparable, an important question emerges alongside that of developing new measures, which is how to effectively *use* these measures in policy-making. Traditionally socio-economic indicators have been used to inform policy in three ways: to monitor progress in socio-economic outcomes; to inform policy design and implementation; and to evaluate policies (see e.g. Barca and McCann, 2011; HM Treasury, 2014). In other words, indicators are useful to understand how countries are evolving (the "what" question); why such changes are observed, including the role of policy (the "why" question); and how policies can be better designed and implemented to improve performance (the "how" question).

Well-being indicators differ from traditional socio-economic indicators in two important ways:

- First, they include areas that were absent from the standard measures used by policy makers. For instance, elements such as social connections and the quality of living together became of interest to policy makers and official statisticians only recently. Similarly, life satisfaction and affect data did not feature prominently among the indicators collected by NSOs or used by governments to monitor progress, while they are now seen as one important stand-alone dimension of well-being and better lives.
- Second, because well-being indicators encompass one multidimensional concept ("well-being") into a single *consistent measurement framework*, they offer the potential of informing policy on a coherent set of targets and instruments needed to achieve these targets. Therefore, while well-being indicators fulfil the traditional role of socio-economic indicators to inform on the "what", "why" and "how" of policies, they do it with a fundamental value-added, which is that of applying a *consistent framework* across the board.

It is important to be clear that measuring well-being does not necessarily imply a radical change in *the goals* of policy. Policy makers have always considered the wider impacts of proposed policy changes on their constituents. However, this analysis has not traditionally been systematic in nature. The main feature of the systematic measurement of well-being is that it allows policy makers to join-up policies at all stages, starting from the identification of policy priorities, to the choice of policy options, to the design of policy programmes, and to policy evaluation. This Annex spells out in more details how these stages can be informed by well-being measures.

Three jobs for well-being indicators

Well-being indicators help performing three tasks that are central in policy-making:

- **Alignment** of outcomes across government agencies and across the policy process
- **Analysis** of policy options and their consequences
- **Accountability** for results.

Figure A.1 below illustrates where and how a policy-integrated well-being framework fits within a traditional model of the policy cycle.

Alignment

"Joining up" government so that different agencies and arms of government operate effectively together in pursuit of the same goals is a key challenge for public management. Government agencies often operate in silos, focusing on the outputs for which they are directly accountable and without reference to the wider impacts of their actions. Even when armed with the best of intentions, there is always a risk that government agencies are institutionally predisposed to focusing on the outcomes for which they are directly responsible. For example, health agencies tend to focus on the direct health impacts of their actions when setting priorities, despite the fact that spill-overs from other policy areas and society-wide patterns on health outcomes are large. Policy spill-overs also operate in the other direction, with health as a major determinant of outcomes in other

Figure A.1. **Well-being indicators and the policy cycle**

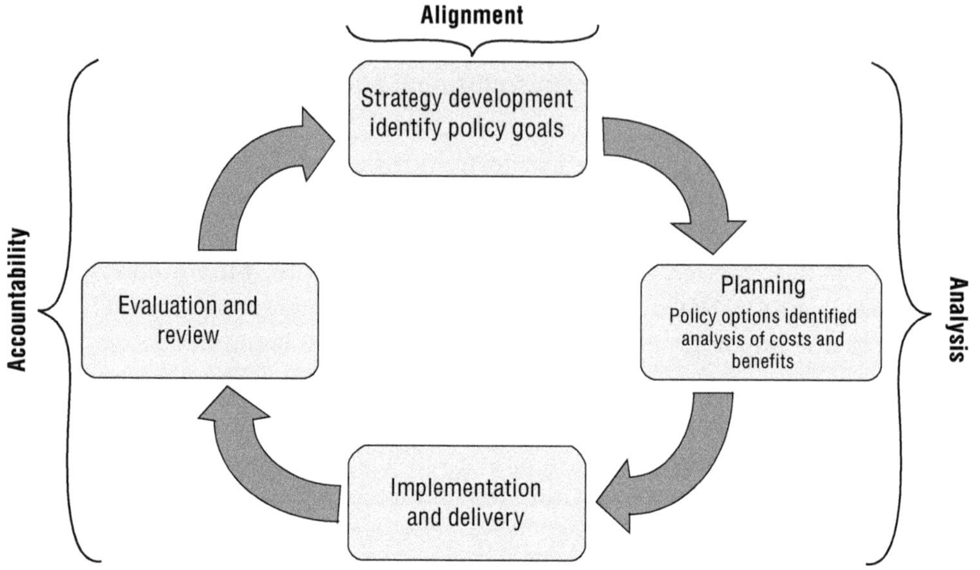

policy areas. Health status is, for example, a major driver of labour force participation, educational attainment, and work life balance (via caring responsibilities). Similar spill-overs occur in nearly all policy areas.

Transcending the silo-approach is, however, challenging. First, it is generally easier for agencies to identify the cross-sectoral drivers of the outcome for which they are directly responsible than to identify all the ways in which the outcome in question impacts on other domains of well-being. For example, there is a large (and policy-influential) literature on the social determinants of health status, but very little in the way of systematic assessments of how health care policies drive other outcomes. Second, even where agencies actively try to co-ordinate across sectors, there may be a lack of consistency in the range of outcomes considered and how these are discussed in each department.

A well-being measurement framework can assist in addressing these two key challenges. By setting out an explicit framework for the range of outcomes to be considered, the framework can ensure a basic level of consistency across the whole of government. While measuring well-being does not in itself identify priorities, it does provide a common set of criteria to help with the policy process of setting priorities. This framework can provide a "checklist" for the kind of outcomes that matter the most when setting policy priorities, and provides a common language for agencies to discuss these consequences. This, in turn, supports more sophisticated analysis of policy options (see below).

While measuring well-being can provide the basis for setting a common set of policy goals across government, it will be most effective in this regard if it is integrated into the policy process itself. This can be achieved in a number of ways. At the more formal level, a well-being framework can form the basis for the accountability procedures for government agencies. A number of high profile public management initiatives such as *Virginia Performs* in the United States and *Scotland Performs* in the United Kingdom have taken this approach (*Scotland Performs* is discussed later in this Annex).

However, even without going this far, a well-being framework can have a large impact. The process of developing a national well-being framework can be a valuable vehicle for generating interactions between public agencies focused around outcome domains if the relevant agencies are directly involved in the process. Similarly, requirements such as the integration of the well-being perspective in Regulatory Impact Analysis (RIA) required for proposed new regulations and legislation has the potential to be effective in aligning agencies to consider a common set of criteria.

The Israeli experience

Alignment has been a major focus of the Israeli initiative to develop indicators of well-being, resilience, and sustainability. Senior civil servants from the relevant agencies were appointed to lead teams of experts to develop indicators for the different outcome domains (e.g. the Ministry of Health for the health domain, the Ministry of Public Security for the personal security). Each expert team was required to be cross-sectoral in nature, bringing in staff from other government agencies as well as academic experts on the subject matter in question. For example, the environment domain was headed by the Ministry of the Environment Protection, but involved staff from the Ministries of Health, Economy, National Infrastructures, Energy and Water Resources, Transport and the Nature and Parks Authority. In effect, the process of developing indicators has been structured so that senior civil servants would have joint conversations around what the ultimate outcomes for policy in each area should be, and how their different agencies affected these outcomes.

Analysis

The analysis of policy options and their consequences is important at both the strategic level (i.e. deciding what goals should be a priority for policy) and at the technical level (i.e. where the costs and benefits of specific policy options need to be identified, and decisions taken on which option to pursue). The systematic measurement of well-being supports the analysis of policy options at both levels. With respect to identifying policy priorities, monitoring well-being may offer an indication of where policy makers should concentrate their efforts. The identification of policy-priorities is informed by a range of elements within the framework:

- The assessment of well-being performance to highlight strengths and weaknesses (with a perspective that can be cross-comparative, over time or across sub-groups of the population).
- The study of people's preferences on the various well-being dimensions, to understand where people see the greatest value-added in well-being from policy change.
- The understanding of levers of action for policy.

In well-functioning democracies, people usually express their *preferences for "well-being"*, i.e. for the type of society they would like to live or even just for a better life for themselves, by casting a ballot or by engaging with politics in several ways. However, in practice, there is a very imperfect connection between the actual agendas of governments once elected and people's desiderata. Yet, policies' acceptance and effectiveness crucially depend on public legitimacy. Using a well-being framework to elicit citizens' views on well-being can complement traditional political processes by informing the policy platforms presented to citizens to vote on, and increase policy legitimacy if this reduces the gap between citizens desires and policy priorities. In addition, understanding people's goals and behaviours beyond the narrow boundaries of the standard economic models may provide policy makers with more efficient instruments for achieving a given objective.

People's preferences for well-being have been long studied in the literature. They can be elicited in a variety of way, through surveys or questionnaires, experiments and administrative records. Most of these studies elicit people's preferences in relation to one or two well-being dimensions, often non-market goods (e.g. health status or environment). However, increasingly more surveys are done with the aim of establishing people's ratings or rankings over a large number of well-being dimensions (e.g. Benjamin et al., 2013). The alternative to eliciting people's preferences by the means of an empirical analysis is to deliberate about what matters the most through consultative approaches (e.g. Alkire, 2008). What matters the most is to note that it is possible to get a deeper understanding of people's values and preferences, and that this information may be of interest for governments when establishing their priorities. Chapter 4 of this report provides an example of this sort of analysis.

Well-being can also be used to identify the best policy instruments available to improve on well-being. Traditionally, evidence-based policy making consist of using statistics for informing policy design and implementation and for informing policy evaluation (e.g. OECD 2013b for an illustration with respect to subjective well-being data). Policy-integrated frameworks make it possible to perform these traditional tasks in an innovative and comprehensive way, by leveraging on the *interconnectedness* of the well-being dimensions.

The *design and the implementation of policy* must be driven by a sound understanding of the mechanisms and pathways that generate the outcomes of interest. For instance, improving educational outcomes requires understanding the role of educational policies as well as that of other policies (e.g. labour market) and non-policy drivers (e.g. family's socio-economic background, peers effects, etc.) on pupils' learning. Similarly, increasing employment requires understanding the impact of various labour market policies, educational policies, macro-economic policies as well as of factors that are broadly exogenous to policy (e.g. demographics, technological progress, globalisation, etc.). Well-being outcomes are simultaneously determined by a common set of determinants. For instance, educational outcomes and employments will be jointly determined by educational and labour market policies, as well as other factors. In practice, a well-being approach has the potential of delivering policy packages that act on different levers (simultaneously or sequentially) to obtain the desired goal, or one set of goals. For instance, it may tell policy makers that to improve people's competencies over the life cycle it is important to implement specific policies in the education sector, in the labour market as well as in regional and urban policies.

The Israeli experience

Israel is at the start of the process of measuring well-being, and thus there has not been an extensive attempt to apply a well-being framework to the analysis of policies. However, some work has already taken place. As part of the process for developing the indicators of well-being, resilience, and sustainability, extensive consultation with the Israeli public has been used to elicit information on the public's preferences for well-being. This has taken the form of online consultation (with around 1,600 respondents) and workshops targeting those groups in society likely to be under-represented in an online response process (with around 400 participants). Information from this consultation process will feed into the choice of indicators, and will inform decisions about where to set priorities among the different domains of well-being. Beyond this, the National Economic Council could have a role in providing analysis of the Israeli indicators each year when they are released. This implies that the notion of well-being will play a core role in the analytical phase of Israeli policy. However, it is currently too early to assess how this will work in practice.

Accountability

Accountability for results is fundamental to efficient and effective governance. This is true at all levels, from the accountability of the government of the day to citizens via the democratic process through to the specific performance agreements of agencies governing what services they will deliver, to whom, and over what time frame. Accountability is also the ultimate rationale for the evaluation of policy interventions *ex post*, and is an important input into strategic priority setting.

With respect to *monitoring* outcomes, well-being indicators may inform on country's (or any smaller geographical entity) performance across a wide range of elements that constitute people's well-being. For instance, the OECD *How's Life?* dashboard (see Chapter 1) provides information on country's performance on 11 well-being dimensions. This information is made available looking across countries, over time and for both averages and specific population groups. These are the three different perspectives through which the dashboard answers the question "is life (getting) better"?

Cross-country information on well-being tells how countries perform in various dimensions. On a first basic level, this type of information answers the question of which countries are offering better lives. On a second, more sophisticated, level, however, cross-country comparisons of well-being also inform on what are the sets of dimensions in which country tend to do well *simultaneously* (e.g. the likelihood that countries performing well in education, also perform well in health). The latter, which captures the *joint correlation of outcomes at country-level*, is a distinctive advantage of looking systematically at the broad notion of well-being.

Monitoring well-being performance *over time* helps understanding whether life is getting better in any specific community. As for cross-country comparisons, the possibility of looking at how countries evolve in more than one dimension over time allows an assessment of the extent to which countries whose performance is improving in one dimension are also improving in another dimension.

Monitoring well-being performance *across population groups* answers the question of whether life is better for some groups of individuals sharing a given characteristics than for others. As in the previous examples, it also makes it possible to examine whether people doing better in any particular dimension also do better in other dimensions (*joint correlation of outcomes at individual level*).

Evaluating policy means assessing *ex post* the impact of a given policy. Once again, there is a huge difference in carrying out this evaluation by looking at the possible or actual impact of policies on a very limited set of criteria (for instance the objectives of a policy programme, e.g. reduce unemployment turn-over when introducing active labour market policies) or looking at the impact of the same policy on the broad range of well-being dimensions (e.g. increase job security, increase workers' competencies through higher firms investment, etc.).

The Israeli experience

Israel has stated that the intention of indicators of well-being, resilience, and sustainability that it is developing will be a central input into the strategic outlook presented to the government each year by the National Economic Council. The indicators will be produced each year by the Central Bureau of Statistics, and then passed to the National Economic Council for analysis. The process is strengthened by having the indicators prepared by the national statistical office (with all the implications for the independence of official statistics that this carries Although it is too early to say how this process will impact on the public's perception of policy-making in Israel, the approach does pick up on important factors that are associated with the successful application of a well-being approach to policy in other countries: tying well-being measurement to decision-making in a meaningful way.

Well-being and policy: country experiences

Despite the increasing acceptance of the need to measure well-being, the range of examples of the application of well-being measures to policy is relatively narrow. This reflects the reality that only recently has it been possible to measure well-being with a high degree of confidence in the validity of the measures; and the fact that there is a time lag between the start of measurement and when enough observations have been accumulated to make substantial policy inferences. There are, however, several examples of policy frameworks in OECD countries that are broadly comparable with Israel and that put the notion of well-being (or an expanded notion of living standards) at the centre. Four of these are described below: these were selected based on their potential to provide useful insights to the Israeli policy process.

United Kingdom

One high profile initiative in this field has been the United Kingdom project to measure national well-being launched by Prime Minister David Cameron in November 2010. This project has three core elements. First, the Office for National Statistics was directed to develop measures of national well-being. As a result of this, the ONS launched a large scale programme of public consultation to identify what things were important to the well-being of citizens. The resulting framework has similar scope to the OECD *How's Life?* framework and the Israeli indicators of well-being, resilience, and sustainability. Figure A.2 below is the result of the second stage of the ONS project, which involved collecting and publishing indicators of the different domains of well-being. It presents the 10 well-being domains that comprise the ONS framework along with the 41 headline indicators used to measure well-being.

The third stage of the UK project has been to implement a well-being focus in policy development. The UK approach has been to encourage individual government agencies to explore how their policy analysis might change if well-being were to be the focus. The Cabinet Office has been instrumental in co-ordinating this work, and has taken an intellectual lead in assisting departments in adopting a well-being centred approach to policy. The result of this work has been a wide range of individual policy initiatives that have been designed or evaluated with a well-being focus. These include setting objectives in public health policy, evaluating adult education courses, evaluating a national citizen service scheme, informing the social impact analysis of major transport schemes, and contributing to the design of active employment assistance (UK Cabinet Office, 2013).

Figure A.2. **United Kingdom national well-being measures**

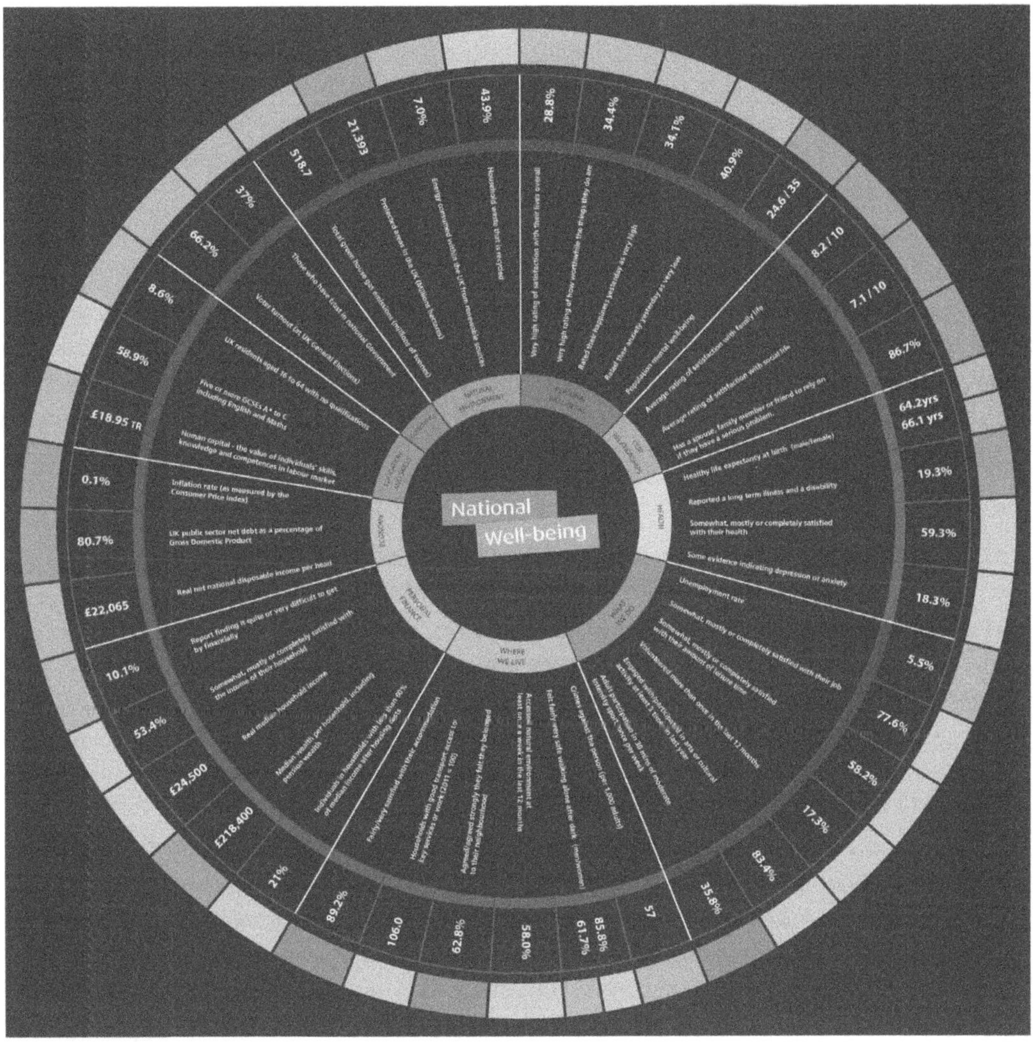

Source: ONS, *www.neighbourhood.statistics.gov.uk/HTMLDocs/dvc146/wrapper.html.*

New Zealand

A different example of a framework that embeds the notion of well-being in policy advice was introduced by the New Zealand Treasury in mid 2000s.[1] The Treasury's Living Standards Framework has five distinctive features: i) multidimensionality, e.g. the determinants of living standards encompass non-material dimensions; ii) the recognition that freedoms, rights and capabilities are important for living standards; iii) the consideration of the distribution of living standards across different groups in society; iv) the sustainability of living standards over time; and v) the importance attributed to subjective measures of well-being as a useful cross-check of what is truly important to individuals. The framework encourages analysts and policy makers (within the Treasury and beyond) to think in an integrated way across policy objectives, to consider their trade-offs and complementarities and to have regard to all of the impacts of a given policy or programme.

While Treasury's advice has been initially framed in terms of the wider considerations of the Living Standards Framework, the Treasury's most recent focus has been on implementing the Framework by developing a practical tool that could be used on a daily basis for Treasury's policy advice. In particular, the tool should help:

> *to think about the living standards impact, rather than (…) something that is adopted as a checklist or compliance exercise. It also will never be a substitute for all the analysis that lies behind good quality policy advice. Rather, it is intended to be a tool that challenges its staff to consistently and systematically consider holistically how any particular piece of policy advice fits within the broader vision that the Treasury aspires to achieve.*

So far, the Treasury's living standards tool has been trialled on five key policy issues (economic growth, macro-economic vulnerability, sustainability for the future, social capital, and equity). In practice, the use of the framework implies that advice on priorities to lift economic growth, for instance, needs to pay attention to the distributional consequences of the suggested policies, and to impacts on other policy objectives. Similarly, it implies that policies should be gauged in terms of their capacity of increasing "opportunities and capabilities for participation in society".

Box A.1. **The New Zealand Living Standards Framework: How to evaluate the impact of policy on equity?**

The New Zealand Treasury's Living Standards Framework suggests that the impact of policies on equity should be assessed on the basis of questions such as:

- Within the groups which will be affected by a proposed policy change, what are the important dimensions of equity and how are they likely to be affected? For example, does a policy change raise the issue of procedural fairness, or does it affect how we protect vulnerable members of society?
- Will a proposed policy change inadvertently damage equity? For example, does a policy affect some groups in society in a way that reduces their chance to participate?
- If a policy increases equity, are there trade-offs with other of the living standards dimensions? Could the policy be improved in a way that minimises these trade-offs? If a policy impacts negatively on equity, is there an alternative that avoids this impact?
- Has the analysis considered all types of equity (such as procedural fairness, opportunities and barriers), and all the relevant aspects (e.g. income, health, education) that are important for this policy?
- What are the short and long term impacts of a policy on equity?

Source: New Zealand Treasury, *www.treasury.govt.nz/abouttreasury/higherlivingstandards*.

Austria

In Austria, several initiatives have been launched to measure and monitor well-being beyond GDP. One of the most prominent is the *Growth in Transition* (*Wachstum im Wandel*) initiative led by the Ministry of Environment (in co-operation with other government agencies and think-tanks), launched in 2008. *Growth in Transition* is a platform to strengthen dialogue about ecologically and socially sustainable growth to enable the transition towards a resource-efficient and environmentally compatible economy. At the end of 2012, the initiative organised an international conference which concluded with a broad 10 point programme including suggestions to foster: i) sustainable development, ii) quality of life and workplaces, iii) measurement of well-being, iv) renewable energies, v) efficient natural resource use, vi) civic engagement in the political process, vii) generational fairness and social connections, viii) quality of urban and rural living spaces, ix) appreciation of natural assets, and x) sustainable agriculture.

Since 2004, *Statistik Austria* (the central statistical office) has also published regularly an indicator report to monitor progress on the goals formulated in Austria's *Sustainable Development Strategy* by the Ministry of Environment. It also launched in October 2012 a new dataset (*How's Austria – Wie geht's Österreich?*) comprised of 30 headline indicators in three areas: material wealth, quality of life and environmental sustainability.

Finally, the Ministry of Economy together with WIFO (a prominent Austrian research institute) recently published a study (*More than Growth – Mehr als Wachstum*), which complemented the *OECD How's Life* indicator set with additional indicators judged especially relevant for Austrians. Responses to a specifically commissioned household survey provided specific rankings of the importance of indicators and dimensions for the well-being of Austrian people. Based on this information, weights were constructed and the indicators aggregated accordingly.

Information from *Mehr als Wachstum* was used to inform the 2013 *OECD Economic Survey* of Austria. The *Survey* was explicitly structured around well-being, with the outcome areas from the OECD Better Life Initiative and the weights from *Mehr als Wachstum* used as a framework for the analysis in the review. This was then used to identify the main drivers of well-being in Austria, and to focus on the reforms and recommendations that would contribute the most to improved well-being.

Scotland

Since 2007 the government of Scotland has organised its strategic goals around a policy-integrated outcomes framework: *Scotland Performs*. In doing so, the Scottish government built on the *Virginia Performs* framework used by the State of Virginia in the United States. *Scotland Performs* measures and reports on the progress of the government of Scotland in creating a more successful country, where success is defined as progress against 16 national outcomes covering key aspects of health, justice, environment, economy, and education. Although the framework does not mention well-being explicitly, the outcomes used to define "success" correspond very closely with those used to measure well-being elsewhere – such as in the OECD *Better Life Initiative*. Further, as is clear from Figure A.3 below, the Scottish framework is outcomes-based (i.e. concerned with good end-states) rather than output-based (i.e. concerned with measuring the volume of services produced).

One noteworthy difference betwee *Scotland Performs* and the New Zealand Treasury's *Living Standards Framework* or the Austrian initiative discussed above, is that *Scotland Performs* is directly integrated into the accountability arrangements for the various agencies responsible to the Scottish government. In other words, the framework does not simply provide guidelines for analysts in various agencies, but rather is used as an explicit reference point for developing targets and outcome measures for government agencies. For example, the main targets for NHS Scotland (the arm of the British National Health Service directly accountable to the Scottish government) for 2012, 2013, and 2014 are linked directly to the *Scotland Performs* framework.

Figure A.3. **The *Scotland Performs* framework**

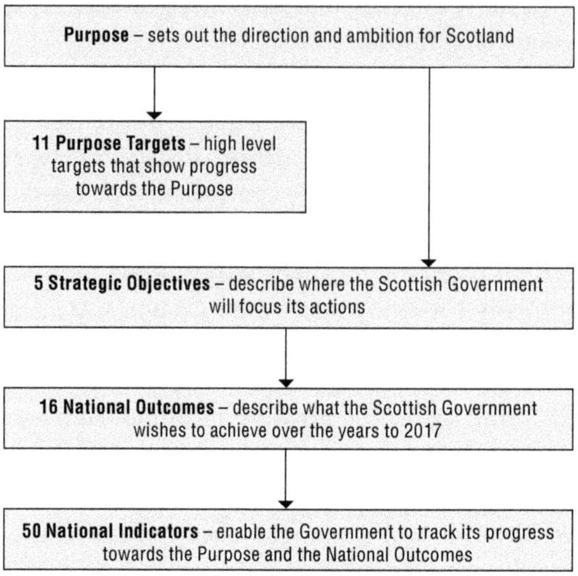

Source: Scottish Government, *www.gov.scot/About/Performance/scotPerforms*.

Challenges in applying a well-being approach to policy

Despite an increasing body of knowledge and practical experience on applying well-being measures to policy, challenges remain. This is not only because measuring well-being requires a large amount of information, but also because much of the gain from a well-being centred approach to policy requires analysing policy issues across a wider range of outcomes (analytically or qualitatively).

Specific challenges include:

- The large number of dimensions that these frameworks potentially cover. Given that policy makers are especially interested in the policy levers shaping these dimensions, and that these drivers may differ across the population, this entails measuring, analysing and evaluating a large number of variables.
- Good measures do not exist for all elements of well-being, and even where good measures do exist, it does not follow that they are collected in a systematic manner by national statistical offices. A well-being centred approach to policy will inevitably have implications for the data collected in order to inform policy.
- The limited availability of analytical models or empirical analysis dealing with the processes driving various well-being dimensions. The knowledge gap is even bigger when considering how well-being dimensions vary together *over time* and as a joint function of key assets such as natural, human, social and economic capital (OECD 2013a).
- The difficulty of articulating a centralised framework (e.g. in the hand of Treasury or central government) with agency -specific frameworks, and the difficulty of combining high-level objectives and instruments with sectorial objectives and policy tools.

With respect to the first of these challenges, it is particularly important to find the right balance between comprehensiveness and simplicity. The New Zealand Treasury strikes this balance by focusing on areas where government decisions are deemed to have a key influence (i.e. areas that reflect Treasury's role in the Government's policy process, areas that make a major difference to living standards, or areas where the Government faces competing objectives). This approach brings the Treasury to identify *five areas as priorities* for improving New Zealand living standards (mentioned above). *Scotland Performs* has a wider range of outcome areas (16) and indicators (50), which necessitates an additional layer of seven "Purpose Targets" in order to identify priority areas.

The second issue – data availability – can in principal be addressed easily, at least with respect to outcomes for which adequate approaches to measurement are known. In practice, however, it can be challenging for national statistical offices to reallocate resources towards new measures and, even if additional resources are forthcoming, there are costs in changes which effect existing time series.

With respect to the third challenge, i.e. limited evidence on policy and non-policy drivers of well-being outcomes, important work is being undertaken by the OECD in the context of its Inclusive Growth project and the New Approaches to Economic Challenges initiative. This work aims to identify key sets of policies that move selected well-being dimensions in the same direction.

The importance of a "whole-of-the-government" approach has been emphasized before for having great potential, but has also proved very hard to implement in practice (see for instance Christensen and Laegreid, 2007). However, there are also examples of successful ways to co-ordinate policy efforts across different agencies and decisional levels, and of the significant pay-off that these efforts can deliver (OECD, 2013c).

Conclusion

It is difficult to draw strong conclusions about "best practice" in applying well-being measures to policy. Although several countries have applied a well-being approach to policy, the total number of countries involved is small, and it is too early to draw strong conclusions about the impact on policy of such an approach. Nonetheless, even at this stage, two key lessons emerge from the case studies reviewed in this Annex.

The first important point is that the involvement of a central agency (the Treasury in New Zealand, the Ministry of Economy in Austria, the Cabinet Office in the United Kingdom) is essential if well-being is to have an impact on policy. This reflects both the crucial role that central agencies play in setting the agenda for other government agencies, but also the fact that the issues to which a well-being approach is most useful are those that a central agency deals with on a day to day basis. Aligning the actions of different government agencies to pursue joint outcomes and evaluating the impacts of different policies on different outcome are areas where a well-being centred approach can add significant value.

The second key point to emerge from the case studies considered here is the importance of how well-being is integrated into policy process. This can be done formally (*Scotland Performs*) or by leadership from central agencies (New Zealand, the United Kingdom). Both approaches highlight that measurement is not sufficient in and of itself. Tying well-being measures into the policy process in a systematic way is of fundamental importance if these measures are to have an impact on the quality of decision-making.

Although Israel's indicators of well-being, sustainability and resilience are still in their early stages, it is evident that the emerging Israeli model will differ in some important ways from the case studies discussed above. The success of the Israeli approach will therefore be of high interest to other OECD countries considering how to apply well-being indicators in policy. In particular, the collaborative process of cross-agency teams being responsible for identifying outcomes and indicators has much potential to support alignment of outcome across government agencies.

Note

1. The Australian Treasury uses a conceptually similar framework for assessing policy, but has not gone so far in measurement.

References

Alkire, S. (2008), "Choosing Dimensions: The Capability Approach and Multi-dimensional Poverty", *MPRA Paper* No. 8862, Oxford.

Barca, F. and P. McCann (2011), "Outcome Indicators and Targets – Towards a New System of Monitoring and Evaluation in EU Cohesion Policy", *Methodological note presented at the High Level Group on the Future of Cohesion Policy*, Brussels, *http://ec.europa.eu/regional_policy/sources/docgener/evaluation/doc/performance/outcome_indicators_en.pdf*.

Benjamin, D., M. Kimball, O. Heffetz and A. Rees-Jones (2012), "What do you think would make you happier? What do you think you would choose?", *American Economic Review*, 102(5), pp. 2083-2110.

Campbell, A. (2012), "The National Performance Framework and Scotland Performs", Scottish Parliament Information Centre.

Christensen, T. and P. Laegreid (2007), "The Whole-of-Government Approach to Public Sector Reform", *Public Administration Review*, Vol. 67(6), pp. 1059-1066.

Gleisner, B., M. Llewellyn-Fowler and F. McAlister (2011), "Working towards higher living standards for New Zealanders", *New Zealand Treasury Paper* 11/02, New Zealand Treasury.

HM Treasury (2014), *The Green Book: Appraisal and Evaluation in Central Government*, first published 18 April 2011, last updated 19 November 2014, London.

Kettner, C., K. Koberl, C. Mayrhuber, S. Karmasin and N. Steininger (2012), Mehr als Wachstum, WIFO monograph, Austria.

Lebensministerium (2010), *Wachstum im wandel*, Lebensministerium Vienna, *http://wachstumimwandel.at/*.

Ministry of Environmental Protection (2014), *Well-being Indicators for Israel*, Jerusalem, *www.sviva.gov.il/English/Indicators/Documents/Well-Being-Indicators-for-Israel-April2014.pdf*.

New Zealand Treasury, (2015), *Higher Living Standards*, Wellington, *www.treasury.govt.nz/abouttreasury/higherlivingstandards*.

OECD (2013a), *How's Life? 2013: Measuring Well-Being*, OECD Publishing, Paris, *http://dx.doi.org/10.1787/9789264201392-en*.

OECD (2013b), *OECD Economic Surveys: Austria 2013*, OECD Publishing, Paris, *http://dx.doi.org/10.1787/eco_surveys-aut-2013-en*.

OECD (2013c), *OECD Guidelines on Measuring Subjective Well-being*, OECD Publishing, Paris, *http://dx.doi.org/10.1787/9789264191655-en*.

OECD (2011), *How's Life?*, OECD Publishing, Paris, *http://dx.doi.org/10.1787/9789264121164-en*.

ONS, *www.neighbourhood.statistics.gov.uk/HTMLDocs/dvc146/wrapper.html*.

Scottish Government (2015), *Scotland Performs*, Edinburgh, *www.gov.scot/About/Performance/scotPerforms*.

UK Cabinet Office (2013), *Well-being Policy and Analysis, An Update of Well-being Work across Whitehall*, Cabinet Office, London, *www.gov.uk/government/collections/national-wellbeing*.

ORGANISATION FOR ECONOMIC CO-OPERATION AND DEVELOPMENT

The OECD is a unique forum where governments work together to address the economic, social and environmental challenges of globalisation. The OECD is also at the forefront of efforts to understand and to help governments respond to new developments and concerns, such as corporate governance, the information economy and the challenges of an ageing population. The Organisation provides a setting where governments can compare policy experiences, seek answers to common problems, identify good practice and work to co-ordinate domestic and international policies.

The OECD member countries are: Australia, Austria, Belgium, Canada, Chile, the Czech Republic, Denmark, Estonia, Finland, France, Germany, Greece, Hungary, Iceland, Ireland, Israel, Italy, Japan, Korea, Luxembourg, Mexico, the Netherlands, New Zealand, Norway, Poland, Portugal, the Slovak Republic, Slovenia, Spain, Sweden, Switzerland, Turkey, the United Kingdom and the United States. The European Commission takes part in the work of the OECD.

OECD Publishing disseminates widely the results of the Organisation's statistics gathering and research on economic, social and environmental issues, as well as the conventions, guidelines and standards agreed by its members.

OECD PUBLISHING, 2, rue André-Pascal, 75775 PARIS CEDEX 16
(30 2015 06 1 P1) ISBN 978-92-64-24602-7 – 2015

www.ingramcontent.com/pod-product-compliance
Ingram Content Group UK Ltd.
Pitfield, Milton Keynes, MK11 3LW, UK
UKHW051505290926
15471UKWH00008B/1436

9 789264 246027